Excerpts from 666

I lost consciousness...I don't remember exactly what happened. There had been two stewardesses standing next to me; but when I awoke only one was there! I picked her up off the floor and she rushed to the pilot's cabin. When she came out she was ashen white...and put her hand to her mouth to hold a scream.

chapter 1

* * *

I felt a tap on my shoulders as I half knelt on the floor. I turned and saw a hand with a scepter...a scepter with six, sparkling stars... and I arose...and followed.

chapter 2

* * *

"...As much as I hate the word, we need an elective Dictatorship... a benevolent authority who will make the laws and see that they are enforced by military rule if necessary. It is our only hope for survival."

chapter 3

* * *

Rumor had it that the sophisticated cameras could photograph a man lighting a cigarette on a cloudy, rainy night from 100 miles high and could measure the growth of beard on his face.

chapter 4

* * *

"To put it bluntly, George, the one way to somehow resolve our population problems was to eliminate people—not bury them— disintegrate them. Miracle 1 did that for us. Special Bibles were printed..."

chapter 5

* * *

Faye looked so small and helpless as she lay on the hospital cart. The crisp white sheets were tucked around her. We followed an orderly as he pushed her down the long corridor towards the door marked NO ADMITTANCE. BIRTH CORRECTION PERSON-NEL ONLY.

chapter 6

* * *

Just as Brother Bartholomew's car passed under the Arc de Triomphe a wild-eyed youth broke through the restraining barriers, a pistol in his hand. Those around him said he was hysterically shouting, "ANTICHRIST...ANTICHRIST!"

chapter 7

* * *

Above are some of the intriguing portions you will read in the first 7 chapters of **666**. But you'll read more! For there are 15 revealing chapters that will keep you in suspense right up to the very last page of the book!

1

DEDICATION

"...O Lord, thou art our father; we are the clay, and thou our potter; and we all are the work of thy hand."
(Isaiah 64:8)

The Master Potter, the Lord, often molds our lives by using individuals who help to shape us and our beliefs.

Consequently this book is dedicated to those who have had an important part in shaping my life.

To my mother, now with the Lord, whose quiet love and deep abiding faith in Christ started me seeking the Way of Life.

To my sister, Elsie, and my brother, Lafayette, who joined me in my new found salvation while a youngster at Montrose Bible Conference.

To the many dedicated speakers at Montrose Bible Conference, Montrose, Penna., who were faithful in the preaching of the Word of God.

To The Church of the Open Door (Philadelphia and Fort Washington) and its Pastors, from Dr. Merril T. MacPherson, Rev. Idwal Thomas, Rev. Jack Murray to Rev. Milton P. Achey and Rev. Richard S. Coons for fearlessly preaching the Word of God without compromise.

To Jim Boutilier, now with the Lord, whose untiring zeal for Christ was a tremendous inspiration to me.

To Mrs. Ruth MacPherson whose close walk with the Lord reflected through the years a shining testimony that made me a stronger Christian.

and to

To my dear wife, Mary, whose love and devotion is beyond all measure.

666

by Salem Kirban

Tyndale House Publishers
Wheaton, Illinois

Coverdale House Publishers, Ltd.
London and Eastbourne, England

Distributed in Canada by
Home Evangel Books, Toronto, Ontario

Library of Congress Catalog Card Number 71-109942
ISBN 0-912582-05-7
Printed in U. S. A.

First Printing ....March, 1970
Second Printing ....June, 1970
Third Printing ....November, 1970
Fourth Printing ....February, 1971
Fifth Printing ....September, 1971
Sixth Printing ....January, 1972
Seventh Printing ....October, 1972
Eighth Printing ....April, 1973
Ninth Printing ....June, 1973
Tenth Printing ....October, 1973
Eleventh Printing ....December, 1973
Twelfth Printing ....June, 1974

ACKNOWLEDGMENTS

To Dr. Gary G. Cohen, Professor of Greek and New Testament at Biblical School of Theology, Hatfield, Pennsylvania, who carefully checked the final manuscript and supplied the Scripture references.

To Bob Krauss, artist, who skillfully designed the front cover and did finished art throughout the book.

To the following photographic sources who made their pictures available for use:

United Press International
Wide World Photos, Inc.
Time Magazine
Black Star
Yoichi R. Okamoto
Aluminum Company of America
NASA
The Matson Photo Service
Magnum Photos, Inc.
Life Magazine
Textron's Bell Aerosystems
National Observer
Joseph F. Morsello
H. Armstrong Roberts

Sovfoto
New York Times
Ewing Galloway
University of Akron
North American Rockwell
Camerapix Nairobi
The Bettmann Archive
American Museum of Natural History
General Telephone & Electronics
American Telephone & Telegraph Company

To The Church of the Open Door for allowing us the use of their sanctuary for photographing several scenes. And to models Sharon Boutilier and Jack Matthews.

To the Batsch Company for excellent craftsmanship in setting the type in this book.

To Dickinson Brothers for printing 666 with all possible speed and quality.

CONTENTS

WHY I WROTE THIS BOOK

It was Hughes Wagner who said,

> If a person is a socialist or a communist, I will know it in twenty-four hours; if he is a member of a labor union, I will know it within a few days; but if he is a member of a Christian church, it may be years before I will ever learn of it.

A majority of the scientific advances have been made in the last 50 years of human history. Man has reached the moon and now is setting his sights on other goals in space.

Yet man still has not learned to cope with his problems right here on earth.

In spite of our technological advances war is more prevalent, unrest is more apparent, moral decay has never been more shocking and famine is more widespread.

Never before in human history has there been a greater need for the Gospel of the saving grace of our Lord Jesus Christ.

And never before in human history has there been, comparatively speaking, less of an effort to reach the teeming billions with the Word of God.

While the Bible still remains the best seller there is a question on whether it is the best read.

One popular author recently stated, "There's more sex in — — — — — [his current book] than in any of my other books, but paradoxically it's less noticeable. People are getting to take sex for granted."

This particular author is guaranteed $500,000 a year for his novels. Most of his novels are filled with sex in its rawest form and six of his books have sold a total of 70 MILLION COPIES! This is a sad reflection on the depraved conditions of today's world.

Yet in spite of this, missionary activity is slackening off for basically two reasons. Fields that were once open are now closed...there is a growing lack of interest among churches to stress the missionary ministry and the need for evangelism.

Many churches that once contended for the faith have now departed to what they believe are "greener" pastures. They have merged with the goliaths of churchdom...and are now preaching another gospel while excusing themselves with claims of "making the Gospel relevant to this day and age." They have watered down the message of man's sin and God's redemption and have replaced it with a social gospel that attempts to cure the ills of society... with a little sprinkle of Bible thrown in.

Tithes and offerings brought to the church are now being funneled into all types of recreational and social activity to "relate" to today's needs.

The music of the church has shifted from the holy hymns of adoration and praise to the howling hopping of the "new Christian beat" that breeds a surface conversion that many times dies out because of its implantation into stony ground.

It's the popular thing to belong to goliath churches of

today...to "tell it like it is"...to keep up with the times religiously.

In many circles the word FUNDAMENTALIST is sneered at, laughed at and held in contempt. And those churches who would hold true to the Word of God become suddenly unpopular. Satan becomes very active and their very existence is fraught with problems.

Yet in these End Times it will be this David that will emerge the victor as the Goliath of churchdom finds itself looking up from earth wondering where all those odd Fundamental Christians have suddenly disappeared.

They will have an explanation. Make no doubt about it! And gullible people worldwide will fall for their reasoning and follow their leading.

> "And for this cause God shall send them strong delusion, that they should believe a lie" (II Thessalonians 2:11).

And why did I write this book — 666?

While many people will not read the Scriptures or anything that has to do with church materials...most will read a novel...a novel built with suspense, photographs, intrigue ...and a novel that has to do with the FUTURE.

I hope that 666 has all of these elements but most of all it attempts to tell in novel form how events may occur during the Tribulation Period.

How important it is for us today as Christians to obey the admonition:

> "Let your light so shine before men, that they may see your good works, and glorify your Father which is in heaven." (Matthew 5:16)

For God tells us in II Corinthians 4:3, 4

> "...if our gospel be hid, it is hid to them that are lost. In whom the god of this world hath blinded the minds of them which believe not, lest the light of the glorious gospel of Christ, who is the image of God, should shine unto them."

Every born-again Christian should be an *active,* daily witness for his Lord and Saviour.

It is my hope that 666 may be used as a witness. Where many will not accept a tract...or perhaps they will accept a Bible, but not read it...they may gladly accept a novel...one that tells about TOMORROW.

And it is my prayer that in so accepting the novel 666, they will become convicted of their sin, realize their need of our Saviour, and accept Him as their Lord and soon coming King.

The novel 666 is not a pleasant book to read. It is alarming and filled with tragedy. Yet it leaves a Blessed Hope! And while the book vividly paints a frightening picture, the events of time may show that it is not even half as terrifying as the Scriptures themselves reveal.

It was Harold L. Lunquist who said, "They tried to stamp out the fire of God in Jerusalem, but they scattered the embers all over the world."

Now, more than ever before, the world and its pseudo-religionists will attempt to crush the faint burning embers underneath the heel of their social church.

May you and I burn brightly for God in order that the glow of our life might continue burning embers of redeeming light until that day arrives when the King of Light shall appear to claim His own.

Salem Kirban

Huntingdon Valley, Pennsylvania 19006
U.S.A.

January, 1970

IN EXPLANATION

This book - **666** - is a novel. Therefore much of it is fiction. However, it is important to note that **very much** of it is also **FACT**.

Using the Scriptures as our basis...it is a **fact** that there will be Rapture (when born-again Christians meet Christ in the air in the "twinkling of an eye" 1 Corinthians 15:52, 1 Thessalonians 4:16, 17).

It is a **fact** that after this occurrence there will be at least a seven year period of great trials and tribulations.

This novel - **666** - revealingly takes many of today's little known discoveries and in story form shows how **antichrist** and his associates may apply them to achieve their own sinister goals. Such items as the picturephone, the ruby laser and the flying belt as well as other inventions already exist, although they have not yet always been perfected to the point we relate them in our novel. Where the story line corresponds with prophetic Scripture...actual Bible verses are given next to that paragraph.

What many people do not realize is that events of today are already paving the way for a world dictator! Christians should no longer express blind support. The days are critical and it is time Christians become concerned and active in what they believe. It's time for responsible patriotism. And there is a difference! Blind support allows the leaders of our nation to ban prayer in schools, release a floodgate of pornography and encourages censorship of press and television media.

On the next few pages are true reproductions of actual excerpts taken from the newspapers in 1969. Read them carefully. It may serve to awaken you regarding the End Times...and how close we are to the time when antichrist will be welcomed by the millions who will hail him as their hero and leader.

How important it is for Christians to be ready for the Second Coming of Christ as these days of the End Times approach!

> "Watch therefore, for ye know neither the day nor the hour wherein the Son of man cometh." (Matthew 25:13)

Surgeon Talks Of Preserving Human Brains

Beverly Hills, Calif. — (AP)— A neurosurgeon who reports he has kept more than 100 monkey brains alive outside the skull for up to several days says human brains might be preserved some day and "trained" as computers.

Dr. Robert J. White of Case-Western Reserve University at Cleveland said he was able to communicate crudely with the isolated monkey brains through electrical signals.

Electrodes were implanted before the brains were removed, he said. . . . through the e . . . brain wave . . . ed.

White told . . . ed by Res . . . Blindness, I . . . "communica . . . brains thr . . . nerves left i . . . electronic in . . . the approp . . . serves visua . . . ions."

A WORLD OF 4 BILLION PREDICTED FOR 1975

Special to The New York Times

TUNIS, Nov. 8 — A wider use of all available contraceptives to meet the rapid increase in world population was urged this week at the meeting of the International Planned Parenthood Federation being held this year in Gammarth. The meeting started Wednesday and will continue through next week.

A report presented to a federation session said that "at today's rate of increase in world population, there will be four billion people by 1975, and nearly double, or seven billion . . . ople, by the year 2000." The present population of the world is estimated at 3.5 billion.

Federation members from 63 countries represented at the meeting not only urged wider use of contraceptives, but called for research into new ones and expansion of their distribution.

Mrs. Agnette Braestrup, a Danish pediatrician, was elected president of the federation, succeeding Lady Rama Rau of India, who had been its head for the last six years.

Limit Couples To 2 Children, Pauling Says

ATLANTIC CITY, Nov. 9. — Dr. Linus C. Pauling, two-time Nobel Prize winner, said Sunday said family size should be limited to two children to prevent overpopulation of the world.

Speaking at a news conference during the 88th annual conference of the Geological Society of America, he said this could be accomplished by voluntary abortion, sterilization, birth control and education.

Dr. Pauling said the world's population must be reduced to one billion from its present 3.5 billion and that the United States should keep its population under its present level of 200 million.

He said that man was changing his environment in ways that can affect his genetic makeup and said, "X rays and dental and medical work, television screens, air pollution and food additives can have effects not completely understood on the process of human inheritance.

"The changes we seem to be causing can only be harmful."

Surgeon's Report
Monkey Brains Kept Alive Outside Skull

BEVERLY HILLS, Calif., Nov. 9 (AP).—A neurosurgeon reported Sunday he had kept more than 100 monkey brains alive outside the skull up to several days.

He raised the possibility that human brains might be preserved as "biological computers."

Dr. Robert J. White of Case-Western Reserve Universty at Cleveland said he had been able to communicate crudely with the monkey brains by means of electrical signals sent through electrodes implanted before the brains were removed by surgery. The signals were followed by increased brain wave activity, as monitored by the electrodes.

Dr. Whit . . . a seminar . . . sponsored by Research to Prevent Blindness, Inc., that he also had sent electrical impulses to one of the monkey brains through eye and ear nerves left intact.

"I found that such an impulse traversed all the intricate intracerebral fiber pathways and arrived at the appropriate portion that serves visual or auditory retention of inherent electrical r . . . s . . . gly sugg . . . hat

THE PHILADELPHIA INQUIRER, MONDAY MORNING, NOVEMBER 10, 1969

Society Must Dictate Size of Families, Survival Study Warns

By PATRICIA McBROOM
Of The Inquirer Staff

The human race should work toward a zero rate of population growth by the end of the century if it is to have any chance at a decent life for all, according to the National Academy of Science.

Achieving this goal means that society will have to have a say in how many children a couple can have.

These are among the conclusions reached by the prestigious Academy after three years of study on man and the earth's resources.

In a document released Sunday, the Academy set down in broad scope steps that must be taken to help insure survival of the human race.

Prepared by an eight-man panel, the report covers food production, mineral resources, marine resources, sources of future energy and, above all, population — projected over the next foreseeable sources of new food forseeable over the next 100 years.

"Population control is the absolute primary essential without which all other efforts are nullified," the panel concluded.

Dr. Preston Cloud, chairman of the panel said in a preface to the report, Resources and Man, that "serious dangers besets us already and greater ones loom in the future. People are in trouble, even around the lands.

"While this appears to be the part of earth's ultimate capacity, humans in population probably will never reach that point, said the panel, because social destruc-

tion and manifold human problems that now pass for population control at best eliminate only unwanted births," said the report.

To achieve real control will "require profound modification toward the goal, the Academy scientists ed at a level considerably under the current population.

"Ultimately this implies that the community and society as a whole, and not only the parents, must have a say about the number of children a couple may have."

The panel said that, contrary to popular belief, the oceans do not appear to harbor great mineral wealth.

"There is little basis for assuming that many marine minerals and chemical resources are a source now for energy will be of large usable volume or that for many essential substances, there are any marine resources at all."

Food from the sea could be increased about 2½ times over the present production, consid-

erably less than what has been projected by others.

But while food from the sea is an excellent source of protein, said the report, it is a poor source of calories. Only the land can supply the needed food. The Panel estimated a future agricultural need of eight times the current production.

As for energy, the Academy scientists said nuclear energy must be developed as quickly as possible, and a breakthrough in atomic sciences is needed to supply the world with an inexhaustible source of uranium 235, which could severely restrict nuclear power in a few decades.

Petroleum liquids and natural gas is used now for energy will be depleted in 50 to 65 years, said the panel.

Among its conclusions, the panel placed priority on developing safe breeder or fusion reactors to supply nuclear energy.

City to Remove 'Eye in Sky' Crime Detector

OLEAN, N. Y., Dec. 26 (AP). — The police chief of this western New York city says an experimental crime surveillance system with cameras mounted on street lights worked "beautifully" during the day. But the system will be removed anyway.

Police Chief Michael Luty said the system has cut the number of burglaries in the business district where it is employed.

But William O. Smith, who won election as mayor after charging in his campaign that the system would be too expensive — up to $70,000 — calls it an "eye in the sky."

INVASION OF PRIVACY

He said its relentless, quiet surveillance smacks of an invasion of privacy.

Eight cameras are mounted on lighting poles in a three-block area of this Cataraugus County communit   22,000.

Noise Level Could Become Lethal If It Continues to Rise, Expert Says

Washington—(UPI)—The racket may not be killing you, On the other hand, maybe it is—slowly, insidiously.

The din that assaults our ears almost non-stop is shattering our tranquility and hurting our health.

Noise pollution is getting worse every year. Nothing very effective is being done about it. According to Sen. Mark O. Hatfield, (R-Ore), the United States is the noisiest of modern societies.

The consensus at an American Medical Association Congress in Chicago was "that noise ...

must be made aware that offensive noise can be controlled and must be made angry enough to do something about it."

Noise has been defined in many ways. It is unwanted sound, sound without value, restricted sound, sound that hurts, harms, distracts, destroys sleep, invades, privacy, frightens, irritates or simply annoys.

Dr. Vern O. Knudsen, chancellor emeritus of the University of California and a student of acoustics, the science of sound, says:

Council for Science and Technology, a White House agency, notes that "growing numbers of industrial racket, because millions researchers fear that the dangerous and hazardous effects of intense noise on human health are seriously underestimated."

There is no doubt that industrial din has inflicted loss of to 50 years ago "were comparatively quiet places in which hearing on millions of workers. At least a million workers now living suffer from some degree of deafness. The federal council estimates that another 6 to 16 million are exposed to noise levels which may ruin their hearing in the future.

lowable level of industrial noise, vision sets, the endless ringing of telephones; the din of the pile drivers, bulldozers, power haws, lawn mowers;

The conversation-killing sound of dull music piped into eleva- tors or restaurants; the night noises that sound like pistol shots but may only be back- fires; the round-the-clock squawking of auto horns.

Everybody says-noise can be muffled—if we are willing to pay the price. Other countries have included national sound in- sulation regulations in their building codes. These nations feels that if a person

triggered calamities.

But more alarming than in- dustrial racket, because millions more persons are affected, is the steeply rising level of "com- munity noise" which afflicts everybody.

According to the federal coun- cil, old-fashioned dwellings of 40 to live." Thanks to modern con- struction techniques we have "some of the noisiest buildings in existence."

Myriad Noises

We hear unmuffled scooters, ...

Ailments which may have been caused or at least aggra- vated by noise include ulcers, heart diseases, allergies, and mental illness. Foreign reports have been attributed sexual im- potency to high noise levels in factories.

Racket can drown out alarm signals or shouted warnings or verbal instructions vital to safe- ty.

Paul N. Borsky of the Colum- bia University School of Public Health, says that a person noise propagators ...

No Clean Air Found in U.S.

Pollution to Kill by '90, Scientists Say

SCOTIA, N. Y,, Dec. 20 (AP).—The way some scientists see it, the choice will be simple. Wear a special breathing mask, or die from pollution.

That's the prospect for life in the Northern Hemisphere by 1990 if the present pollution rate continues, according to scientists at the Atmospheric

and much plant life will be killed off.

—In 20 years, man will live in domed cities.

Even now, the scientists say, there is no more clean air left in the United States. A six-year search was conducted by members of the research center, which is

been increasing at a rate far greater than the air is able to cleanse itself.

The last vestiges of clean air the center noted in the United States was near Flagstaff, Ariz., but it disappeared six years ago when, Hulstrunk said, air pollution from the California coast reached

deadly for humans at 35,000 particles.

At the fatal point, Hulstrunk says, the only solution now apparent will be domed cities.

"We can put on a semi- spacesuit and roam around a deserted and dead country. The people will be inside and all living things outside will be dead. Technology will have

Evening Bulletin

WITH SUNDAY MORNING EDITION

DAILY HOME DELIVERY 60

PHILADELPHIA, PA. 19101, WEDNESDAY, NOVEMBER 26, 1969

Army Orders Witnesses
Not to Discuss Massacre

2d Eyewitness Account
Former Soldier Tells of Slaying 10 In South Vietnamese Massacre

New York — (AP) — A former soldier said in an NBC News interview telecast last night that he killed at least ten South Vietnamese civilians, including a woman and a two-year old boy, in the village of My Lai on "a direct order" from an officer.

NBC correspondent Bill Matney identified the veteran as Vernardo Simpson of Jackson, Miss., where the interview was taped earlier.

It was the second eyewitness account made available so far. Paul Meadlo of West Terre Haute, Ind., in an interview Monday told of killing dozens South Vietnamese civili

Court-Martial Ordered

Lt. William L. Calley, been accused of the mur 109 South Vietnamese in March, 1968 incident and court-martial has been ordere Some Vietnamese survivors say that the death toll was 567.

The following is the Simpson interview as broadcast on the Huntley-Brinkley Report and recorded in New York:

Simpson: Well, that afternoon we got briefed on this go-ing into the village by our company commander, Captain (F nest) Medina. That we w —that when we leav village, that there anything standi gers, women pigs, chick we set 9 or

[illegible overlapping clipping: BRAVE NEW WORLD OF THE 1990S

What will medicine and health services be like in the 1990s? Drugs to blunt curiosity and initia-tive will be available for use—or misuse. All parts of the body except the brain and spinal cord will be replaceable by transplant surgery. Seventy per cent of cancers should be controllable. The aging process will be delayed and even partially reversed. Such, in any event, is the opinion of 40 medical experts in a report issued by Britain's Office of Health Economics.]

man and a child, running away from it, towards the huts. So, I told them to stop in their lan-guage and everything, and then they didn't, and I had orders to shoo 'em down and I did this. T hat I did, I shot them, nd the little boy.

bout how old was two years old.

nds do you uring that swept

nt?

magazines,

say that you — ate, you accounted y for about ten.

Yes.

Q. Were any of the men in the company reluctant to follow

Continued on Page 27, Col. 6

Secretary Going Before Senate Panel

By The Associated Press

A military judge yesterday or-dered potential witnesses in the court-martial of Lt. William L. Calley, Jr., on charges of mur-dering 109 South Vietnamese ci-vilians to discuss their evidence only with principals in the trial.

Lt. Col. Reid Kennedy, senior trial judge at Ft. Benning, Ga., where Calley will be court-mar-tialed, ordered the prosecution to notify all potential witnesses of the restriction on public dis-closures.

Media Given Time

Kennedy's order came at a hearing where prosecution and defense counsels asked him to ban news interviews with per-sons who might testify at the court-martial.

Kennedy said he would allow "a reasonable time" for news media to impose self-restraints that would assure an impartial trial.

Secretary of the Army Stanley R. Resor and top Army officials briefed the Senate and House Armed Services Committees to-day about the alleged massacre at My Lai on March 16, 1968. The briefings were closed, but Pentagon officials said a copy of Resor's statements would be released later.

Resor, asked by newsmen about quoting Rep. Gerald R. Ford (R-Mich), the minority leader, as saying top Army offi-cials knew about the incident during the Johnson Administra-

Washington Merry-Go-Round

U. S. Trains Egyptians In Poison Gas Use

By JACK ANDERSON

Washington — Pentagon officials aren't advertising it, but the Army is instructing foreign specialists in chemical and biological welfare.

A total of 550 aliens from 36 nations—including Egypt, Yugoslavia and South Vietnam—have taken two-to-36-week courses at the Army's Chemical School at Ft. McClellan, Ala.

Although fewer than half-a-dozen Egyptians have learned about poison gas in the U.S., these key officers reportedly used their American know-how to help plan the poison gas attacks upon Yemen in 1967. Representatives of the International Red Cross Verified that Egyptian pilots dropped canisters of poison gases from two Soviet-built MIG fighters and nine Ilyushin bombers over Ketaf, a remote Yemen community. Some 150 villagers gagged, coughed and bled to death.

The Egyptians, like other foreign specialists, supposedly were taught only "defense" against the hideous sprays and germs. As part of the courses at Ft. McClellan, however, they received expert instruction in the poisonous qualities of the gases, how these gases can be disseminated and which gases are most effective under various conditions.

Trained in Defense

The U.S. has trained Arab and Israeli officers alike to "defend" themselves against poison gas attacks from each other. In addition to the Egyptians, specialists from Iraq, Jordan, Lebanon and Saudi Arabia have attended the Army's Chemical School.

The only Communists who have been admitted into the secret chemical classes at Ft. McClellan are the Yugoslavs. However, close allies, such as the British, Australians and Canadians, have been given a deeper insight into our chemical and biological warfare technology at the super-secret Dugway Proving Grounds, Utah — site of nerve gas tests on animals.

Congressional incredulity over American storage of nerve gases abroad and the shipment of lethal gases inside the U.S. has now raised doubts about the training of foreign troops in gas and bacteriological lore. For the Pentagon has seeded the world with poison gas and germ warfare experts.

NEWSMEN RECEIVE VATICAN WARNING

Those Showing 'Incorrect' View Will Lose Rights

Special to The New York Times

ROME, Nov. 19 — The Vatican threatened today to withdraw accreditation from any correspondent deemed to have demonstrated an "incorrect attitude" toward the Pope, the Holy See or the Roman Catholic Church.

The threat was issued in an explanatory note accompanying forms sent to Rome correspondents to be completed for a new system of accreditation for coverage of activities of the Holy See.

Official Vatican sources sought to discount the significance of the warning. They asserted that they could not think of a single example of an "incorrect attitude" in Vatican dispatches in the last half-dozen years that would justify the withdrawal of accreditation.

America's Terrifying Arsenal

Germs Could Knock Out 60 Million In Single Raid by 10 Aircraft

The Evening Bulletin
PHILADELPHIA
Tuesday, July 8, 1969
28   B

Third of Several Articles

By COL. R. D. HEINL, Jr.
(Military Analyst)

Fort Detrick, Md.—(NANA)— The world has lived uncomfortably with chemical warfare since the first German gas attack in April, 1915, but has so far been spared the ultimate horror of germ warfare.

Maintaining that state of affairs is the ultimate justification for the U. S. Army's biological laboratories here on the rolling green Maryland countryside.

Despite secrecy and security far tighter than that which surrounds our nuclear armaments, potential enemies of the United States among the 15 other nations which have chemical biological warfare (CBW) programs know that the American biological arsenal contains agents capable of inflicting as many million casualties as a thermonuclear attack.

It was estimated in 1960 by a U. S. Army biological warfare expert, Maj. Gen. Marshall Stubbs, that ten aircraft, each dispensing 10,000 pounds of biological agents over the U. S., could kill or incapacitate 60 million people. Our enemies understand that such a situation could just as readily apply to Communist China or to Russia.

Not All Germs Suitable

Not every germ or disease is suitable for military use. Basically, the scientists (like those here at Fort Detrick, look for to 75 percent of unvaccinated victims), and Q-fever, a non-lethal incapacitant which brings on a week or more of high fever, chills, headache and muscle pains.

Four virus agents complete our biological inventory. These are: Breakbone, or dengue fever, intensely uncomfortable but rarely fatal; Rift Valley fever, likewise uncomfortable but not lethal; psittacosis (parrot fever) and Venezuelan equine encephalomyelitis, also generally non-fatal and therefore apparently well-suited to incapacitate a hostile army or population.

Warning Device Sought

Besides the development of BW agents, Fort Detrick is heavily committed to defense and safety measures in the field of biological warfare.

A very substantial percentage of Fort Detrick's research budget is devoted to what might seem the needle-in-a-haystack project of and developing a rapid, automatic, portable detection and warning device which would instantly register the presence of enemy BW agents in the atmosphere.

At present, Army scientists say this is the laboratory's top priority.

Need for a warning device is underscored by the fact that the service gas mask provides as complete protection against biological attack as against chemical attack. The high-quality filter mask doubles against germ attack.

any known BW agent.

Since air dissemination and ingestion through the respiratory tract are the unique means of transmitting military BW agents in the atmosphere, agents, loading them into shells, bombs and rockets, and storing our large reserve stocks of biological munitions in some 250 heavily-constructed "igloo" revetments throughout the base.

Underground Storage

Production of the biological rick takes place at Fort Detrick supplies developed at Fort Detrick three floors of Pine Bluff's ten-story main producing and filling facility are sunk below ground. Safety is for obvious reasons Pine Bluff Arsenal, Ark. Originally a chemical warfare plant, Pine Bluff now devotes well over half its capacity to manufacturing BW program. The biological laboratories in negative air pressure. The work itself is done within frontight biological safety cabinets by scientists or technicians using elbow-length surgical gloves fitted to airtight portholes.

Entrances have decontamination locks where germ-killing ultraviolet rays bathe persons entering and leaving.

All the sewage and exhaust air at Fort Detrick is heat-treated at temperatures guaranteed to kill all biological agents.

The plumbing lines are welded; you can walk the laboratories without ever seeing a standard plumber's joint or elbow.

Next: Emotion Muddles Logic in Debate.

The Evening Bulletin
PHILADELPHIA
Friday, December 12, 1969

Hundreds Flee As Nerve Gas Leaks in West

Dugway Proving Ground, Utah — (AP) — Some deadly nerve gas leaked from a one-ton container to the earthen floor of a storage building yesterday and about 300 persons were removed from the area.

The Army said a team of specialists sprayed the ground with a chemical which rendered the agent, known as GB, harmless.

In March, 1968, 6,400 sheep were killed when nerve gas being used in an aerial test spray was blown into nearby Skull Valley.

Sen. Frank Moss (D-Utah) said the new spisode underlined "once again the continuing danger associated with storage and moving of chemical agents such as nerve gas."

Plug Is Damaged

Army officials at this test center initially refused to discuss the matter. Later they acknowledged that while "relocating a one-ton storage container of GB, a filling plug was accidentally damaged, resulting in a small leak."

Dr. Grant S. Winn, a state air quality official, estimated th

New Liberal Mood Is Found Among Fundamentalist Protestants

THE NEW YORK TIMES, SUNDAY, SEPTEMBER 14, 1959

By EDWARD B. FISKE
Special to The New York Times

MINNEAPOLIS, Sept. 13 — Fundamentalist Protestants, generally regarded as the last major holdouts against ecumenical cooperation and the mixing of religion with social issues, have begun to modify their position on both counts.

Informed church leaders believe that the trend, if it continues, could produce one of the first major changes in the American Protestantism since the bitter theological battles between liberals and conservatives in the early 20th century.

On the one hand, fundamentalists—or "conservative evangelicals," as most now prefer to be called—are moving toward liberal policies of open involvement in social issues like race, peace and poverty.

"They're beginning to come out of their shells," said the Rev. Oswald C. J. Hoffman, preacher on the "Lutheran Hour" radio program. "They realize that you can't withdraw into a kind of Protestant mo-

delegates from 93 Protestant denominations, was convened by a committee of laymen and clergymen headed by Dr. Hoffman, a Missouri Synod Lutheran. The Rev. Billy Graham, the evangelist, was honorary chairman and a major speaker.

The majority of the participants came from traditionally fundamentalist denominations, such as the Southern Baptist Convention. The rest represented the conservative wings of mainline liberal bodies like the Episcopal Church.

The two groups were united in their acceptance of the traditional fundamentalist position. This includes adherence to such doctrines as heaven and hell, the second coming of Christ, the literal existence of Adam and Eve and the divine inspiration of the Bible.

Such teachings were generally abandoned by most of the new conservative counterpart when, in the late 19th and early 20th centuries, a split occurred between fundamentalists and the so-called modernists. Participants in the congress here have also challenged such ideas as the literal truth of Genesis.

mittee, expressed hope that the the 1973 evangelism thrust" on the "1973 evangelism thrust" would lead to cooperative efforts in other areas. "Evangelism is something all of us can agree on," he said. "It can be Christ as well as His divinity."

The conquest "new breed" of evangelical that is now emerging is represented by the Rev. Leighton Ford, a 37-year-old Canadian evangelist who is the brother-in-law and heir-designate of Mr. Graham.

At some of his rallies he conducts "love-ins" and asks members of the congregation not only to make a "decision for Christ" but also to fill out a card committing themselves to a specific act of social involvement.

At the meeting here delegates responded warmly both to an appeal by a caucus of the 40 black delegates to work against racism in America's Protestant churches and to widespread conservative evangelist from Brooklyn.

Delegates here have generally agreed that the move toward social action had been precipitated by the nation's ra-

the Rev. Alan G. Reutter, a young Presbyterian pastor from Richland, Wash. "They're asking whether it works. This Dr. Hubbard, who is a Conservative Baptist and chairman of the Urban Coalition in Pasadena, Calif.

At the same time, even those who accept the need for social involvement have not worked out its full theological implications. "Some still regard social action as primarily a tactic for getting people to listen to the Gospel," said Dr. Hubbard.

Black participants also emphasized that the concern for social involvement was so new

though mankind is sinful, the world was still created by God and this must be good, said Accompanying the new mood has been a movement away from traditional forms of individual piety, such as opposition to movies and card playing, and have characterized the fundamentalist position for decades.

"We need a new model of Christian piety," said Mr. Skinner. "The question is not whether to miniskirt or not to miniskirt. It's whether you are available to your fellow man."

---

14   The South Bend Tribune

CHRISTIANITY GOES MODERN

Affirmations Made Between Rock, Folk Music

By GEORGE W. CORNELL
Associated Press

NEW YORK — The hall is big and mostly dark, except for the garish, oscillating patterns of colored light flashing on the wide screens at either side and behind the throbbing clamor of the band.

Across the broad, dim interior, streaked with racing, phosphorescent beams, about 1,000 young people sit in little groups at white-topped tables, absorbed in the electric rock sounds and the shimmering psychedelic glow.

The the loud music stops, and a lean, thick-haired guitar player, in bright blue shirt and white pants, with a red kerchief at his neck steps to the microphone and tells how a relationship with Christ got him off dope.

"It's a fantastic experience," he said. "Jesus gives you a way. He sticks with a man. He's for you, and once you tune in with him, you just keep wanting to know and love Him better."

Rock Reverberations

Bam, thump and strumming strings. Again, the amplified rock reverberations flood the room; the flowing chromatic lights trace phantom designs on the panels, and a shapely girl in a miniskirt steps up to sing a ballad.

Each night after Graham's service in Madison Square Garden, where he is devoting special attention to young people, swarms of them migrate a block up the street to keep the mood jumping until midnight.

"It's a culture shock to most religious people," says Rev. John Guest, the wide-belted, wavy-haired young British Anglican priest who runs the program, and who looks and dresses like a swinger himself.

"Religion is generally regarded as something that belongs only in a staid, musty environment, but what we're saying here is that it fits into the secular world," he said. "It's a new scene."

Conversation About Religion

In between the rock and folk music, and the brief, simple affirmations of faith from the mi-

Nixon Prepares Plan To Draw Population Away From Big Cities

By JAMES K. BATTEN
Inquirer Washington Bureau

WASHINGTON, Dec. 25.—With a worried eye on America's exploding population, President Nixon is quietly preparing a series of major proposals for channeling growth away from the big and troubled cities.

In his State of the Union speech in January and in a subsequent message to Congress, Mr. Nixon is expected to press for a high-priority campaign to build new cities and expand the nation's towns and smaller cities.

If he does, it will be the first time an American President has suggested positive, calculated steps to reverse the historic flow of people into the big metropolitan centers and spread them more evenly across the national landscape.

FEAR 'STRANGULATION'

This drastic re-direction, Mr. Nixon is said to believe, is essential if the nation is to avoid urban strangulation in the 30 years between now and the end of the 20th Century.

In the decades of the 1970s, the 1980s and the 1990s, experts now are warning, U. S. population is almost certain

Pope Indicates He Will Share Power

Continued From Page 1, Col. 7

U. S. Is Fast Becoming Elective Dictatorship, Sen. Fulbright Says

WASHINGTON, June 19 (UPI).—Sen. J. William Fulbright (D., Ark.) said on Thursday the United States was well along the road toward "an elective dictatorship."

The chairman of the Senate Foreign Relations Committee opened debate on a controversial resolution asserting Congress' role in the making of foreign policy. It was expected to last through next week.

FOREIGN POLICY

Fulbright warned that the United States was "already a long way toward becoming an elective dictatorship, more or less complete over foreign policy and over those vast and expanding areas of our domestic life which in one way or another are related to or dependent upon the military establishment."

RESULT OF EMPIRE

If the nation continues its role of involvement and unilateral military action overseas, he said, "then the future can hold nothing for us except endless foreign exertions, chronic warfare, burgeoning expense and the proliferation of an already formidable military-industrial-labor-academic complex — in short the militarization of American life."

"If in short, America is to become an empire," Fulbright said, "there is very little chance that it can avoid becoming a virtual dictatorship as well."

The Evening Bulletin
PHILADELPHIA, Monday, December 22, 1969

Guillotine Is Still Legal In France; Used Sparingly

By RODNEY ANGOVE

Paris — (AP) — In a locked closet within Paris' Sante prison lies a collection of heavy beams and packing cases, a seven-foot wicker basket, a paillike large coal bucket, and a flat velvet-lined silverware box containing a polished trapezoidal blade with finely honed edge.

It is the famous French guillotine.

No, Dr. Guillotine did not invent it. He merely promoted it in Parliament. No, he did not himself pass under its blade, although he did serve a brief prison term for political reasons.

The guillotine became famous in the revolutionary 1790s, but was being used as early as 1521, according to an engraving in the Nuernburg, Germany, museum.

It was the press that brought ... to public executions.

THE NEW YORK TIMES, FRIDAY, OCTOBER 31, 1969

20,000 Poison Bullets Made and Stockpiled by Army

By ROBERT M. SMITH
Special to The New York Times

WASHINGTON, Oct. 30—The Army has produced and stockpiled more than 20,000 poison bullets.

It is reliably reported that the bullets contain Botulinum—a toxin that produces an acute, highly fatal disease of the nervous system.

A secret memorandum prepared in 1966 by Chemical Corps officers for Secretary of the Army Stanley R. Resor said that thousands of the bullets had been produced and stockpiled at Pine Bluff Arsenal, in central Arkansas.

There is no evidence that the bullets have been used.

It is not known whether the United States is still producing the poison bullets. However, in recent private conversations with other Government officials, Defense Department personnel have indicated that the bullets are, at the least, still stockpiled.

Assassination Weapon

Officially, the Defense officials have shied from the questions of officials in other departments as to what the "special" weapons at Pine Bluff Arsenal are; they refer to them in only the most general terms.

Reliable sources say that the 1966 memo divided the poison bullets into two types—38-calibre and "separable." It is not clear what "separable" means. The sources say the memo reported that considerably more than 10,000 bullets of each type were stored at the arsenal.

Knowledgeable sources indicate that the poison bullets could logically serve only one purpose: assassination. To kill an enemy leader with a poison bullet, it would be necessary to do no more than nick him; he would very likely die of botulism, the disease induced by the powerful toxin.

It is not clear whether the United States produced poison bullets before 1965. However, that is the first reference to the bullets that sources familiar with Army weaponry say they have seen.

The year 1965 was when the United States began to send large numbers of combat forces to Vietnam. In 1964, there were 23,300 American troops in Vietnam; in 1965, there were 184,300.

The Hgue Convention of 1907—which the United States has signed—prohibits the use, but not the manufacture, of poison weapons. This injunction is repeated in the official Army guide to the rules governing warfare, Army Field Manual 27-10, "The Law of Land Warfare."

"It is especially forbidden," the manual points out, "to employ poison or poisoned weapons." At another point it notes: "It is especially forbidden to employ arms, projectiles or material calculated to cause unnecessary suffering."

The Pine Bluff Arsenal has both biological and chemical production facilities. In the biological area, five officers, four enlisted men and 323 civilians are engaged there in a $7-million-a-year operation centered in a 10-story tower.

The Army has described the biological plant at Pine Bluff as a "pre-production facility." It says that the arsenal produces biological agents to develop the technique and "hardware" necessary to mass-produce the germs if they are needed.

The operation, the Army says, also involves storing some of the germs and toxins (the dead but poisonous byproducts of bacteria) in refrigerated "igloos." The iglos, in the north and central portions of the arsenal, are reinforced concrete huts covered with two to three feet of dirt.

There are 273 igloos at the arsenal, plus 32 warehouses, 16 sheds and 72 concrete magazine, but it is not known how many of the igloos are used to store biological agents. Pine Bluffs also stores lethal chemical agents.

Presumably the poison bullets are stored in the concrete magazines.

Specific information on biological agents is secret. However, Representative Richard D. McCarthy, Democrat of upstate New York, an outspoken critic of American chemical and biological warfare policy, has said the disease bearing weapons the United States develops, tests and in some instances stockpiles would produce — besides botulism — antarax, tularemin, Q-fever and Venezuelan equine encephalitis.

Another Army manual, Technical Manual 3-216, "Military Bilogy and Biological Agents," discusses the disease botulism in some detail.

The mnaual says that the mortality rate of botulism is 65 per cent in the United States. However, Americans contract the disease by eating contaminated and improperly cooked food. Presumably, the mortality rate would be higher if the toxin were introduced in a concentrated form and through a bullet wound.

The Amry manual says that the symptoms of the disease appear in 12 to 72 hours and that "antitoxin therapy is of doubtful value, particularly when large doses have been consumed." The disease is not contagious.

The manual also says that "through repeated purification procedures [the toxin] has been obtained in a crystalline form and is one of the most powerful toxins known."

"Botulism is an acute, highly fatal disease," the manual continues. "It is characterized by vomiting, constipation, thirst, general weakness, headache, fever, dizziness, double vision and dilation of the pupils. Paralysis is the usual cause of death."

The National Security Council is now in the final stages of a review of the United States' chemical-biological warfare policies. An interagency staff report has been prepared on chemical-biological warfare, and the report is currently being discussed by high officials of the Pentagon, State Department, Arms Control and Disarmament Agency and other agencies.

President Nixon plans to meet with the National Security Council in early November to consider the issue and to try to formulate a chemical-biological warfare policy.

Plea to Tax Churches Weighed by Top Court

Suit Cites Ban on Aid To Religion

WASHINGTON, Nov. 19 (AP). —The Supreme Court considered Wednesday a plea that it reverse a practice as old as the nation and expose churches and synagogues to real estate taxes.

Edward J. Ennis, American Civil Liberties Union lawyer, presented the proposition that he said was "so obvious it is hard to expand upon"—that tax exemption is an aid to religion banned by the First Amendment.

BILL OF RIGHTS

Speaking for Frederick Walz, an almost recluse lawyer who owns a small lot on Staten Island, N.Y., the white-haired civil liberties lawyer said "the plain words, the first ten words of the Bill of Rights" make tax exemptions for property used entirely for religious purposes unconstitutional.

Only "the great political power of the religious organizations of this country," Ennis said, has permitted tax exemption in the face of the First Amendment's command that "Congress shall make no law respecting an establishment of religion."

VALUE OF RELIGION

But J. Lee Rankin, corporation counsel of New York City, argued in response that the tax exemptions are "recognition of the value of religion in sustaining this country."

Legislatures, he said, have the power to decide which groups shall pay taxes, and there is no constitutional reason why churches should be separated from other "charitable" organizations that are also exempted.

Rankin, a former U.S. solicitor general, contended that across-the-board t a x exemptions for all religious groups keeps government "neutral" in religious matters.

VALUE OF PROPERTY

Should the states be required to tax the churches, he said,

VIRUS IS PROPOSED FOR A BIRTH CURB

DURHAM, N. H. (AP) — A University of New Hampshire botanist says that all women could be sterilized by an airborne virus, and those who wanted to have children could then receive an antidote.

Dr. Richard W. Schreiber says that the virus and antidote could be developed in three years at a cost of $5-million.

He said his system would require married couples to "make a human decision" to have a family, reversing the present approach that requires them to "work not to have children."

The antidote would be administered by injection and would be good for six months or less, he said.

Dr. Schreiber asserted that his system was justified by trends that show man is "fatally close to breeding himself out of existence."

Explanation Of Terms Used In This Book

Antichrist

A name taken from I and II John. In Daniel he is referred to as the little horn and the vile person; In II Thessalonians as the Son of Perdition; and in Revelation as the Beast out of the sea.

Satan so completely possesses the man as to amount almost to an incarnation. Scriptures appear to indicate that he, as Judas Iscariot, will become indwelt by Satan.

Antichrist will oppose Christ, the saints, and the Jews. He will be first hailed as a Man of Peace and given unlimited power by the European countries, the United States and Israel. At his rise, Antichrist will be only a man, but with satanic power. His sudden, sensational rise as the saviour of a world threatened by destruction will mark the beginning of the Time of the End.

His later attempt to annihilate the Jews will bring about his defeat at Jerusalem by the return of Christ. All prophecy up to the return of Christ will be fulfilled in his day.

The False Prophet

Antichrist will be the political ruler who will work the works of Satan. *The False Prophet* will be the religious ruler who will undergird the work of the *Antichrist*. Both get their power from Satan.

The False Prophet never will attempt to promote himself. He will never become an object of worship. He will do the work of a prophet in that he directs

22

attention away from himself to one who he says has the right to be worshipped (the Antichrist).

The False Prophet will imitate many miracles of God. He will cause fire to come down from heaven imitating the miracles of Elijah in order to convince the nation Israel that he (The False Prophet) is the Elijah whom Malachi promised was yet to come! Having achieved this deception the False Prophet will declare that since this miracle (bringing fire from heaven) shows that he is Elijah . . . then, therefore, the Antichrist is truly Christ and should be worshipped.

He will also build a statue, and through some satanic miracle cause this statue (image) to talk and somehow come to life. When the people see this miracle they will fall down and worship the Antichrist believing him to be Christ.

Mark of the Beast

During the second half of the seven year Tribulation Period the Antichrist (who previously was setting himself up as a Man of Peace) will suddenly move against the Jews and all those who have accepted Christ as Saviour during the first 3½ years of this Period. In Revelation 13:16, 17 we read that ". . . he (False Prophet) causeth all, both small and great, rich and poor, free and bond, to receive some mark in their right hand, or in their foreheads: And that no man might buy or sell, save he that had the mark . . . "

Therefore those who refuse to submit to the authority of this system by having this mark (the Mark of the Beast), either starve to death slowly, or else are slain by the representatives of the government, who will treat as traitors all who refuse to accept this identifying mark.

Rapture

This refers to the time, prior to the start of the 7 year Tribulation Period, when believing Christians (both dead and alive) will "in the twinkling of an eye" rise up to meet Christ in the air.

" . . . if we believe that Jesus died and rose again, even so them also which sleep in Jesus will God bring with Him. For this we say unto you by the word of the Lord, that we which are alive and remain unto the coming of the Lord shall not precede them which are asleep.

For the Lord himself shall descend from Heaven with a shout . . . and the dead in Christ shall rise first: Then we which are alive and remain shall be caught up (RAPTURE) together with them in the clouds, to meet the Lord in the air: and so shall we ever be with the Lord" (I Thessalonians 4:14-17).

Second Coming of Christ

This is one of the most prominent doctrines in the Bible. In the New Testament alone it is referred to over 300 times. His First Coming was over 1900 years ago when He came on earth to save man from sin. The Second Coming is an event starting at the Rapture and comprehending four phases: *First,* at the Rapture Christ takes the believers out of this world to be with Him (I Thessalonians 4). *Second* Christ pours out His judgments on the world during the 7 year Tribulation Period. *Third,* Christ at the end of the 7 year Tribulation destroys the Antichrist and his wicked followers (Revelation 19). *Fourth,* Christ sets up His millennial Kingdom prophesied so often in the Old Testament.

IN EXPLANATION

1. "NOW IS THE DAY OF SALVATION" and no one should wait. The Bible does not encourage anyone to wait. Nevertheless, some disobediently do wait, and by God's grace get saved on the next day—or week—or year. This in no way detracts from God's command that all should turn to Him today. "Now is the Day of Salvation" (2 Corinthians 6:2), for the Scriptures make it clear that our life is like a vapor that vanishes away and for us tomorrow may never come (James 4:13-15).

2. A "Second Chance"? We deny that there is any "Second Chance" after death. Death, then the judgment. After Armageddon, at the Judgment of Matthew 25:31-46—when all the surviving people of the world (alive after the Tribulation) are gathered, there is no hint of a "second chance."

   At the Judgment of the Great White Throne, after the Millennium (Revelation 20), there is no Second Chance.

   However, after the Rapture (1 Thessalonians 4:13-18), those who are *not* taken up with Jesus are *still* alive on earth. They live into the awful Tribulation years—and many who live into this period will indeed turn to Christ (Revelation 7:13-14*).

   The vast majority of those who live past the Rapture will follow the Antichrist and *remain* lost (Revelation 13:7-8).

   Those, however, who do turn to Christ at this time will be saved (Revelation 7).

   No "Second Chance"—as long as you live you are still on that "First Chance."

*The Greek of Revelation 7:14 says that these have come out of "the Great Tribulation." Although not reflected in the King James Version translation, the definite article "the" is present in the Greek text.

When the Rapture of the believers occurs—this will usher in the seven years which are called the Tribulation.

In 2 Thessalonians 2:11 we read: "And for this cause God shall send them strong delusion, that they should believe a lie."

In this way, God will permit a person to rule on this earth who will promise and work miracles and wonders in his day.

This will be so convincing that people will think that he is a true world saviour and will actually be believing a lie.

Understanding the above, you will be better able to understand this book, which written in novel form, attempts to show what may occur when the saints of Christ rise.

Chapter 1

I Saw The Saints Rise

Bill and I had just finished covering the Presidential conventions. And it was with a sigh of relief that we boarded our flight in Chicago bound for the West Coast.

It seemed as though not a day passed without a major news event and my job as a reporter on the Los Angeles Times kept me running in circles.

There was always some cleric spouting words of peace and some "funny people" sitting on top of mountains waiting for the destruction of the world.

One thing I hoped for and that was that my wife would leave me alone and quit pestering me to attend church on Sunday. It was my only day of peace . . . and I needed a rest after those two political conventions.

As my eyes closed in a half sleep I could still hear her saying, "George, come on, get up out of bed and come to Church with the children and me." And I would just turn over and say, "Helen, leave me alone in peace, I see enough hypocrites throughout the week."

27

And she would always reply, "Alright, George, I'll leave you alone. There's a Bible by your bed and the bookmark's at I Corinthians chapter 15. Please read it and I'll see you at the Rapture."

That Helen could be a comic sometimes . . . I thought . . . half asleep . . . why is it every Sunday she had to hand me that same line . . . "I'll see you at the Rapture"? Did she really believe that stuff?

As our plane soared into the heavens and the sunlight came breaking through I glanced out over the fluffy white clouds below, stretched out in my seat, and while I slowly sipped a cocktail I mused to myself . . . Rapture . . . what a fairy tale. Why as a reporter I knew the world was getting better and better . . . new advances in technology . . . heart transplants an every day occurrence . . . our first rocket ships had landed on the moon and there was talk of a regular commuter service. It looked like Pan American would get the first scheduled airline flights. Why people were even living longer. At the medical convention I covered just a few days ago they had unveiled their first replacement bank of human parts. I remember viewing long cases of arms, legs, hearts, livers and kidneys. Doctors were talking about the success of their cancer replacement program . . . a program that made it possible to remove cancer ridden limbs and replace them with new ones from accident victims. And for the first time a serum for arresting cancer had proved 100% effective!

In my mind . . . there was no doubt about it. This old world was on the upswing. Why even people were living longer. And there was talk of discarding old bodies and having brain transplants. This was the 21st century—not the Middle Ages. That's why I couldn't understand Helen's old fashioned concepts about God. She was one of the few I knew and her type of church was on the way out. Most churches had kept up with the times. But Helen's old church keeps singing, "The Old Rugged Cross" as though they really believed it.

I remember someone once saying . . . "in unity there is strength." And this country was sure getting unified. Helen was horrified but I was happy when I covered the United Church Fellowship in Rome. It

I know thy works, that thou art neither cold nor hot: I would thou wert cold or hot. So then because thou art lukewarm, and neither cold nor hot, I will spue thee out of my mouth. (Revelation 3:15,16).

was an historic occasion. Two very important things happened. The Protestants finally acquiesed on some silly old notions they had held on to and united with the Catholic church. And that's the way it should be. They now call it the CHURCH OF THE WORLD. Their theme was "Heaven on Earth for the World." It was a marvelous banner and a real thrill to see all the Protestant denomination leaders and all the Catholic leaders join hands on the platform singing their newly written hymn as the congregation of over 5000 clergy joined in . . .

> Praise God from whom all blessings flow
> God's in His heaven on earth below
> Let men unite, cast out all fears
> For heaven is earth for endless years!

It was a catchy tune and set the pace for the entire convention . . . and that tune spread like wildfire all over the world. Even the President adopted it as the official United States hymn in the interest of world-wide harmony. It was a brilliant gesture on his part!

The second great thing that happened at the United Church Fellowship in Rome was the election of a new world leader. And in one of the major news events of the year . . . the Pope relinquished his position so a prominent statesman in the United States could be elected honorary leader of the CHURCH OF THE WORLD. Brother Barthomolew was a dark horse. He seemed to rise up from nowhere . . . and I can't describe it . . . it was like magnetism. He had resolved the Arab-Israeli conflict and gave the Jews peace. And it was he who had almost single handedly stopped the war in China. The United States had been fighting them for 5 years and it seemed like another Vietnam. Russia was just about ready to step in on the side of China. Brother Bartholomew secretly flew into China . . . and from what I heard miraculously cured Leader Chou from almost certain death. He walked unharmed through Shanghai. Some even said that he had given sight to the blind, hearing to the deaf and made crippled men walk straight.

And in the latter time of their Kingdom, when the transgressors are come to the full, a King of Fierce countenance, and understanding dark sentences, shall stand up. And his power shall be mighty, but not by his own power: and he shall destroy wonderfully, and shall prosper . . . (Daniel 8: 23,24).

China had never seen anything like it. And when he returned to the United States with a peace proposal in his hand — the Americans loved him — he could have asked for anything and got it!

And he did ask . . . and he did get it!

That's the only thing that bothers me. He seems so powerful . . . and yet as I've interviewed him . . . he seems so kind . . . so considerate . . . so dedicated to world peace which he says can only come about through a one world government.

Perhaps he may be right. Anyway he was kind enough to give me the exclusive story about his part in forming the Federated States of Europe and how he convinced our President to join the organization.

With that, the stewardess asked if I wanted another cocktail. I said no . . . which reminded me of dear old Helen again. To her drinking was a sin. How can it be a sin . . . I reminded her . . . when the cocktail lounge at the United Church Fellowship Building in Rome was filled with high clerics all drinking. And all she would say was . . . "You'll see, George . . . just you wait . . . they're tools of the Devil."

How ridiculous I thought . . . but why argue with my wife.

It was then . . . as I was half daydreaming . . . that Bill asked me a funny question . . .

"George, do you believe in flying saucers?"

"In this modern day and age, Bill, do you still believe those fairy tales?"

Then we which are alive and remain shall be caught up together with them in the clouds, to meet the Lord in the air: and so shall we ever be with the Lord. (I Thessalonians 4:17).

"Well, not really, but I've never seen the heavens look so funny. Look way over there at that unusual formation of clouds."

"Bill, why don't you take a drink . . . maybe you'll see some more clouds!"

With that I left him to his cloud watching and I went back to my half-dozing day dreaming.

Brother Bartholomew was a man of action. And the people loved him. Our war with China, which he stopped, had seen over 250,000 of our prime young men killed in action. Oh . . . we killed over 2 million Chinese . . . but that seemed like a drop in the bucket.

So it was a real tribute to him and the United States when he was elected Honorary Leader of the CHURCH OF THE WORLD. The people were grateful. And the President in deference to his abilities had summoned us to the White House to make an announcement "of great import to the peace of the world."

I'll never forget that announcement as over 1000 reporters stood on the White House lawn on a warm, sunny day. The President was all smiles. Next to him was Brother Bartholomew. TV cameras were everywhere. This was the first time the WORLD NETWORK OF TELEVISION was telecasting. This was a new network that Brother Bartholomew had brought about. It was his belief that if all news media could be controlled to send out GOOD, then *evil* would not prevail and the world would understand each other and get better and better.

Now, why hadn't I thought of that idea? So far the Federated States of Europe had joined the WORLD NETWORK as well as the United States, Canada and South America.

And now the President was speaking:

> Ladies and Gentlemen . . . all of you know how hard I have worked for world peace. But there comes one far better than I who has achieved that which I thought would never be possible. The Bible tells us that faith can remove mountains. And with us today is one who I firmly believe is God's man for this hour—a Saint on earth—Brother Bartholomew. Through his good works he has demonstrated that he truly can remove mountains. I am happy to announce to you today that Brother Bartholomew has convinced both Russia and China to join the WORLD NETWORK of television and to work for mutual understanding of all nations. Because of his work in China in ending their war and because I feel that the leaders of the world tomorrow will be leaders in God's church I am directing to be built within the year a new 50 story WORLD CHURCH HEADQUARTERS building in the heart of Washington, D.C. on the Capitol grounds.

This was the most sensational news of the year! And the reporters scampered to their phones!

This convinced me that the world was getting better and better every day. I was going to really give it to Helen . . . tell her all about this fantastic new development . . . about world leaders finally recognizing God and asking a holy man to be the leader of the country . . . for the world. This was really heaven on earth . . . and I was witnessing it.

> And for this cause God shall send them strong delusion, that they should believe a lie. (2 Thessalonians 2:11).

But I knew it—that day I rushed home to tell Helen the news first hand—you would think she would have been thrilled. Instead she just sat down on the couch and cried and kept repeating to me, "George, you just don't understand, you just don't understand. This is the beginning of the END!"

And I must confess, I didn't understand. How could anyone understand her and her Bible . . . especially Revelation with its trumpets and seals and horsemen . . . what a fairy tale!

How glad I was to be in on all this momentous news as it was happening—great advances in medicine, a cure for cancer, a united world church, a world leader appointed right from the United States and now a world church headquarters right in Washington, D.C.

Brother Bartholomew had confided to a few of us what his next project was and it seemed unbelievable . . . for no one thought that the Jews in Israel would ever find peace. They were constantly harrassed by enemies all around them. Russia threatened to bring their massive armies down and even their horsemen and swallow them up. It was like the perils of Egypt all over again. But over the doorway to Brother Bartholomew's office was something that was symbolic of his whole leadership.

> WORLD PEACE IS HEAVEN . . .
> WHERE PEACE ABIDES
> HEAVEN IS THERE ALSO

The turmoil of Israel was threatening world peace. And the Presidential conventions conveyed this element of unrest. It seemed that there was no suitable candidate in either party. Both parties appeared deadlocked.

Vote after vote was taken but no standard bearer was chosen. And then I remembered that grand old white haired man stand up at the Republican convention and given a standing ovation. He was one of the former leaders of the Presbyterian Church who was instrumental in bringing his church into the CHURCH OF THE WORLD at the Rome meetings.

> "Gentlemen," he said, "It is evident that when man proposes, God disposes. I have watched man after man propose a leader for your party and for the Democratic party . . . and man has not succeeded.

May I be so bold to suggest that now God should have his way. Let's have a new UNITED CONVENTION of Democrats and Republicans and let's give God a chance. I move that we so do, and elect Brother Bartholomew as our DUAL representative as PRESIDENT of the United States and HONORARY HEAD of THE CHURCH OF THE WORLD!"

I'll never forget that day. The delegates went wild with excitement. And I was amazed as I watched them join hands and circle the auditorium singing ". . . let men unite, cast out all fears . . . for heaven is earth for endless years." And now that convention was over. Brother Bartholomew was elected unanimously. And I was going home. I almost missed the plane. These new supersonic jets carry 1000 people but I was the last one to get a seat. I was happy I had made the late afternoon flight. I would be home shortly. And I had a lot to tell Helen!

Just then Bill shouted excitedly, "George look out that window . . . I tell you that's not just a cloud. I've never seen the sky so funny looking. It's as though it was opening up . . . **And there shall be signs in the sun, and in the moon, and in the stars; and upon the earth distress of nations, with perplexity; the sea and the waves roaring. (Luke 21:25)**
George IT IS OPENING UP . . . PEELING BACK LIKE A SCROLL . . . George what's happening?"

He was shouting now . . . and I felt embarrassed. But I looked around and everyone in the plane was standing up and pointing with excitement. And then it happened . . . Almost like a twinkling of an eye. **In a moment, in the twinkling of an eye . . . the dead shall be changed. (I Corinthians 15:52).**

It seemed like the plane got much lighter . . . turned abruptly and went into a dive from 80,000 feet high.

I lost consciousness . . . I don't remember exactly what happened. There had been two stewardesses standing next to me; but when I awoke only one was there! **Then shall two be in the field; the one shall be taken, and the other left. Two women shall be grinding at the mill; the one shall be taken, and the other left. (Matthew 24: 40,41).**

I picked her up off the floor and she rushed to the pilot's cabin. When she came out she was ashen white . . . and put her hand to her mouth to hold a scream.

Just then the intercom came on and we heard a voice . . .

"Ladies and Gentlemen . . . something rather unusual has happened. We are not sure what . . . but please be calm . . . everything is under control. Our pilot has vanished . . . perhaps some mysterious celestial illness. This caused the abrupt dive . . . but your co-pilot now has full control of the aircraft. Please keep your seatbelts fastened."

Why should that make the stewardess shout with fear . . . I wondered . . . and then I looked around me and she pointed with trembling hands . . .

"LOOK . . .," she screamed, "HALF OF THE PASSENGERS ARE MISSING!"

I'll never forget the chills that ran up and down my spine. HALF OF THE PASSENGERS ARE MISSING. It wasn't half . . . but it looked as though 100 or so just disappeared. And I turned to tell Bill.

BUT BILL WASN'T THERE!

And suddenly it came to me.

I WAS HERE!

When we landed, I rushed to my car. Crowds were collecting at the airport because many flights had been cancelled due to crew members not reporting for duty. I got on to the clogged highway . . . clogged with driverless cars . . . was the world going crazy? It seemed as if a multitude of sleepy drivers had all at once decided to stop no matter where they were. Most had pulled to the side of the road; but nowhere were any of these drivers to be seen. A train was half-way across a highway!

I just had to get home. Tears poured down my cheeks . . . and a cold sweat engulfed me.

I drove up the drive. Thank God, Helen's car was still there. She was home.

I rushed in the door and shouted, Honey I'm home . . . are you alright?"

No answer.

Again I shouted, "Helen, where are you? I'm home! Where are the children?"

No answer.

Frantically, I ran through every room shouting, "Helen, Helen!"

And my own voice came echoing back through the empty halls!

And then a voice of the past seemed to echo in my mind . . . "Alright, George, I'll leave you alone. There's a Bible by your bed and the bookmark's at I Corinthians, chapter 15. Please read it and I'll see you at the Rapture."

For the Lord Himself shall descend from heaven with a shout, with the voice of the archangel, and with the trump of God: and the dead in Christ shall rise first: Then we which are alive and remain shall be caught up together with them in the clouds, to meet the Lord in the air: and so shall we ever be with the Lord. (I Thessalonians 4: 16,17).

"THE RAPTURE! That's it! This is the RAPTURE!

And my Helen and my children are gone!"

Quickly I ran into the bedroom and there it was—the Bible was still on the bedstand. I hurriedly opened it at the place of the bookmark.

Hurry, read, hurry, read. I must hurry. Why can't I read? The tears were flowing down my face. My eyes were so filled that the print seemed blurred . . . but I had to read what it said. Time was so precious. Why didn't I read this book before . . . when there was so much time. Why? Why?

Finally my eyes focused through the tears . . . and I read . . . I Corinthians 15:52,53.

"Behold, I show you a mystery; We shall not all sleep, but we shall be changed.

In a moment, in the twinkling of an eye, at the last trump; for the trumpet shall sound, and the dead

I got on to the clogged highway...clogged with driverless cars...was the world going crazy?...A train was halfway across a highway!

shall be raised incorruptible, and we shall be changed . . . . "

It must be true! It must be true! Everything Helen said must be true! That Bible . . . that talk about accepting Jesus Christ as personal Saviour . . . that talk of Christ dying on the cross for our sins . . . to give us eternal life . . . that talk of the Tribulation period. ALL OF IT MUST BE TRUE! I was hysterical, sobbing, kissing the picture of Helen. Then the phone rang!

That jangled, harsh ring jarred me from my hysteria. With a crying voice I answered it . . .

"Hello," I said.

"Hello, is this George?"

"Yes."

"George, this is Tom Malone at WORLD NETWORK TELEVISION. Brother Bartholomew has called a news conference for tomorrow in CHURCH OF THE WORLD Headquarters in Washington. He has some important peace moves to discuss and also will explain this weird disappearance of some heretics. I want you to be there to cover the story for us."

"OK, Tom I'll be there. Goodbye."

And with a sigh of relief, I hung up.

The world was getting better and better. This so called Rapture must be a hoax. Why did I let myself get excited? This was God's way of punishing those who did not unite in a world church—that's why Helen disappeared and her following.

WHERE PEACE ABIDES . . .
HEAVEN IS THERE ALSO!   Revelation
Chapter 17

World peace was just around the corner.

I had many questions to ask Brother Bartholomew tomorrow.

But Brother Bartholomew would have the answers!

And that's all that mattered!   2 Thessalonians 2:1-12

Chapter 2

The Great Reassurance

The last rays of sunlight were painting a fantasy of beauty as they hit the earth.

But as I drove to the airport those rays revealed the ugliness of the world...and the sudden shock of the recent disaster. I passed a car still aflame and a woman in apparent distress running for her life.

Was this all a bad dream? Would I awaken and find that everything was back to normal?

When I arrived at the airport I was soon brought face to face with the reality of it all. People were running around in a state of confusion. It was impossible to park in the airport parking lot so I swung my car to the side of the road and walked to the main entrance of the terminal.

As I entered the terminal I could hear the public address system blaring over and over again the news. It's funny how politely they couch their words as though today's disaster was just a temporary inconvenience.

I passed a car still aflame and a woman in apparent distress running for her life.

MAY WE HAVE YOUR ATTENTION, PLEASE! BECAUSE OF CURRENT CONDITIONS, ALL FLIGHTS ARE TEMPORARILY CANCELLED. NEW SCHEDULES WILL BE POSTED JUST AS QUICKLY AS POSSIBLE. PLEASE RETURN TO YOUR HOMES AND TUNE IN TO YOUR EMERGENCY RADIO FREQUENCY BAND FOR FURTHER INFORMATION.

I groaned when I heard the words, "ALL FLIGHTS ARE TEMPORARILY CANCELLED." But then I heard my name being called.

GEORGE OMEGA PLEASE REPORT TO AMERICAN AIRLINES TICKET COUNTER

Quickly I pushed my way through the crowd. The sea of faces seemed hostile to me as if to say, "Who was I...someone special?"

Hopefully, and yet in my heart I knew there was no hope, I looked for Helen, my wife, and my two children, Sue and Tommy.

But all the faces were strange to me...and quite dejectedly I finally reached the ticket counter.

"Hello, my name's Omega. You called me on the intercom."

"Yes, Mr. Omega, we had a call from Washington to clear you for immediate passage. Right from the top man...Brother Bartholomew himself. You must be pretty important. Anyway, the plane is on the runway. Take ramp 6. It's a special emergency flight."

"Fine. Thanks a lot," I replied, "but how will I know which plane?"

"Can't miss it, Mr. Omega, just look for the number on the tail. It's number 666!"

For some reason, I don't know why...but a chill went up and down my spine. What was it that disturbed me? There was something odd about that number but somehow I just couldn't place it. Was my imagination playing tricks on me? It had been a long hard day...so I chalked it up to overstrain and hurried towards the gate.

As the jet soared into the heavens I could see the patchwork of destruction down below. It was as though someone had tipped a stack of dominoes...as we used to do when we were kids. Everything seemed in a state of confusion. Turnpikes were clogged with autos that seemed to merge together into one welded mass. Nothing moved. What little farm land there was appeared overrun with cars trying to reach their destination.

The sun was slipping slowly over the horizon now and the shades of darkness seemed to carry a message of impending doom.

I was never one for extra sensory perception...but somehow I felt like I was standing at the brink of a large chasm... and I was to have a front row seat in history's holocaust of horrors.

The words of the ticket agent echoed through my mind... "You must be pretty important...just look for the number on the tail. It's number 666."

Funny, I never considered myself important. How I became projected into a place of prominence was because I happened to be at the right place at the right time.

It was on a trip to the Middle East. I wasn't a religious person but my wife had begged me to take her and the children to Jerusalem.

I dreaded the trip but I decided to combine business with pleasure. I left my wife and Sue and Tommy in Jerusalem while I flew to Bagdad to check up on some startling news reports...reports about a man who was performing miracles and who, they said, had no father.

Upon returning to Jerusalem I could tell that my wife was unhappy and I asked her why.

"George," she replied, "somehow the face of this nation has changed...changed so drastically that I'm afraid the Rapture might occur any minute...and you still have not accepted Christ as your personal Saviour. George, please, complete our family circle."

Little Sue gripped my hand and Tommy just looked down at his feet. I knew Tommy only did that when he was about to cry. Plaintively Sue looked up and said, "Please, daddy, please take my Jesus."

If ever I was close to making a decision for this Christ... it was then. But revealing news I had uncovered in Bagdad cast more doubts on Helen's religion...as far as I was concerned.

"Look, Helen, I appreciate your concern and the kids, too. But I've just discovered some things that change the whole picture. Just be patient. By the way, what makes you think this Rapture is so close?"

Helen looked at me with tears in her eyes as she told how the face of the Holy Land had drastically changed. The once quiet hills of Judea were now covered with ugly concrete apartment houses hastily erected to make homes for the flood of Jews. Bethlehem was a thriving industrial town belching smoke from automobile and ammunition factories. Smog covered the once familiar scene of the Shepherd's field where the angel of the Lord came and said,"...behold, I bring you good tidings of great joy...." The kibbutz at Ein Gev was working at what seemed insurmountable odds to rid the Sea of Galilee of industrial pollutants that had killed the once famous "St. Peter's fish."

Then Helen leaned on my shoulder and sobbed, "George, even the Garden Tomb has disappeared. And do you know what's in its place? A big super 8 lane highway that starts at Tel Aviv, goes through Jerusalem and ends at Haifa. All that's left is a little marker on the side of the road that says, 'Here once was a Tomb where some Christians believed their Christ was buried.'"

A jolting air pocket awakened me from my sleep of memory. How I wish I could relive those days with Helen in Jerusalem. But it was too late. Soon I would again meet Brother Bartholomew. I had confidence in him. Many had asked me what he looked like. To me he looks like a prophet. In him there is no hypocrisy, and his followers love him. Tall, well shaped, his hair is not too long, just long enough to portray that fatherly appeal...that appeal of confidence. His eyes are bright blue, crystal clear. I have seen him laugh. I have seen him weep. And to me his extraordinary attractiveness and divine perfections surpass the children of men in every sense. He is most eloquent. And if there was such a thing as divine...this man Brother Bartholomew is divine!

The landing in Washington was uneventful...that is, until I stepped out and seemed swarmed over by a bunch of reporters and photographers. How odd, I remember thinking, why me? I am a reporter. Why would anyone want my picture?

One of my photographer friends caught my eye, "Hey, George, look this way. I need a good shot for my paper."

"What's the big event, fellas?" I'm not important. Is this a joke?"

With that Tom Malone grabbed my arm. He was an important cog in the WORLD NETWORK TELEVISION conglomerate.

"Tom, what gives and why all this publicity?"

"I'm sorry, George, you weren't informed earlier...and I can't tell you yet, but Brother Bartholomew has some big plans for you...that's why you're in the spotlight. Right now we have to rush to the TV station. BB is having a nationwide ON THE AIR press conference."

"BB, who is that?"

"BB...that's our short nickname for BROTHER BARTHOLOMEW...but don't ever use it in his presence. It offends him. With his plans he will have to be some sort of god!"

THE PRESS CONFERENCE

The TV studio was huge. In fact it was the biggest one in the world. There were 6 tiers of cushioned seats curved in a semi-circle so everyone had a front row view of the speaker. This intimate arrangement seated 666 people. The first rows were reserved for Brother Bartholomew's cabinet and a select number of reporters and photographers. Special microphones were worn at the lapel of each reporter. The room was entirely dark...except for one spotlight that focused on Brother Bartholomew.

As I entered the studio I sensed the quiet, reverent hush. The thick carpeted rugs cushioned my footsteps. An usher led me to the front row and he quickly adjusted a microphone to my lapel. A glint of recognition seemed to come from the face of Brother Bartholomew.

Suddenly the red ON THE AIR sign blinked away the darkness and the announcer broke the silence while a world listened.

LADIES AND GENTLEMEN, THE PRESIDENT OF THE UNITED STATES

As though he had the situation well under control Brother Bartholomew started speaking. I had often said that if

bullets were flying all around him and if his boat were sinking, Brother Bartholomew could speak one word and the bullets would cease...he could take one step and walk on water. There was something special about this man...something that demanded respect and inspired confidence. His voice broke my thoughts...

GOOD EVENING AMERICA and the WORLD! This is a night to remember.
To some it may be a night of confusion,
a night of disaster
a night of despair
But it is none of these.
No this night,
Tonight
IS A NIGHT OF DESTINY
And because I want you to know all of the facts I have decided against a prepared text. Instead I have selected 6 of America's best reporters to question me on today's events...events known by some as RAPTURE...but which were indeed phenomena easily explained.

The announcer then said, "Thank you, Mr. President. Our first question is from George Omega."

I was shocked. No one had prepared me for this. This certainly was going to be unrehearsed. What would I ask? Certainly I couldn't jeopardize my career now. My remarks would be seen by hundreds of millions across the world. Hesitatingly I stood up and in my mind I framed a question, then spoke: "Sir, all of us must agree that something most unusual happened today. People have just seemed to disappear. My wife..." I couldn't go on. My voice choked up. Brother Bartholomew intervened and broke the embarrassing silence:

> *Friends,* I told you this would be unrehearsed. George Omega is a trusted advisor to me. I value his guidance. What he is trying to say is that in this rapture occurrence his wife and two children have disappeared. I have already instituted a search for them. It would seem the Darts of Satan would attempt anything to undermine the quest for peace...even to strike at a wife and two tender little children. But, George, rest at ease, we will not fail.

It was as though Brother Bartholomew was making a holy command. His voice had a reassuring ring as he proceeded to answer my question.

> Friends of the World. Yes, even BROTHERS OF THE WORLD, for in this time of need, all of us must be BROTHERS. It would seem from time immemorial people have been telling us the sky is falling. But has it fallen yet? Of course not. Remember in June 1969 when the San Francisco CHRONICLE reported that a planet was about to hit the earth. That was 31 years ago. Did it occur? Of course not. And in December 1943 Edgar Cayce predicted Atlantis would rise again. Has anyone seen Atlantis?

The audience laughed.

> Cayce said Japan would go into the sea; New York City would disappear. But these events have not

occurred! We must emulate Alexander the Great. An eclipse of the sun occurred just as Alexander was preparing to engage in a major battle. The event spread panic among his troops. Alexander was a man of courage. To him the eclipse was not an omen of doom but a benediction of blessing. He inspired his army to go on. The next day he won a smashing victory over his enemies. I ask you this one question...if this so-called RAPTURE occurred, why are our outstanding clergy still here? Bishop Arthur has just arrived from Europe. Brother Arthur, please stand up and tell us what you have discussed with me.

Bishop Arthur stood up. I had heard about him, but had never met this man who Brother Bartholomew respected. I understood he was a cleric who came from France. Some referred to him as the progressive cleric. He had a godly appearance, seemed humble, yet had piercing eyes that commanded attention.

Beware of false prophets, which come to you in sheep's clothing, but inwardly they are ravening wolves. (Matthew 7:15).

Thank you Brother Bartholomew. May I first say the world has always had its "Chicken Littles" to cackle and crow about the sky falling down on our heads.

But may I remind you of I Corinthians 10:13 which tells us: "There hath no temptation taken you but such as is common to man: but God is faithful, who will not suffer you to be tempted above that ye are able; but will with the temptation also make a way to escape, that ye may be able to bear it."

And the next verse, my friends, is most important! "Wherefore, my dearly beloved, flee from idolatry."

The audience was spellbound as Bishop Arthur continued:

The event you witnessed today which some call the RAPTURE is simply a temptation. But God is telling us here that He is faithful and He will make a way to escape. We are also told that those who believed this heretical doctrine of the RAPTURE are idolators. Why the word RAPTURE does not even appear in Scripture. And I have quoted these verses from the beloved original King James Version of the Bible. This is not a new version, my friends. Putting aside faith, would it not seem strange to you that if there were such an event as the RAPTURE, that we clergy who are closest to God and have the mind of God would STILL BE HERE ON EARTH? The fact is WE ARE HERE. And every outstanding clergyman is *here*. WE HAVE NOT DISAPPEARED. The disappearance of many seems to be a biological secret that we cannot at this moment yet explain. But in due time, it will be revealed. But this much I can tell you, God has allowed these events to occur for a purpose. RIGHT NOW, those of you who have a Bible, turn to Revelation 1:7. It reads:

Behold, he cometh with clouds and every eye shall see Him.

There is no doubt we are living in a day of clouds. And right now every eye, through the scientific miracle of our TV space stations, is witnessing a most momentous event.

QUICKLY NOW, read verse 16:

And he had in his right hand seven stars...

And his countenance was as the sun shineth in his strength.

LOOK NOW AT BROTHER BARTHOLOMEW. LOOK AT HIS RIGHT HAND!

There was an audible gasp in that huge auditorium. All eyes focused at the spiral of light that shone on Brother Bartholomew. Slowly a smile came across his face. No one had noticed it before. But in his right hand was a shining gold septer. And emblazoned in diamonds was a cluster of stars.

The air was electric.

Slowly Brother Bartholomew arose and waved the scepter as if to impart a blessing on the audience. The reflecting light from the diamonds seemed to cast a halo around his head.

I am come in my Father's name, and ye receive me not: if another shall come in his own name, him ye will receive. (John 5:43).

And somehow I knew no further explanation of today's event was needed. We were standing in the presence of God's messenger.

The silence was broken by the click of heels as the smartly dressed U.S. Marine Band snapped to attention and broke into the martial strains of HAIL TO THE CHIEF.

It had been a hard day. Emotionally I was wrung out and drip dried. Bed was a welcome sight and soon the day's events faded into slumberland.

I awoke to the sound of church bells. It must be Sunday. For once I planned to attend the National Cathedral in Washington. After breakfast I hopped a cab and within a few minutes was at this imposing entrance.

A guard stopped me.

"May I have your ticket, please?"

"Ticket for what?" I asked.

"I'm sorry, sir, you may not understand," he replied. "National Cathedral, as is the case with many churches, is now a museum of living history. Six months ago Brother Bartholomew proposed this wonderful opportunity at the suggestion of Bishop Arthur."

Then it all came back to me. Of course, how could I be so forgetful? I purchased a ticket and entered.

There were many displays, some enclosed in glass, other set in a scenic panorama. They captured history and events as they were in 1969 and 1970. This was now the year 2000 and the last 30 years had seen some very radical changes. That's why Bishop Arthur thought it wise to use the mostly empty churches for a worthwhile cause.

A crowd was gathered in the area the National Cathedral pulpit once stood. I later learned this one exhibit was among the most popular. For it was an exhibit of something that now was almost non-existent.

It is called THE LIVING TREE exhibit. It is one of the last remaining trees in the world. It looks rather small and frail and leaves have an autumn appearance. In the background a painted mural of a forest shows the visitor how the tree once looked in its natural environment before the pollution disaster that almost wiped out all vegetation from the earth.

A wise scientist, seeing the handwriting on the wall, had carefully placed this tree in a germ and pollution-free environment for posterity.

Suddenly my heart leaped forward!

Could I believe my eyes?

Was it all a dream? The rapture couldn't have occurred. There looking at the LIVING TREE was Helen...there was little Sue and Tommy. I was sure it was them.

Tears welled up in my eyes. I cried out...HELEN, HELEN ...but I was so overcome, only an awkward sound came out. SUE...TOMMY...YOU'RE HERE! THANK GOD YOU'RE SAFE.

Quickly I pushed my way through the crowd. The puzzled looks on their faces didn't disturb me. Suddenly the path was wide open. They were still looking at the LIVING TREE.

HELEN! SUE! TOM! I shouted.

The family turned.

And to me it seemed like the bottom of the world collapsed as I dropped my head in unbelief.

For the faces I saw were not Helen, not Sue, not Tom. The silhouettes were close resemblances. But these were people I did not know.

I felt a tap on my shoulders as I half knelt on the floor. I turned and saw a hand with a scepter...a scepter with six, sparkling stars...and I arose...and followed.

Was it all a dream? The rapture couldn't have occurred. There looking at the LIVING TREE was Helen...there was little Sue and Tommy. I was sure it was them.

Chapter 3

The Sinister Plot

Brother Bartholomew was a man of compassion. He understood my grief and disappointment at the Living Tree exhibit.

Half in tears my voice cracked as I said to him, "Sir, I don't know how I can go on!"

"I understand, George," he replied softly, "it reminds me of the philosophical clock which spent great time meditating upon its future. It reasoned that it had to tick twice each second, 120 times each minute or 7200 times every hour - in 24 hours, 172,800 ticks. This meant 63,072,000 times every year, calculated the clock. And in ten years it would have to tick 630,720,000 times! At this point it collapsed from nervous exhaustion. But when it revived, it saw in a moment of insight that all it had to do was *one tick at a time.* So it began, and now, after a hundred years, it is still a respected grandfather clock. What I'm trying to say is this, George, there are perilous times ahead... but we must live one minute at a time meeting each challenge as it presents itself. Otherwise this country and the world will be lost."

The next day Brother Bartholomew summoned me to his office at the White House. I could tell there was something on his mind as I hesitatingly sat down. He seemed in deep thought and I was afraid to disturb him.

My inner fears were quickly dispelled. I looked up at Brother Bartholomew and smiled. I knew then that everything would turn out all right. The next day Brother Bartholomew summoned me to his office at the White House. I could tell there was something on his mind as I hesitatingly sat down. He seemed in deep thought and I was afraid to disturb him.

"George," he began, "I need a trusted advisor, one who can be my right arm, one who has had some touch with the Rapture problem and yet one in whom I can place complete confidence. George, I want you to be that man."

I was stunned. Me, an ordinary reporter. Why had Brother Bartholomew taken a sudden liking to me and thrust me into the place of prominence. What would this mean?

"Sir, I don't quite understand, why me?"

"Good question, George. You haven't tasted leadership. There are too many leaders in my Government with big ambitions. I need a down-to-earth individual to become my Presidential advisor. I've watched you ever since you first interviewed me in the Middle East. And somehow, I knew one day I would be relying on your assistance. I have big plans, George, very big plans . . . plans that may seem fantastic to you now. But I want you to be a part of these plans. All I can tell you now . . . is one day the whole world will know Brother Bartholomew. And humbly I want to serve my Father in Heaven."

This was what impressed me about Brother Bartholomew . . . and yet somewhat confused me . . . his constant reference to God as though he had a holy calling. And yet I must admit, it was because of this that I replied, "Yes, Mr. President, I will accept."

"Good, I knew you would."

With that he rang a buzzer and Tom Malone entered. He was no longer a television executive. Malone was now Presidential Secretary and quite efficient. While rather tall I noticed his head always dipped slightly forward. It gave him a rather apologetic appearance. It also made him not quite as tall as Brother Bartholomew. In the days to come Tom and I were to become fast friends. It would be a mistake that I would regret.

"Tom," Brother Bartholomew instructed, "summon the Mayors to my office tomorrow for an open press conference . . . all of them . . . New York City, Miami, Philadelphia, Los Angeles and Chicago . . . and, oh yes, Dallas. I want to brief George on the state of the Union as well as make public the problems we face."

Brother Bartholomew gave frequent press conferences. In private he told me that the public must always be informed on every step. It was what he called, "communication." After all, he reasoned, an informed public will accept all types of news if they know about it. It was a good way to keep down revolts and problem areas. BB must have taken a course in psychology for he understood people . . . knew how to agree yet disagree, how to quell factions and make them the best of friends. It was this type of leadership that projected him so quickly to the Presidency.

The United States was now made up of six cities. I remember the history books of the 1970's. I called it the Golden Era. Hardly any problems, a few rebellious youth, age of the mini-skirt, a small war they called the War in Vietnam, and many, many hundreds of important cities. But now with the population explosion . . . only six cities were left. What once were Indianapolis and Fort Wayne, Dayton, St. Louis and Minneapolis were now called CHICAGO. City after city had been merged into this Midwest conglomerate. The country-side was gone. These small towns were now suburbs of CHICAGO. PHILADELPHIA had swallowed up Harrisburg, Pittsburgh, Scranton and Williamsport. NEW YORK CITY extended as far north as Portland, Maine. LOS ANGELES went as far east as Denver. One patch of farm land remained. The state of Kansas was declared farm area. Topeka and Wichita were leveled to make the complete state a farm oasis. The rest of the United States was basically the six major cities.

Brother Bartholomew summoned in a group of reporters, and announced to them my appointment as his Presidential Advisor. From then on the world about me seemed to change. I was greeted everywhere with a hallowed respect. It was as though I was an advisor to god. A few reservations about this new appointment crept into my mind, but each time I would hastily dismiss them as fantasy. This was a new age and I had complete confidence in Brother Bartholomew.

The meeting the next day brought me closer to the problems of the day. As the TV cameras focused in on the meeting of city mayors the striking voice of Brother Bartholomew caught my attention.

My fellow citizens and honored mayors. We are facing a crisis in our cities today . . . a crisis of which each citizen must be aware. This informal meeting of mayors, I hope, will bring you current on these problems and what you and I can do about it. It was Sir Julian Huxley who said in 1969 that the 1980's would be a perilous time. It is now the year 2000 and it is very evident he knew what he was talking about. It took initially thousands of years to reach the first billion human beings by 1700, only 130 more years to add the second billion by 1830, 30 years to add the third billion by 1960, 15 years to add the fourth billion in 1975. And now in the year 2000 our population is almost 7 billion. To be exact 6 billion, 6 hundred and 66 thousand.

Therefore, I have asked my Presidential Advisor, George Omega, to brief you on two recent edicts we have recommended to Congress. This will be a good way for you to meet the new man in my cabinet in whom I place utmost confidence. . . George Omega.

"Thank you, Mr. President. Honorable mayors and citizens of the United States. Here are the two new laws to take effect upon confirmation by Congress:

1. TRANSPORTATION BILL
   This bill seeks to solve both   And he shall...think to change
                                     times and laws.... (Daniel 7:25).

the air pollution and transportation crisis that plagues our country. The bill recommends the abolishment of all automobiles over the next two years. Automobiles will be used after that only by members of local and national government.

2. BIRTH COUPONS
The rapid rise of population has made voluntary birth control ineffective. Passage of a bill is recommended to control births, issuing birth coupons to a limited number of eligible, healthy young adults.

These are the first of many bills Brother Bartholomew will introduce to Congress this year. Thank you, Mr. President."

And with that, I sat down, somewhat horrified at what I had read. I had not seen the script earlier. It was thrust into my hands just moments before we went on the air. While these were Brother Bartholomew's recommendations, the entire nation was looking at me. I was the one who announced the edicts. I had a lurking suspicion that it would be I who would soon become the unpopular one.

Television news was most important in these chaotic days. NBC alone was budgeting over $5 million per week for news coverage. Live color signals via satellite was costing $25,000 for the first ten minutes and $1000 for each additional minute . . . and this was reaching every city in Europe. Film crews were earning $2000 per week.

Brother Bartholomew arose and addressed the assembly of mayors. He called on the mayor of New York to present his report. The mayor, a handsome and quiet young man had the air of efficiency as he described the almost impossible conditions of his city.

"Mr. President, some still think of New York as a Dream City, but I believe a more appropriate word would be "nightmare." Three-fourths of our population is on welfare. We haven't seen the sun in weeks! New York City belches into the air 10,200 tons of sulphur dioxide, 1200 tons of dirt and 28,000 tons of carbon monoxide daily. Robberies have increased to such a proportion we have assigned civilians in each block as patrolmen with power of arrest. They also may act as jury and judge. It is our only way to combat this age of lawlessness. Our sewage plant has backed up to the point of a health disaster. Over 1300 million gallons of raw waste

This know also, that in the last days perilous times shall come.
For men shall be lovers of their own selves, covetous, boasters, proud, blasphemers, disobedient to parents, unthankful, unholy.
Without natural affection, truce-breakers, false accusers, incontinent, fierce, despisers of those that are good.
Traitors, heady, highminded lovers of pleasure more than lovers of God. (2 Timothy 3:1-4).

still pour every day into surrounding rivers and ocean. And there are over 20 million cars in New York! New York is a disaster area, Mr. President. I am afraid the next step is the Titanic lifeboats scene — every man for himself. Everybody is trying to get into their lifeboat to survive. It's everyone for himself. May I suggest a pure democracy or republic cannot work in this day and age. As much as I hate the word, we need an elective Dictatorship...a benevolent authority who will make the laws and see that they are enforced by military rule if necessary. It is our only hope for survival."

And with that the mayor of New York sat down. For a moment there was silence. All of us knew conditions were getting out of hand. Ever since a Vice President's speech 30 years ago in November, 1969, when it was implied that television media needed some type of governmental control . . . the populace was more open to acceptance of wider federal regulations. And Congress, embroiled in political favortism, simply could not act fast enough to meet the crisis of the day. Certainly something had to be done, and done quickly. Everyone knew what had to be done. But none had the courage to say it. Now it was said — so everyone not only in the United States but in all the world could hear. America was on the road to a dictatorship . . . a benign dictatorship. It was her only hope of survival. America was no longer unsinkable. Like the Titanic, it was approaching the iceberg of disaster. It must act now before an unruly population in a rush to save themselves catapult an entire nation into a chaotic revolt from which it would never recover.

As the other mayors droned on with their reports, all similar in their brink of disaster content, my mind wandered. What was this world coming to?

Could it possibly be true that we were saying goodbye to a free elective system? There seemed no other way to turn. Funny, how America grew so fast technologically, turned a virgin farmland into ugly, gasping industrial complexes . . . something like a cancerous growth that soon revolted spreading disaster wherever its tentacles reached. The 1976 World's Fair had as its theme AMERICA, LAND OF FREEDOM AND PROGRESS. And now, just 24 years later, both of these facts were to become just a bad dream. I remember my parents telling me how proud they were to sing "America The Beautiful." There were no more "fields of amber grain" nor "purple mountain majesties." The early riots of young people in the late 1960's had triggered a nation of irresponsibility. Then some thought it shocking that youth should dictate to teachers, have freedom in love and sex without marriage. Their freedom came but it became a hollow victory for they lost purpose in life and never found the utopia for which they were seeking. The sex filth I view today openly on the streets, in specially built communion booths in churches — they call it the communion of love — was simply too shocking for me to think further upon.

Now it seemed we had made full circle. Like the decline and fall of the Roman Empire we were going to be swallowed up in our own wickedness . . . unless a saviour came along. Somehow I feel, Brother Bartholomew is that saviour. How privileged I am to serve him.

The meeting was drawing to a close and the Mayor of Los Angeles was making a proposal.

"Mr. President, all of us are aware of how critical a problem our nation faces. Such a problem calls for drastic steps to be taken immediately. As mayors we have individually met with leaders in our constituency and collectively we agree that an elective dictatorship is urgent right now . . . if we are to exist. Ancient Rome elected a dictator in times of extreme urgency. It is with this same thought in mind that our mayors have been unanimous in asking that you be entrusted by Congress with dictatorial powers, subject of course, to recall by a majority vote of the 6 mayors. And to this end we have forwarded such a bill to Congress."

No one apparently was surprised. The inevitable had come. There was no other way. There just had to be a strong man if we were to survive.

And I stood upon the sand of the sea, and saw a beast rise up.... (Revelation 13:1).

Brother Bartholomew then stood up. Everyone had confidence in him. Every problem he tackled in the past he had accomplished and resolved excellently. True, not everyone could be satisfied but recent polls placed his popularity at a high 76% . . . much higher than any other President enjoyed under less chaotic circumstances. I am sure he realized this as he spoke.

Let me first say that I indeed am gratified by the confidence you have placed in me . . . and also very humbled . . . for I am a new citizen to your country.

My Middle East origins and birth were most unique and now I can see the reason for them. For this simple upbringing away from the clutter of humanity has, I believe, prepared me for my mission on earth. I do believe that I do indeed follow God's will, and under God nothing is impossible.

Suddenly the door burst open. A flushed Tom Malone rushed in with a paper in his hand, quickly mounted the podium and handed it to Brother Bartholomew. Brother Bartholomew quickly glanced at the sheet and retaining his composure continued: "I have just been handed a memo from Senator Mason who is in Congress which is now in joint session. He has advised me that Russian troops are moving in the direction of Israel. He has also assured me that Congress will quickly approve the TOTAL POWERS LAW for the Presidency."

The audience was bristling with whispers. What many had feared was already beginning to happen. Russia would no longer wait for Israel. And now powers greater than the Gulf of Tonkin resolution were about to be granted to the President of the United States. But there was no other way.

And thou shalt come up against my people of Israel, as a cloud to cover the land; it shall be in the latter days, and I will bring thee against my land, that the heathen may know me, when I shall be sanctified in thee, O Gog, before their eyes. (Ezekiel 38:16).

Brother Bartholomew spoke again: Gentlemen, after this meeting I will be ordering my Presidential Advisor, George Omega to fly to Russia with a plan for peace.

Brother Bartholomew, with steel-like composure and firmness during a crisis, continued:

But now I have another proposal which will help resolve the problems confronting our population which, despite the present emergency, I might as well announce now as planned. As wonderful as our computers are, our rising population makes it difficult to record each individual by a name plus a Social

Security number, a Medicare number, a Birth
Guarantee number and a Food allotment number. I
am therefore recommending to Congress that each individual be assigned one number. That one number
will be carried by him through life. By this one number identification system we will save billions of
dollars, be better able to control crime, offenders of
our population and food laws. At first this may seem
drastic and harsh. . .

But you have appointed me because I have resolved the problems of our day. And this is the only
way to reach the road of sensibility and peace. I am
most confident Congress will pass favorably on this
recommendation and on others that I will issue upon
receiving the TOTAL POWERS confirmation from
your elected officials. Thank you.

It was all over and I rushed over to congratulate Brother
Bartholomew, as did all the Mayors and important government officials.

Then, quite worn out, I headed for my office for a little
relaxation before lunch. On my desk was a package. It was
tied with string and falling apart. Suddenly my heart leaped.
That handwriting. I recognized it instantly. It was Helen's.
She was alive!

But then I saw the postmark . . . it was dated before that
dreadful Rapture date. It seemed as though this box had
followed me around the country and months later it had been
at last finally delivered to me here in Washington.

Quickly I tore it open. Crumpled newspapers were used
as packing. Funny, they were very old newspapers from a
little town called Tunkhannock, Pennsylvania. There was a
column titled "From our Early Files" and bits of news as
they occurred in 1908 and 1928.

1908
Rev. Wolcott, of Mehoopany, has organized a
Bible class of about 20 men. They meet in the
classroom of the M.E. Church.

Funny, how memories come back. Bible classes hadn't been held anywhere since 1975. The religious leaders felt this was a restriction of individual freedoms. The early 70's were filled with so many new versions of the Bible that soon they lost their impact on the people. It became unpopular to even have a Bible. Church leaders admonished their congregations to be more concerned about the social conditions of today than the fairy tales of yesterday. I glanced back down at the paper.

> 1928
> Several cars went through town Tuesday
> morning, occupied by members of the
> Roosevelt Highway Association going to Erie.
> The leading car was driven by a woman
> smoking a cigarette.

So that's when it all started . . . the growth of the automobile to where now it was a curse and a threat to human existence. And if those people thought a girl smoking a cigarette was an oddity those day, they should have lived today. This was the age of unisex. And somehow I was uncomfortable in it. Little did I dream two years ago that Birth Coupons would become a reality but rampant sex without marriage had overpopulated the world much quicker than biologists had earlier predicted. Cigarettes had long ago been abolished by law but the law looked favorably on a new item which resembled a cigarette but placed the user into a highly euphoric condition. Some Senators had argued however, that even though this was a drug, it was beneficial in this age of crowding and over population to have at least half of the population in a placid, half drugged attitude. As bad as the situation was it was the most acceptable way to somewhat quell what could become an insurmountable problem.

After throwing out what seemed like a boxful of paper suddenly I spotted at the very bottom a little black book. Instantly I knew what it was and quickly I glanced around the room to see that no one was looking. I reached in to lift it out . . . but then I remembered . . . all trusted advisors are also watched by a trusted TV spy system. Each room had hidden monitors. But I knew where mine was simply becuase it was in need of minor repairs. A slight beeping sound was being emitted . . . a sound normally too soft to hear. But one day soon after the Living Tree episode when I thought that I had found Helen I had knelt down at my desk to pray. No sooner had I knelt when Brother Bartholomew called me in and suggested that prayer would best be answered by faith in his ability to solve not only the problems of the world but my personal problems as well.

How did he know I was praying, I wondered. When I returned to my office I was determined to find out. And I did. The small television monitor was part of a plaque that read PRAYER CHANGES THINGS.

Quickly I grabbed the box which Helen had sent. I walked out of the office and rushed to my apartment. In the privacy of a small closet I tenderly lifted the black book. It was more than a book. It was a Bible purposely very small so it could be hidden. For they had long ago become a rarity. I knew I must at all costs hold on to it and read it. Yet I knew that doing so might later cost me my life. I had full confidence in Brother Bartholomew but somehow I felt he must not know of my find.

On the way back to the office I stopped for a quick bite of lunch. Even this had changed. No more thick, juicy steaks or corned beef sandwiches like my father had been fond of. Scarcity of land made it impossible to graze cattle and the population explosion had placed all meat at a premium. Hardly anyone could afford it at $600 a pound . . . for this represented to most a week's wages. Besides the substitute foods weren't too bad once you got used to them. Science had developed new foods from unexpected sources in the race against starvation. Worms, toads, termites and grasshoppers are now made to look and taste like ham. Special spinning processes take crude oil, mix it with bacteria to develop protein cakes. Protein cakes are chicken, steak and ham flavored. For lunch I settled on the special of the day . . . ham protein cake with french fried grasshoppers and a cup of coffee.

As I entered the office, Tom Malone stopped me.

"George, Brother Bartholomew would like to see you on that Russian announcement. And when you're through there, stop in to my office for a briefing."

With my schedule so hectic there was little time to think about Helen and my two children. And it appeared that my schedule would become even busier in the near future.

Quickly I stepped into Brother Bartholomew's office. He was looking out the window but as though he knew I was coming he said, "Hello, George, did you have a nice lunch?"

"Yes sir, thank you . . . Tom Malone said that you wanted to see me about the Russian situation."

"That's right, George, sit down."

And with that he left the window and sat behind his desk. On his desk was a plaque. It appeared like mine but as I looked at it . . . it was different for it read THINGS CHANGE PRAYER. He saw me look at it and spoke before I could ask.

"THINGS do change prayer, George. For we must be doers not only hearers. Do you recall James 1:22. It goes like this: 'Be ye doers of the word, and not hearers only.' It's in your Bible, George, the one you took home with you at lunch and opened in your closet. You see, George, I know, but don't be fearful, everyone should read God's Word. The trouble is that not many can read it with understanding. I believe if my people will pray, then things will change. And as their leader I have the power over THINGS which will CHANGE PRAYER into rejoicing."

I was stunned. How did he know I had a Bible? I must be more careful in the future. Well, anyway, he couldn't read my thoughts . . . or could he?

"Enough preaching, George, I really called you in to confirm to you that I am sending you to Moscow and to the other capitals of Europe. Premier Alexi Bazenoff is getting itchy feet over Israel and I have a personal message that may surprise him. I want you to carry that message. I've alerted Air Force One to fly you."

"Very well sir, I can go immediately. I can stop by Tom Malone's office for the briefing."

"Very good, George, but won't you want to say goodbye to Faye before you leave?"

My face turned ashen. My knees felt as though they would buckle from underneath me. Faye! How did he know? In fact in my anguish over Helen and Tommy and Sue, I had forgotten about Faye. Faye, my daughter by a previous marriage, had not been one for religious formalism. My first wife had died in a plane crash. Faye was in her teens at the time. When this tragedy occurred she went to New York to complete her studies, and then she married Bill Sanders, a rising young executive. Helen had often talked to her and to Bill about Christ but they shrugged it off with, "We'll enjoy life now . . . there's plenty of time."

Brother Bartholomew was speaking again, "Yes, George, I know about Faye and about Bill. They're safe in New York. We've located them. Why not go into Tom's office and talk to them on the Picturephone."

Quickly I ran to Tom's office. It seemed prophetical that Tom had already known, for he was dialing New York for me. Suddenly a picture came on the tube. It was Faye picking up the phone in her apartment and as I picked up the phone she saw me and in joy filled with tears she shouted: "Daddy, oh, daddy, it's so good to hear from you! Where's Mom?"

She always called Helen, Mom, because she loved her even though she wasn't her real mother. Faye said that Helen had certain spiritual qualities about her that she wished she could attain.

As best I could I explained the Rapture incident, and that since then I couldn't locate Mom or little Sue or Tommy. The conversation ended after 15 minutes with a promise we

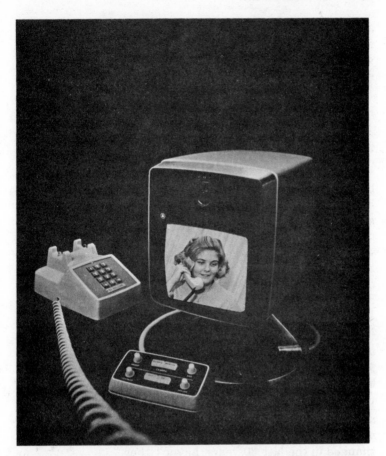

would get together for a reunion the minute I came back from Russia.

I was walking on Cloud Nine as I hung up the receiver.

I felt I was a part of life again. Not everything was gone. I still had Faye and Bill. The link had not been broken.

But as Tom Malone briefed me on my Moscow mission somehow deep within me dwelt a feeling that I was to become an instrument in a sinister plot. If I had known then what I now know I could hardly have kept on living. But the die had been cast. And I was part of the mold.

Chapter 4

Flight To Moscow

Tom Malone was to accompany me to Russia, whether as an aide or an informer, I did not know. But I was prepared for any event and decided that caution on my part was the better part of valor.

We arrived at the airport a little ahead of schedule so Tom and I sat down for a cup of coffee. For lack of desire to say much I commented, "Flight operations have certainly changed in the last 30 years, haven't they."

"Quite so, George. When I was a boy in the early 70's we were all thrilled about the 747. My parents called it a new air age. I can remember it held up to 490 passengers and was three-fourths of a football field in length. Its average cruising speed was 625 miles an hour. It was a bargain at $20 million each. And the amazing things were those tractors which wheeled them from the terminal to the runway. They were $125,000 each."

"Funny thing, Tom," I replied, "I was just thinking about my grandparents . . . they just wouldn't believe the world

"...There was grandmom and grandpop looking at the moon."

if they saw it today. Back home I had an old charcoal picture a friend of theirs made on their honeymoon. There was grandmom and grandpop looking at the moon . . . so much in love. It took them 7 days to cross the Atlantic. Now it takes just 2 hours, 20 minutes! Somehow I feel they packed a lot more living into their life, simple as it was. Maybe that's what made life so rich, so meaningful. They had a reason for living . . . and they enjoyed every minute of it."

"George, it was Dorion who said, 'The love of the past is often but hatred of the present.' Could it be that these times disturb you? I recall a story my father told me. One night three horsemen were riding across an Eastern desert. As they crossed the dry bed of a river, a voice called, 'Halt!' They did so and the voice continued telling them to dismount, pick up some pebbles and put them in their pockets. Then the voice said, 'You have done as I commanded. Tomorrow at sun-up you will be both glad and sorry.'"

"Mystified, they rode on, as directed. At sunrise, they reached into their pockets and found that the pebbles were diamonds, rubies and other precious stones. Then they thought of the warning, and they were both glad and sorry — glad they had taken some, sorry they had not taken more."

"George, you are living in an enlightened age. Pick up all the pebbles you can now . . . for somehow I have a feeling that this opportunity won't be knocking too long."

I didn't know what to make of Tom. Sometimes he was like a philosophical patronizing father.

A military officer notified us our flight was ready. Quickly we boarded the Boeing SST. This was the President's own plane built to fly 2000 miles per hour. This luxury craft had special offices and extra roominess so that it only carried 50 passengers. All types of electronic gear, special cameras and exotic equipment were aboard. Some referred to it as the Spy in the Sky. Rumor had it that the sophisticated cameras could photograph a man lighting a cigarette on a cloudy, rainy night from 100 miles high and could measure the growth of beard on his face.

*This was the President's own plane built to fly 2000 miles per hour
...we had reached 60,000 feet.*

Tom quickly settled down for the flight by ordering a cocktail. Many times I would have done the same thing. But since the Rapture occurrence, perhaps I had become somewhat religious. When Tom offered me a drink, I declined. As Tom stretched wearily back into the seat, took a few sips, I could feel one of his little lectures coming on.

"You know, George, there's a rule of thumb in transportation that every time you cut travel time in half you double the volume of traffic between two points. This was true thousands of years ago after man first caught a horse and rode him. And its true now. No wonder Brother Bartholomew had to abolish cars from the scene. We were being overrun by them. This is no longer a 24 hour world. It's a 12 hour world. That's it, George, a 12 hour world! Man is now able to fly to any major airport in the world in just 12 hours — just half a day. Think of it."

With that the "droop snoot" nose of our SST eased up and locked into position. Within minutes we had reached an altitude of 60,000 feet. This was 25,000 feet higher than the commercial jets of the early 70's. At 60,000 feet additional engines — more powerful than the engines of the Queen Elizabeth II ocean liner — sent the craft forward at mach 2.2 speed.

Tom took me up to the cabin to look at the controls. I noticed one dial suddenly flashing a red warning signal. The plane nosed down into a sharp dive. It was like dropping suddenly in an elevator. I felt sick, lost my balance and slid half way back to the tail. Tom accompanied me, cocktail and all. It was a silly, yet frightening sight. Shaking and wet with perspiration I made my way back to my seat. Tom filled me in on the details.

"Sorry, George, I should have known. You see at 60,000 feet or higher solar radiation and solar flares become a real hazard to planes. That flashing light warned us that our radiation meter had encountered dangerous conditions. That's why it was necessary to swoop down to 40,000 feet."

Time had certainly been shortened. Just 2 hours 20 minutes to London and just 45 minutes more to Moscow. I fell asleep and the next nudge I felt was Tom telling me to freshen up and shave. We would be landing in Moscow in 10 minutes.

Tom briefed me on protocol. Said our guide would be Tamara. She would make sure we said hello to the right people in government, and pronounced their names correctly.

When we arrived at the deplaning ramp instead of a welcoming committee it looked like a funeral. Black crepe hung over the terminal entrance. I could see that the delegation of officials awaiting us all had black armbands. Alexi Bazenoff did not seem to be in the delegation. This was most unusual.

We came down the ramp, shook hands with all the dignitaries and then proceeded to the microphone stand that was awaiting us. Brother Bartholomew had already provided me with the script to read at this welcoming ceremony.

Fellow Brothers,

In less than 3 hours I have flown from America to Russia. This feat alone must make us brothers.

Brother Bartholomew has asked me to come to Russia to convey his deep wishes for cooperation. The United States has long had a policy of co-existence. But this Administration has now adopted the policy of cooperation. We are with you in your plans, as well as in your aspirations. Our sincere hope is that our discussions with your leaders might prove fruitful for world peace. Thank you.

There was polite clapping and we entered the waiting limousines. Tamara introduced herself. She was a solidly built, determined-looking Russian of 35, daughter of the director of a large Moscow factory. Quite jokingly I said, "I didn't know our arrival would have a funeral welcome."

Quite apologetically she replied, "How foolish of me. You couldn't have known. It happened so quickly. Some of our best men including Premier Bazenoff's son were captured by the Israeli army, tortured and their bodies thrown into the Dead Sea. Our whole nation is up in arms. I'm afraid there's going to be a war. Plans are being made to erect in the Bell Tower of Ivan the Great the enormous Tsar Kolokol, the King of Bells.

...well-drilled soldiers marched past the coffins.

We entered Red Square. The vast cobblestoned rectangle was echoing to the stamp of thousands of feet as well-drilled soldiers marched past the coffins. The familiar Kremlin wall runs the entire length of Red Square and its twenty towers give credence to the banner which says GLORY TO THE PEOPLE — THE BUILDERS.

Tamara reminded us that Russia is not a state, but a world. And within its borders, the Soviet Union — offers a breathtaking geographical sweep being the globe's largest unbroken land mass under a single flag.

Noting our ignorance of their country Tamara suggested that we have an orientation lunch together. Our meeting with Premier Bazenoff was not until 3 so we agreed.

Tom was much impressed with Russia. Apparently he knew some things I didn't know. I got the feeling that Russia was not really our friend and that Brother Bartholomew had a plan in mind . . . a plan to once and for all dismiss this threat to the United States. I was soon to find out.

Tamara told us more of her country.

"From its western extreme near Kaliningrad, the U.S.S.R. stretches some 6000 miles eastward to Bering Strait. There are 149 separate languages spoken by peoples of U.S.S.R. And our country covers 8,650,000 square miles. Moscow alone has 20 million residents!"

"What about Siberia?" I interrupted.

"Siberia is a gold mine of wealth. With Russia's recent discovery of weather control, Siberia is now the bread basket of our nation. You probably remember a time when temperatures were as cold as -96° Fahrenheit but that's a thing of the past. There are still trees here in Siberia! You don't find this true in America, do you? And Russians are better fed than most Americans. When is the last time you had real roast beef? Tonight you will feast on roast beef Stroganof. We Russians have harnessed the sun giving Siberia an even 70° climate year round. It has been a life saver during these difficult days. In the days of your President Eisenhower you sent Mr. Nixon to this country. Your country erected a $3,600,000 exhibit in Sokolniki Park to show us how America lived. But your technology has outraced your common sense. And now Russia is better fed, better clothed and the size of our population while a problem is not as great as yours. You see years ago our State limited the number of children born in each community. We saw what was coming."

I was forced to reluctantly nod affirmatively . . . and as I did Tamara's winning smile brought back memories of Helen. I reached to touch her hand. Somehow she knew and understood the anguish that was mine.

Tamera left us at a guest room in the stately Kremlin halls. We had an hour before our meeting with Dr. Ivan A. Kapitsa, Dean of Soviet physicists. It was Kapitsa who Brother Bartholomew told us believed in the ultimate convergence of the Soviet and American systems of government. And BB was anxious that we sound him out. Perhaps, he had told us, Russia would merge with the United States. If there is any thinking on these lines, let's grab the initiative.

"...Plans are being made to erect in the Bell Tower of Ivan the Great the enormous Tsar Kolokol, the King of Bells."

Tom seemed to think otherwise. As though he knew it from memory he began to rattle off the Kremlin record of Broken Pacts, as he called them.

"... George, their pact breaking continued through the end of World War II, and through the partitioning of Berlin. The Reds waited until we defeated Japan before conveniently entering the war, then painlessly extracted $1 billion in industrial equipment from Manchuria. They broke every agreement with President Eisenhower; fooled President Johnson. In every war in Vietnam, Laos, and Cuba the Soviet government supplied four-fifths of all of the explosives and 80 percent of all the bullets and mines. President Nixon's Non-Proliferation Treaty was broken by the Reds within one year. And Humphrey and President Ted Kennedy had no better luck. And that was in the 70's. Since then Russia has grabbed up not only Sweden, Finland and Norway but also France."

Tom was right. Something had to be done. Somehow I felt Brother Bartholomew would do it.

A knock on our door signaled us that the time for the big

The long tables of official delegates amazed us. Several hundred dignitaries must have been there. And at each place stood bottles of Russia's best wine and vodka.

meeting had arrived. Tamara led us to St. George's Hall in the Great Kremlin Palace. Inside the hall itself, a huge chandelier illuminated the white marble wall plaques which celebrated the knights who had won fame and honor in the Czarist army. And in the center, of course, there was the usual huge painting of Lenin.

Premier Alexi Bazenoff, wreathed in smiles, quickly came over and gave us the familiar Russian kiss. The long tables of official delegates amazed us. Several hundred dignitaries must have been there. And at each place stood bottles of Russia's best wine and vodka.

We sat down and the proceedings began. Premier Bazenoff spoke first.

"May I first welcome our brothers from America. This is both a happy and a sad occasion. Happy because we are together seeking a common meeting ground with the United States. Sad, because the sinister Jews have slain many of our youth in the prime of their life . . . one of them being my only son."

He choked somewhat as he continued. "Throughout the world their are 88 countries with communist influence, over 1 billion active communist members. This is a rich heritage. To them and to you, we make this toast."

As one, everyone stood and toasted Premier Bazenoff. A hand tapped me on the shoulder. I turned. It was Dr. Kapitsa.

After the introductions Tom and I, taking him aside, peppered him with questions.

"Dr. Kapitsa, why do you believe America and Soviet systems of government will converge?" I asked.

"It's inevitable, Mr. Omega, because only through such a convergence can the two great powers avoid a fatal clash. Look at your government now. It is becoming more dictatorial while ours is becoming more democratic. Your folly in the ABM system made this quite evident. For each anti-ballistic-missile you employed, we too, increased the number of our missiles. We must unite for survival."

Brother Bartholomew had given Tom Malone a sealed envelope before we departed for Russia. Now Tom handed it to me. It was titled simply MESSAGE TO MOSCOW. Premier Bazenoff called for silence and asked me to step to the podium. I had no idea what I was going to say. Tom instructed me that as Brother Bartholomew's representative I was only to read his message.

> Premier Bazenoff, Members of the Politburo, Citizens of the World. The United States mourns with you the passing of some of your nation's youth.
>
> It recognizes that these are desperate days, days that call for immediate corrective action. For unless the fire of controversy is quickly put out, there will be no world tomorrow.
>
> In your quest for freedom the United States stands with you. Your actions will be our actions. We support Israel's right to exist but we condemn her expansionist policies.
>
> This is one world and together, hands across the sea, we join with you as brother to brother.
>
> Brother Bartholomew

The words came out but I was shocked at what I was reading. How did Brother Bartholomew know that these Russians would be killed even before it happened? And why this reverse stand supporting Russia against Israel?

The Russians were delighted. The applause was loud and long. Something was happening, right under my nose, but for the life of me, I couldn't put my finger on it.

Late that night we walked through Red Square. Newsboys were hawking the news . . . front page headlines declaring how Israel had tortured Russian soldiers, dumped their bodies in the Dead Sea . . . how America announced it would stand behind Russia.

ed me to hurry back with him to the Palace. It
) retire for tomorrow would be a long day. I had
uestions but Tom ignored them . . . he seemed
intent on reaching our room.

As soon as we entered, he quickly closed the door, pulled
up his shirt sleeve to disclose what I thought was a wrist
radio. He quickly adjusted some dials, pulled out two ear-
phones and told me to listen.

I heard voices . . . but they were in Russian. He quickly
pulled a wire from his tie-clasp. Seeing my puzzled look he
explained that the tie clasp was a Translating Unit — the

wrist radio, a transmitting unit. The voice of Bazenoff was now coming through clearly but not in Russian. It was in English.

"Lenin could have never thought of this plan. Even the Americans were fooled. My son got too close to a Chinese border. The fool. He was always too ambitious anyway, and getting democratic. It's better he's dead."

"Brother Bazenoff, how did you arrange for the bodies in the Dead Sea?"

"There were no bodies found in the Dead Sea. It was all a hoax to give us an excuse to march on Israel, gain U.S. support. There are no bodies in those coffins. The coffins are filled with wax life-like dummies.

"But what about your son," an aide inquired?

"The Chinese did good work on my son, used his body as a pin cushion. That's the picture that appeared in the papers. But his body has been sent to the Rejuvenation Laboratory. We are working on a new discovery . . . a discovery that will bring my son back to life."

The shock of these words must have had a humorous effect on Tom. He switched off the Wrist Radio and burst into laughter. I was stunned. The United States had been fooled and here all Tom could do was laugh.

Was I in a dream world? Could this be true? "Tom," I half shouted, "what's this all about?"

Tom became serious and shocked me all the more. "George, when you've worked for Brother Bartholomew as long as I have, you will come to understand that nothing will surprise him. First, Brother Bartholomew has a most sophisticated spy system, an electronic network that apprises him of every move of the Soviet Union. Just as our Wrist Radio picked up their conversation from a few hundred feet away . . .

Washington Control can pick up conversations thousands of miles away, ferret out the inconsequential, and retain the data of significance. It's a memory bank that surpasses anything in your parent's time. Remember the telephone of your father's day. It had 752 parts. These new electronic systems operate on as few as six parts."

"You mean Brother Bartholomew knew about this plot even before it happened?" "Yes, George, he not only knew about it, in his own way he helped plan it. For years Russia has been aiding Egypt and Syria, supplying them with arms. They were a source of constant irritation to Israel. Brother Bartholomew knew something would break . . . he just wants it to break in his favor. And it will. How, I can't say, but it will."

"But why would he assure Russia of the U.S. support in its problem with Israel?" I asked.

"Let's put it this way," Tom replied, "to calculate the number of moves possible in a game of chess, you would have to start with the figure one followed by 50 zeros. Then you take the number 10 and multiply it by itself that many times. Brother Bartholomew figures . . . why let the Russians be the leader in a chess game that has so many alternative moves. So he makes the first move—supports Russia against Israel. And I predict for Russia it will be the last move!"

I must admit I didn't understand, but then I had a lot to learn and tomorrow would be another long day.

In Russia one could still see the stars in the sky. The air pollutants had not dealt their mask of death in this strange land. My eyelids closed in drowsiness. Somewhere I seemed to hear little Sue. She was kneeling by her bed. My mind wandered to two years ago. I had come home late and tired, tip-toed upstairs, heard her praying, saying, "Dear Lord, please bring Daddy with us at the Rapture . . . if it be thy will. And if not, dear Lord, please give Daddy wisdom and grace when the bad days come. Then, mommy says we'll meet him near Heze . . . Heze . . . something or other tunnel . . . please dear Lord."

Funny how at the brink of sleep how such memories come back. Hezekiah's Tunnel. It was at that tunnel entrance in Jerusalem that Helen cried. She didn't know why but she said somehow this tunnel would have a special meaning to all of us. She insisted right there that we all kneel and pray. I had never knelt before with my family. But her tears reached me . . . and for her sake, I knelt. Soon Sue's hand clasped mine. My small son Tom reached over for my other hand while Helen said a simple prayer. I can't remember all of it but I do remember her small, believing voice saying, "Please dear Lord, if not at the Rapture, make us a family again at Hezekiah's tunnel."

That seemed so long ago. The still night was broken by the tolling of a bell. Was it the enormous Tsar Kolokol, the King of Bells? I did not know. I only knew I was falling asleep . . . asleep in the Kremlin.

Chapter 5

Cloud of Death

Upon returning to Washington Tom Malone and I gave a report on conditions as we saw them in Russia. Brother Bartholomew was very attentive although somehow I got the feeling that he knew exactly what had happened even before we told him.

I could tell he was preoccupied. He got up from behind his desk, slowly walked over to us, pulled up a chair and sat down. Whenever he did this in the past it was always to let us in on some momentous decision.

The world was moving too fast for me and I didn't know whether or not I could stand any more surprises.

He spoke.

"This world has too many religions. That's one of our underlying problems. Do you realize that each of the seven days in the week is designated as the Sabbath by various nationalities and religions. *Monday* is the Greek Sabbath, *Tuesday* the Persian, *Wednesday* the Assyrian, *Thursday* the Egyptian, *Friday* the Turkish, *Saturday* the Jewish and

Sunday the Christian. The population explosion is so critical that there is no longer room for so many diverse thoughts. Something must be done about it."

"Sir, isn't that a bit old fashioned in thinking?" Tom asked.

"Tom, rejecting things because they are old fashioned would rule out the sun and the moon. Let's look at today's world. Thirty years ago who would have dreamed we could reach London in a couple hours by commercial aircraft? Next year jets will make this time seem long — by flying from Chicago to Tokyo in a half hour. We've been able to climate control our cities although we haven't licked the pollution problem. Russia has solved the weather problem in Siberia, and she has floated icebergs down to irrigate the reclaimed land. Pinhead-sized microcircuit radios in stereo are small enough to be inserted in a person's ears. Our laser beams can crumble a mountain in seconds. And while this is restricted information, you and I know this to be possible."

"What are you trying to tell us, sir?" I asked.

"Just this, George, I say we already have inventions enough. Our bathrooms are more luxurious than those of ancient Rome. We jet around the world faster than Caesar could march from Pompeii to Rome. But our basic instincts and thinking processes have ...seal the book, even to the time of the end: many shall run to and fro, and knowledge shall be increased. (Daniel 12:4) not improved. Let us get down to the basics. To change the world we must first change ourselves. Five million patents have been issued by the U.S. Patent Office. But has this helped our world? NO! Everywhere you turn someone is espousing a new religion. Not even the Pope was good enough for the Catholics. They couldn't accept his infallibility. The fundamentalist Protestants have disappeared. And the watered down Protestants have merged with the watered down Catholics into a watered down new religion...a United World Church."

"What does the Bible say about these times?" I asked rather boldly?

"Glad you asked, George. Take a look at your Bible. It's in your coat pocket...inside coat pocket."

Brother Bartholomew must have noticed the surprised look on my face. It had been so long ago that I hid it in a specially made pocket on the inner lining of my coat I had almost forgotten about it. Rather sheepishly I pulled it out.

"Now turn to Psalm 9:17 and read it."

I read it aloud.

> "The wicked shall be turned into hell,
> and all the nations that forget God."

"Do you believe that, George?"

"Well, uh, yes, yes sir, I do, don't I?"

"Of course you do, George. Don't be so fearful. Remember, I trust you or I would not have appointed you to be my Presidential Advisor. The Bible is true...*every word of it*. And never forget that. Many, of course, err in their interpretation of it. That's why it was banned from all except for those whom our country felt would be wise in discernment."

His words rang in my ear...don't be so fearful. Here was a good time to ask him why those churches called Fundamentalist were wrecked, why some still lie in shambles from the destruction caused by Church Renewal mobs.

"The explanation is rather simple, George. It was Max Muller who said 'All truth is safe and nothing else is safe; and he who keeps back the truth, withholds it from men, from motives of expediency, is either a coward or a criminal or both.'"

Tom Malone sat there not saying a word. I wondered just how much he knew about Brother Bartholomew.

Brother Bartholomew continued. "Those which you term Fundamentalists were really heretics who were throwing not only this country but the world into chaos. The Lord knows this world is chaotic enough without a group of people

For the time will come when they will not endure sound doctrine; but after their own lusts shall they heap to themselves teachers, having itching ears. (2 Timothy 4:3)

screaming the world is coming to an end...and filling people's minds with silly tales about a rapture. Anyone who has read the Bible knows Matthew 22:29 states, '...Ye do err, not knowing the Scriptures nor the power of God.'"

"But how do you explain the book of Revelation and that verse about catching up together in the clouds?" I asked rather boldly.

With that Tom interjected, "George, I think we better go. Brother Bartholomew is very busy and has an important meeting coming up."

"No, wait," Brother Bartholomew insisted, "let me put George's mind at ease. First, George, let's make this clear. The Bible is the word of God. There is no doubt in my mind about it. But Fundamentalists were teaching that the book of Revelation was to be interpreted literally."

"Now some of it is literal, some of it is symbolic. Those who can discern the Scriptures know the difference. The Fundamentalists didn't. Take Revelation 9:7-10. Remember it tells about the Fifth Trumpet judgment. Now who ever heard of locusts that looked like horses, wearing crowns of gold, with faces as men, hair of women and teeth as lions and tails like scorpions? Can you imagine interpreting this literally?"

"Well, it does sound a little off beam, sir," I replied.

"Now about that catching away verse. That's found in I Thessalonians 4:16, 17. I can quote it from memory. There's hardly a verse in the Scriptures that I don't know. It goes like this:

> For the Lord himself shall descend from Heaven
> with a shout, with the voice of the archangel,
> and with the trump of God: and the dead in
> Christ shall rise first:
>
> Then we which are alive and remain shall be caught
> up together with them in the clouds, to meet the
> Lord in the air: and so shall we ever be with the
> Lord.

Foolish Fundamentalists termed this the 'Rapture.' It is

no such thing. First, have you or have I seen the Lord descend from Heaven? Of course not. His time has not yet come. But the time is coming. Do you think for one moment that the Lord would allow Christ to finish His work before the judgments that are to come are completed? No, his spirit and his body are with us right now. Soon, George, you will know that Christ indeed does live. But the time for that is not now."

"But, sir, about the disappearance of so many people?"

"George, what I am now about to tell you, you won't believe. It is too fantastic for you to believe...but it is true. Our population throughout the world was getting far out of hand. Religious factions and fanatics were adding to the problems. Something had to be done. I attended a secret meeting in Basel, Switzerland with heads of state and prominent scientists. There a special powder was revealed to us. It is called Miracle 1. When properly mixed with a printing ink, it generates particles of sub-microscopic molecular size. This reaction is called a Quark. And when touched by the human finger, that body heat sets a series of reactions in motion. In short, Miracle 1, in one second disintegrates the body that has come in contact with this powerful powder."

"I don't understand sir."

"To put it bluntly, George, the one way to somehow resolve our population problems was to eliminate people — not bury them — disintegrate them. Miracle 1 did that for us. Special Bibles were printed. I Thessalonians 4:16, 17 were printed in a different ink, an ink mixed with Miracle 1 powder. These Bibles were distributed to all Fundamentalist churches and to all individuals who wanted them. The United World Church issued a memo to all churches asking them not to preach from I Thessalonians, chapter 4. You know the rest. The persistent Fundamentalists did...the very next Sunday. And as their fingers brushed past verses 16 and 17...POOF...they were gone!"

> But evil men and seducers shall wax worse and worse, deceiving, and being deceived. (2 Timothy 3:13)

"Incredible!" I exclaimed!

With that, Tom spoke up. "Sir there are two problems at hand. The Mayor of New York City is giving us difficulty on the Birth Coupon system and the Transportation Bill..."

Brother Bartholomew interrupted, walked over to the side of his desk, flipped a switch. A wall opened. Down came a security control panel with a TV screen. A light blinked and a picture appeared on the screen. In fact there were four screens...each transmitting a different picture. Brother Bartholomew punched the NEW YORK key. The pictures

changed. On Screen 1 crowds appeared filling New York streets. The screen showed hundreds of people waving their fists in demonstration of their protest of BB's actions. On Screen 2 was Mayor Bill Marcon talking to someone in his office. Brother Bartholomew turned up the sound control. Marcon's voice came out loud and embarrassingly clear.

"Bartholomew has to go. BB is too big for his boots.

My people won't stand for this banishment of all automobiles. And Birth Coupons take away their individual freedom."

Another voice in the Mayor's room came on....

"You're right, Bill. BB is too much of a dictator. If we let him get away with it, he'll think he's God. Listen, I have a plan..."

With that Brother Bartholomew turned the set off. I got the impression he knew of their plan even before they planned it.

Tom cleared his throat and spoke again. "As I was saying sir, you know the problem in New York, and the meeting coming up in a few minutes at the United World Church headquarters. Seems some of the ministers are getting cold feet. Starting to take the Bible literally. Seem to think your recent pronouncements on that Birth Coupon and the turning of some churches into museums are a little too much."

"We'll take care of that, Tom, let's go!"

And with that Brother Bartholomew motioned towards the door and we walked out.

This had been some revelation to me. Was I understanding the Bible more clearly? I had heard scuttlebut about Miracle 1. No one knew it by that name. There was reference to a powerful powder, however. Perhaps I had pegged Brother Bartholomew all wrong. The closer I got to him the more he seemed like someone from outer space...someone who knew what the problems were even before they began. Could he be sent by Satan? No, there was too much love in his heart. His constant reference to the Scripture impressed me. Could be he was an angel sent from God? If I only knew the Scriptures better, I thought. And then again, maybe I'm doing too much thinking. BB knows the way. I'll just follow him.

The platform of the United World Church auditorium was crowded. All of the important clergy vied for a seat near Brother Bartholomew. As President he was also automatically head of the United World Church. Tom Malone had quite a problem making sure no clergy was offended. While the denominations had merged, it seemed the best way was to have the leading head of the old Methodist Church, the old United Presbyterian Church, the old Episcopal Church and the Pope's representative from the old Catholic Church... all sit together in a semi-circle with Brother Bartholomew in the middle. The Convocation on Church Union had indeed been very effective in bringing the churches into one unified body.

Bishop Arthur, about whom I had almost forgotten, stood up and addressed the assembly. He was giving a short history of the progress of the church in the last thirty years.

In the last thirty years the churches have made great strides. Some of us have all but forgotten the great service rendered to us by those termed "new evangelicals" in the early 70's. They solved the word problems that plagued our growth. Through their initiative they eliminated the word "saved," substituted for it a much better word, "estranged." "Born again" was changed to an "encounter with God."

"Salvation" and "new birth" became "commitment." And to these pioneers of church union we shall be eternally grateful, because their small first step has made ours so much easier.

Those words struck a chord of remembrance in my mind. I could remember Helen as she was housecleaning singing, "Jesus Saves, Jesus Saves." Was Bishop Arthur's remarks really one of progress? I wondered.

The Bishop continued.

We are called here because there are some who are concerned with the apparent deterioration of the church. Let us remember Christ's admonition to us:

"Ye are all the children of light, and the children of the day: we are not of the night, nor of darkness."

"Yes, Bishop Arthur," Brother Bartholomew interrupted.

"But the next verse in I Thessalonians 5:5 and 6 is important, too. It is this:

> "Therefore let us not sleep, as do others; but let us watch and be sober."

Thank you, Brother Bartholomew. You are so right. Our council at the United World Church feels that as children of light more of our churches should be opened now that the heretics have disappeared. Our people need spiritual comfort and recreation that is geared to their needs. That is why we have called you to address us.

With that the audience as one arose and started clapping wildly.

Brother Bartholomew acknowledged the applause and began to speak.

> May we open with a word of prayer, please.

> Almighty Father, in whom we place our faith and trust, we humbly come before you as a nation in need of spiritual guidance, a nation broken and contrite, whose commitment is to thee and thee alone.

> Bring us that voice from heaven assuring us that promise of Revelation 21:3, "Behold, the tabernacle of God is with men..." Make this earth a new earth, pure and clean.

> And to thee we give all the honor and all the glory, Amen.

It was as though the audience was hypnotized. You could hear a pin drop. The silence was as if God was standing in their presence.

Brother Bartholomew continued.

> I have been deeply concerned about the needs of the church. My offices gave you wholehearted support in the destruction of those churches that nearly singlehandedly caused chaos in our nation

through their false doctrines. We must guard against any such thing reoccuring. And I know that it will not. Our churches must be big. They must meet the social needs of their respective communities. Too long have we endured the teaching of those who were more concerned with sin and less concerned with social welfare. If the church is to survive, and it will, it must be, as Jesus was, concerned about the social welfare of its peoples.

Fundamentalists taught the miracle of the loaves and fishes. It was no miracle. The productive use of oxygen and CO_2 through modern farming have given us such bounties of food from a few loaves which far surpass that so-called miracle of Matthew 14:15-21! Five loaves and two fishes fed 5000 then. Since man has ventured into space we can now pack more into the area occupied by five loaves and two fishes than would feed—not 5000—but 15,000 people!

Is the Bible wrong? No the Bible is not wrong. But those who interpret it wrongly are wrong! I say the miracle is not the miracle of making five loaves and two fishes multiply. But rather the miracle is that Christ was concerned about the SOCIAL WEL-FARE OF THE PEOPLE. And THIS IS THE MESSAGE AND MINISTRY THAT OUR CHURCH MUST RELATE TO TODAY!

The round of applause was deafening. It would have gone on indefinitely, but Brother Bartholomew held up his hand and continued.

Congress has given me elective decision powers. I am making a decision right now. It will take effect immediately. I am appointing Bishop Arthur as my Presidential Consultant on Religion. Hear him. His words are wise. He has proven his faithfulness and concern...concern for the church and for the people.

Furthermore, at his suggestion, I have directed Congress to appropriate funds...whatever funds are

necessary...to reconvert every church in America to
its primary ministry of meeting the social needs of
our time. Bishop Arthur will apprise you of our
plan, aptly called PLAN ADVANCE. Thank you and
God bless you.

With that the audience stood up and sang the theme hymn
of the church. I remember first hearing it at the United
Church Fellowship in Rome.

Praise God from whom all blessings flow
God's in His heaven on earth below
Let men unite, cast out all fears
For heaven is earth for endless years!

Bishop Arthur took the podium and addressed the
audience.

Thank you Brother Bartholomew for your kind remarks. I am both humbled and honored to accept
such a position of responsibility as Consultant on
Religion. My life will be devoted to your cause of
peace and justice. Now to the business at hand.
Brother Bartholomew has asked me to convey to you
briefly PLAN ADVANCE. It is a plan I am sure all
of you will approve. Quite simply it is three-fold.

1. Recreational facilities of all churches will be expanded. Government money will be available to
assure every church of adequate facilities to meet
the social needs of our people.

Every church will be assured of an olympic size
swimming pool, a baseball and basketball diamond
and tennis courts.

2. We must follow Paul's admonition in I Corinthians
8:22 "...that I might by all   Love not the world,
means save some." Our   neither the things that
constitutions must be   are in the world. If any
changed, our barriers made   man love the world, the
less stringent. Churches   love of the Father is not
are encouraged to em-   in Him. (1 John 2:15)
ploy psychedelic lights or whatever worldly fad
that they might attract those not in the church

body. We have organized special teams of "Christian rock" groups to conduct concerts in every church in the nation. We are of the world, we must be with the world if we expect them to come to our world.

3. The church must become more relevant to today's problems. We have adopted successfully in our churches God's direction of complete sexual freedom. We must also be ready to adopt his condoning of mass destruction of life. We cannot cope with present population growth. As a church we must accept and approve certain actions that will wipe out millions of those degenerates who would ruin us all. This is as God has willed. For the survival of all some will have to be eliminated. May I remind you of Lamentations 4:9, "they that be slain with the sword are better than they that be slain with hunger...."

Thank you for your attentiveness. The ushers will give you complete details on PLAN ADVANCE. You may get them on the way out. Let us close in prayer.

I ran out ahead of the crowd anxious to get back to the office. It was going to be a long day.

Tom Malone met me in the hall. He looked as though he had seen a ghost.

Tom, who was so reserved...shook? I couldn't believe it. Whatever this news was, it would be earth shaking.

"What's up, Tom? You're rushing around like a cloud of dust!"

"Have to run, George, but something big is about to happen!"

"WHAT?" I shouted. "Tell me, Tom, please!"

"BB put the finger on New York. They're due for a Dust Cloud Crystal Drop."

"Tom, I don't understand, what's a Dust Cloud Crystal Drop? And what's so drastic about that?"

"George, several years ago scientists discovered that a

river of red dust flows on the trade winds across the South Atlantic and into the Caribbean area. Tropical meteorologists found this cosmic dust forms a belt around the earth. BOMEX, that's short for Barbados Oceanographic and Meteorological Experiment believed that this dust triggered hurricanes. That was in the 70's. Now our scientists know not only that dust clouds exist, more important, they know how to harness them, send them where they want, seed them with whatever they want...and how to control them from space platforms high above the earth. Yet they can pinpoint their direction to within a few feet...and dispense their lethal ability by the flick of one switch.

What I'm trying to say is this, George. Mayor Marcon of New York is giving BB problems. And besides that the population problem up there is getting out of hand. Some people want more than their six feet of personal living space. Others are tired of living 200 floors up and sharing their 9 x 15 apartment with two other families."

"But didn't Bill Marcon himself say in his speech '...we need an elective Dictatorship...a benevolent authority'?"

"Yes, he did, George. But politics makes for strange bed-fellows. And Marcon has some aspirations of unseating BB and taking the Presidency himself. That's why BB carefully primed Bishop Arthur on Lamentations 4:9 and his statements, '...we must accept and approve certain actions that will wipe out millions. ...For the survival of all some will have to be eliminated!' BB leaves for Cape Kennedy tomorrow for a space flight above New York. He will personally trigger MIRACLE 1. It will be injected into a dust cloud. Roving satellites will gently waft the cloud over New York, encircling it with air to prevent it from seeping elsewhere. Within a twinkling of an eye—the people of New York will cease to exist. Miracle 1 will have disintegrated them. Then BB flicks another switch, neutralizes Miracle 1's potency. Presto it becomes just another cloud!"

I was shocked beyond words. Tom started to walk down the hall. I ran after him.

"My God, Tom, Faye and Bill are in New York. Tom, what will I do. You've got to help me!"

"...Roving satellites will gently waft the cloud over New York..."

For the first time in his life, as far as I can remember, Tom's eyes reflected a bit of sympathy, some small understanding for my grief. His wife and children were still alive. He went home to them every night. Thus he could understand the grief that was mine. With Faye and Bill gone, I would have nothing. And with nothing...no hope...I would be of little value to BB. Tom knew he had to do something... and do it quick.

"Look George, quick, get up to New York. I'll tell BB I've sent you up to get a last minute report on conditions."

"But, let me call Faye and Bill before I catch the flight."

"Impossible, George, time is short. All flights to New York have been cancelled. I couldn't even clear Air Force 1 to go into New York today. The ACV's are still running, though. It's your only chance. And while you dash to the docks, I'll be alerting Faye and Bill to be ready."

Tom was right. No time to waste. And the ACV's would be the only way now. How thankful I was that in the early 1980's the Air Cushion Vehicle became an efficient means of sea transportation. Each ACV now carried 800 passengers and 75 cars. They skimmed over the water on a cushion of air. Their cruising speed was 200 miles per hour. I would make New York within the hour from Washington. It was now 3:30 in the afternoon. Tom told me the last return ACV from New York would be tonight at 11:15.

Faye rushed into my arms at the dock in New York. Both she and Bill were waiting for me. It was the first time in a long time that I had seen Faye cry. She had been a highly sophisticated girl. But the events of the last few days had changed all that. Bill was bewildered. Tom had told them I was coming, that it was important they come back with me. He couldn't tell them anything more. And I couldn't either. Somehow I felt Brother Bartholomew knew my every step. And I knew that I might as well keep silent on the fate that was to befall New York — for no one would believe me anyway.

The ACV ride back to Washington was uneventful. Faye unburdened her heart to me. Tears welled in her eyes as she recalled the last Thanksgiving Day that Helen and Sue and Tommy were alive. Helen always went out of her way to witness her faith to Faye. And Faye resented having religion pushed on her. That Thanksgiving, Helen bought an extra large turkey, and some extra foods, foods she knew Faye liked. The turkey was a special protein mixture, molded to look like a turkey, injected with flavorings that were almost as succulent as the old fashion bird-type turkey. We sat around the table. Helen asked us to bow our heads and give thanks. I can still hear Helen's voice,

"Dear Lord,
We are thankful for thy blessings on our
home, for the good food thou hast placed
before us...."

It was then Faye, pushed back her chair, her face flush she shouted at all of us, but particularly Helen.

"Good food! What good food? Thankful for blessings? You have the nerve to thank God for this trash? If God were God would he let us starve and eat junk they call food that's made from crude oil? Would he let us overpopulate so greatly that we live in horrible square cubes two and three hundred stories high? Where is God...if there is a God? You stupid fools. How long will you keep up this masquerade of holiness?"

And with that she stamped out of the house and out of our lives. That was the last I heard of her until Brother Bartholomew revealed her location to me.

As Faye recalled this incident, she started to cry. The silent swoosh of the ACV over the waters was broken by her uncontrollable sobs. "I'm sorry, Daddy, so awfully sorry, Daddy. If Mother were only here. If only she knew how sorry I am. She was so good."

I put my arm around Bill and held Faye tightly. As her head lay on my shoulder and her damp blonde curls brushed by my face, I said, "Don't cry, Faye, I know you're sorry. And somehow, I feel Helen knows you're sorry. We must be brave. There's a strange world ahead. We've got to search the Scriptures. Somewhere there must be a clue."

We arrived in Washington. Faye insisted that we search out the old Bible church where she went to Sunday School. I knew what she would find but I didn't have the heart to tell her.

The government car met us at the dock. I told the driver that I wanted to investigate a church for possible renovations under BB PLAN ADVANCE.

When we arrived at the church, I whispered to Bill to take Faye in alone. I explained that I would follow.

It was quiet. But in my mind the strains of little children singing seemed to echo back and forth....

> Jesus wants me for a sunbeam,
> a sunbeam,
> a sunbeam,
> Jesus wants me for a sunbeam
> To shine for Him each day.

My thoughts were interrupted by sobbing from within. Quickly I dashed inside the weather-worn church. The interior was in shambles...chairs broken, hymnbooks thrown on the floor. It was as though a tornado had swept through the place. This was one of the churches earmarked for destruction because of its teachings. And Bishop Arthur and his group had certainly done an efficient job.

Faye and Bill were kneeling at the communion table. Faye was praying. I only caught the last few phrases.

> "Dear God, thy will be done over this life to be.
> And thank you, God.
>> Amen."

"Life to be? What life to be, Faye?" I asked fearfully.

The interior was in shambles...chairs broken, hymnbooks thrown on the floor....This was one of the churches earmarked for destruction because of its teachings. And Bishop Arthur and his group had certainly done an efficient job.

Tenderly she looked up at Bill. Bill hugged her tightly, softly kissed her on the forehead.

"Dad, we're going to have a baby."

My heart sank. I should have been joyful. Faye had no Birth Coupon. I knew what would happen. And for the first time in what seemed ages...I knelt in prayer...and I cried!

For, behold, the days are coming, in the which they shall say, Blessed are the barren, and the wombs that never bare... (Luke 23:29)

Chapter 6

Invasion from the North

Faye looked so small and helpless as she lay on the hospital cart. The crisp white sheets were tucked around her. We followed an orderly as he pushed her down the long corridor towards the door marked NO ADMITTANCE. BIRTH CORRECTION PERSONNEL ONLY.

Bill was on the verge of tears. Never have I found it so difficult to retain my composure. But I had to, for Faye's sake.

That day I had returned to Presidential quarters, Brother Bartholomew outlined every step I had taken. Said he was sorry Faye was pregnant...pregnant without a Birth Coupon.

And while he had compassion and understanding he was firm in that he could make no exception. It would cause problems. Birth Coupons were rarely issued anymore. Those who had no coupons were forbidden to conceive and give birth. If they did, it was mandatory they enter the hospital immediately, and report to the Birth Correction Center.

It broke my heart to tell Faye. But I had no other choice. I would have to sacrifice a new life so that I could keep Faye and Bill. It was the only way.

We reached the doors. Bill gently kissed Faye. Faye gripped my hand as if to say, "Pray, daddy, pray real hard."

And then she was gone. Only the swinging of the doors broke the silence. Faye screamed...and then I knew the reality of the thing had hit her. And I cursed toward God! Even as I did, I knew it was wrong. The only prayer I knew was the Lord's Prayer and softly my lips formed a plea...

"...lead us not into temptation, but deliver us from evil: For thine is the kingdom, and the power, and the glory, for ever. Amen."

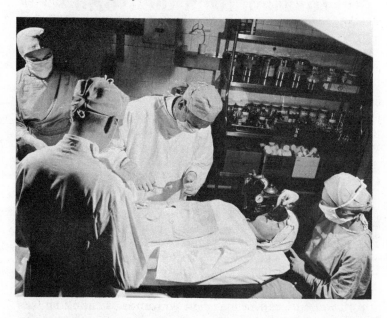

Inside the operating room, Faye lay still, her eyes closed. Her scream came when an intern had injected her with sodium pentothal and she knew that soon her baby would be taken from her. It was all done very efficiently and quickly. The hall was lined with 15 other women, all in a state of semi-consciousness, all without Birth Coupons. In the early 1970's the President had requested that people limit their families. That didn't work. Now Birth Coupons imposed severe restrictions to control population growth. Everyone in government and in religious circles approved. There simply was no other way out of the dilemma.

The doctor pulled the small IBM card from the chart holder above Faye's head. The card read

FAYE SANDERS
Age 27
Father: George Omega
Assigned Number: 061 23 481 2

The mysterious punched holes in the IBM card would tell the doctor what to do. Quickly he took the card, slipped it into a sophisticated electronic machine. The card zipped through several channels. Lights blinked on and off. The card dropped down into a tray. Into another tray dropped a vial and out the side came a strip of instructions. They were crisp, impersonal. No time for bedside manners. There was a job to do and the hallway was lined with similar cases. The doctor read the instruction slip.

FAYE SANDERS
Drug 666X

The doctor knew what to do. Quickly he picked up the vial, inserted it into a thigh injection needle. In a moment it was over. No need for anesthesia. The sodium pentothal was just to induce a light sleep and to calm down a hysterical woman until it was all over. Then it would be too late. 666 was the code number for Birth Eradication. X was the designation for the additional drug compound that prevented all future conception. Not everyone who entered the Birth Correction unit received the X compound. But most did. Many, in fact, wanted it.

When Faye awakened back in her room both Bill and I were at her side. We could not pray here. The ward was filled with fifty women. Each was allowed one hour of recuperation before being sent home. And the carts were being wheeled back and forth with a distressing regularity. When the dizziness passed, Faye got dressed, and we went home.

Faye looked like a defeated woman. There seemed nothing more for her to live for. Soon the drugs would work, quickly, painlessly. The life within her ceased to be.

I could care less about the consequences as I rushed into Brother Bartholomew's office. Once and for all I was going to tell him what I thought about his plans and edicts. I owed it to Faye. No longer could I control my inner feelings.

I opened the door, rushed into his office and stopped in my tracks both shocked and surprised. Temporary scaffold-

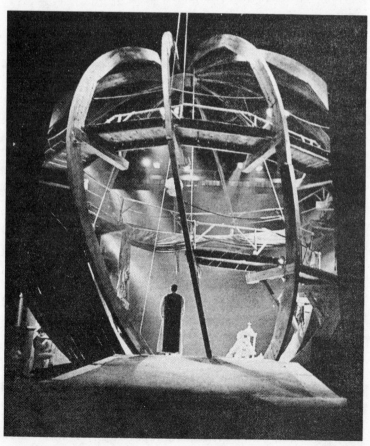

ing was up. There, with his back turned towards me was
Brother Bartholomew. But not in a business suit as I had
always seen him...now he was in a robe with a bright red
cape. And with rapt admiration he was viewing a pure white
ivory carved throne. For a moment I thought I was stepping
into the very presence of God.

He turned, beckoned for me to come up the slightly
inclined ramp.

My face flushed with anger as I shouted, "YOU KILLED
HER! YOU KILLED HER! YOUR LAWS HAVE KILLED
FAYE'S BABY AND HER HOPE FOR LIVING. WHY
DON'T YOU KILL ME?"

He said nothing. He gently held my arm and led me to the
side of the room...as though such business was too holy for
this spot. He pressed a button on the wall. A television
screen eased out. On the screen were three people. Helen,
little Sue and Tommy. They were crying and Helen was
speaking...

"George, darling, I know it's hard to understand.
Please do everything Brother Bartholomew says.
He loves you George. Soon he will be annointed of
God."

I stared in disbelief. I rushed to the screen. The light
slowly flickered into darkness and the sound kept echoing
from the wall...

"He loves you, George. He loves you, George.
He loves you, George."

And the last soft, fading words I heard were...

"Soon he will be annointed of God."

Was I going out of my mind? It must be a trick. Was this
in the Bible?

Brother Bartholomew put his arms around my shoulders
and spoke: "George, there are many things we do not understand. I don't understand why God is going to place His
mantle of service on me. But I accept it. George, pull out
your Bible and let's together read II Timothy 4:5-7.

I took the Bible from my pocket. But my mist-filled eyes could not find Timothy. And even if my eyes were clear I wouldn't have known if Timothy was in the Old or New Testament. Brother Bartholomew quickly leafed past Colossians and Thessalonians and his finger rested on the verses in Timothy. Haltingly I read with him the verses he directed...

> "But watch thou in all things, endure afflictions, do the work of an evangelist, make full proof of thy ministry.
>
> For I am now ready to be offered, and the time of my departure is at hand.
>
> I have fought a good fight, I have finished my course, I have kept the faith...."

"George, don't you think God is an all-knowing God. You weren't much of a Christian before. Your wife was the testimony in your home. How important it is for us now to endure afflictions and to prove ourselves. That's what Paul is saying. None of us know how much longer we have on earth. The problems we face today are monumental compared to 1970 or 1980. But at the end of our course, we must be able to say as Paul, 'I have kept the faith.' Helen would want it that way. And, George, I need you."

I looked up at Brother Bartholomew. He was right. I must get this hatred from my heart. Truly he was sent from God. I again looked forward to working with him to save the world.

The silence was broken by the incessant buzzing of the HOT LINE Picturephone. Brother Bartholomew walked over to it, picked up the receiver. The screen brightened. And there on the picture tube was the Premier of Israel.

Shalom Ben-Mayer had only recently been elected Prime Minister of Israel. A soldier and statesman, he was well respected in his country. I recalled the time I interviewed him right before he won the election. "Do Jews accept Jesus as the son of God?" I asked.

"One God has created us," he replied. "We all have one father. A Christian cannot say exactly the same thing...But we do not accept Jesus as the son of God because we do not think that God has a son...It is the most humane of all religions...the Jewish religion. Our Bible does not begin with the Gospels. Our Bible does not even begin with Abraham being the first Jew. It begins with the first human pair... They were neither Jews, nor Christians, nor Moslems. They were neither white, nor black, nor yellow. We don't know what they were. But all human beings were created in the image of God. This is the essence of our religion."

Seeing from my face that this explanation wasn't really enough, he cleared his throat and continued.

"We have our books of the Torah—you call it the Law. In the third book you call it Leviticus—it is said you should love your fellow man like yourself...In my view, my humble view, Christianity was created by St. Paul, not Jesus. Jesus was a Jew like other Jews. The Jewish religion is not the same as the Christian or any other religion. It is...a nation."

I then asked, "Do you believe that in the continuing development of Israel there is a conscious effort to change the people's character, to have an Israeli character different than that of Jews elsewhere?"

Ben-Mayer had looked at me with a smile on his face and replied, "It must not be an Israeli character, but a real Jewish character, which is one which the Bible said we must have. It was said by Moshe. You call him Moses. His name to us is Moshe. What Moshe said some 3300 years ago is true today as it was then. He said, 'You are a few among peoples, and therefore you must be...'" Ben-Mayer paused, then continued, "Because I can't find an expression in English which is correct, I must say it in Hebrew. 'Am segula.' It means your quality must be much higher than your quantity. You should be spiritually better than any other people in the world. A Jew here may be fanatically religious, or he might be an atheist. I don't go to a synagogue. Yet I am not an atheist. I am convinced that there is one supreme thing—

whether you call it God or any other name it doesn't matter...." And with that the interview had ended.

That was 3 years ago. Now the HOT LINE PICTURE-PHONE shown brightly with Shalom Ben-Mayer's face. Usually smiling, Ben-Mayer's face was drawn and concerned. The Hot Line is only used for emergencies. I could tell this was just that.

"Mr. President," Ben-Mayer was saying, "Intelligence has informed us that Russia is on the move again. Forces from Germany, Poland, Yugoslavia, Iran, Turkey and other Arab states have men and tanks mobilized on all fronts for a great pincer move into our territory. Tanks have massed the full length of Turkey, like an army of horses, ready to devour us the minute the signal is given. We urgently need your help right now."

Brother Bartholomew was calm as he flipped the switch to talk. It was as though he knew every step before it happened.

"Brother Ben-Mayer, I know the situation looks desperate. But here's what I want you to do. Tonight, go on your national television hook-up. Announce that I will arrive tomorrow in Jerusalem to give a special message to the Jewish people right on the Mount of Olives. Announce that I will perform a spectacular feat that will show to the world that the sacred land of the Jews must remain in their sovereignty. Have as many of your people as possible fill the Kidron Valley to watch us. I will speak at 12 noon. Will the sun be shining?"

Even him, whose coming is after the working of Satan with all power and signs and lying wonders. (2 Thessalonians 2:9)

Shalom Ben-Mayer turned to an aide, checked the weather, then said, "Yes, Mr. President, there will not be a cloud in the sky tomorrow."

"Good," Brother Bartholomew replied. "Set the stage for something really big!"

With that the picture faded and Brother Bartholomew

turned to me promising, "George, you are going to see God's power in action tomorrow."

With that he led me down the hall to a room marked CONFIDENTIAL TOP CLEARANCE PERSONNEL ONLY. BB rang the buzzer. We were admitted. The room seemed unpretentious. Except for one corner. There stood a small cabinet with thirty 3" x 8" file drawers, each with a special combination lock...each labeled in what appeared to be a hieroglyphic code.

Brother Bartholomew pointed to the drawer with 3 rows of strange lettering.

[hieroglyphic / coded lettering — three rows]

"Are you sure you want this, sir?" the scientist asked. "We have tested this under laboratory conditions but it may prove more powerful than any of us can anticipate."

"Quite all right," BB replied, "This will be a good opportunity to test its effectiveness under actual conditions."

"You need a full sun and accurate aim, sir."

"Yes," Brother Bartholomew assured the scientist, "I've taken all these things into consideration."

With that the scientist twisted the dial at what seemed an innumerable number of times. The lock clicked open. He pulled out the drawer, and then he set it down on an examining table cushioned in a plush layer of white dense foam rubber.

I was amazed at what I saw. It looked like an ordinary ring...a gold banded ring with a pitch black onyx face and a sparkling center diamond.

"Why, that's only a ring," I exclaimed!

"You mean it looks like a ring," Brother Bartholomew replied. "But under the right conditions it captures the energies of the sun over its black surface, generates unbelievable energy and channels it through the diamond sending-device to become a devestating laser beam of destruction. Properly used it can crumble a building in seconds. The laser was first discovered in the early 1960's. The perfected instrument you now see was only made operational last month, right here in this laboratory."

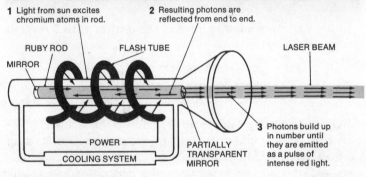

Diagram of Brother Bartholomew's
RUBY LASER RING

1 Light from sun excites chromium atoms in rod.

2 Resulting photons are reflected from end to end.

RUBY ROD   FLASH TUBE   LASER BEAM

MIRROR

POWER

COOLING SYSTEM

PARTIALLY TRANSPARENT MIRROR

3 Photons build up in number until they are emitted as a pulse of intense red light.

Copyright © 1969, Salem Kirban, Inc.

Would wonders ever cease? This seemed impossible!

The scientist who perfected this laser ring went on to explain: "Many years ago a beam from what we call a ruby laser was aimed at the moon, 240,000 miles away. It reached the lunar surface a second later. Working at this speed this laser ring works as follows: When the sun hits the diamond the chromium atoms under the onyx surface turn into an excited state. These excited atoms then generate energy millions of times more powerful than a similar surface area on the sun. Within one minute this destructive power is released into a laser ray through the diamond channel. It will destroy anything in its path. Whoever uses this ring must hold his hand high at 12 noon to absorb the sun's rays and within a minute point the ring exactly at the target in question. There is no room for error."

Brother Bartholomew took the ring and placed it on a finger on his right hand. Then Brother Bartholomew showed

New York City...instant tragedy had struck here. Fringe area casualties did not disintegrate but were killed...and the world had already forgotten.

RUBY LASER RING'S DESTRUCTIVE CAPACITY DRAMATICALLY SHOWN IN SERIES OF 8 PHOTOGRAPHS EACH TAKEN ONE SECOND APART

(1) The test building shown intact.

(2) A puff of smoke appears.

(3) The Ring's powerful rays begin their work.

(4) The right section collapses.

(6) Entire building begins to disintegrate.

(8) Building disappears...as if never there!

(5) Laser Ray's destructive force at its peak.

(7) After 7 seconds...a puff of smoke.

us a series of photographs which revealed the awesome destructiveness of the ruby laser. The scientist then covered the onyx surface with a protective cover. Time was now too precious to take Air Force 1 to Israel. In the early 1990's aerospace craft were made capable of landing at ordinary jet airports. These vehicles were part rocket, part orbiting spacecraft and part airplane. Development was begun way back in 1970 under the then President Nixon's Space Task Group. These Space Shuttles, as they were called, stood 225 feet high, weighed 1.5 million pounds and are capable of carrying 25,000 pounds of cargo and passengers. It would take us to Jerusalem in a little under one-half hour.

I had never ridden in a space craft before. But the take-off was unusually smooth. It seemed no different than an ordinary jet. BB was anxious for me to go on this flight with

him to see how earth looked hundreds of miles up. Within a minute he pointed down toward our floor windows. I noticed nothing but brown masses of earth. He pushed a button marked SIDE DIMENSIONAL. What seemed like a special glass suddenly slid through the paneled window. It was a tremendously clear and sharp magnification. I could see what appeared to be a countryside. Articles of clothing were strewn everywhere, and young people were searching and picking up bits and pieces.

"That was New York City," Brother Bartholomew explained. Funny, I thought, instant tragedy had struck here, and the world had already forgotten. Even I had forgotten.

Twenty minutes later the space shuttle paused over Israel. Down below I saw the entire Holy Land. It was a magnificent sight. I could see that BB was getting excited. It were as though he was coming home.

Our space craft came to a smooth landing at Jerusalem Airport. Brother Bartholomew quickly changed clothes, slipped on his robe and bright red cape, checked his Laser ring, and motioned to the steward to open the door. I remembered the old Bible pictures in my mother's Bible. He reminded me so much of Jesus. It was as though Christ himself were returning to the Mount of Olives, but not on a donkey, in a modern Year 2000 space craft. Incredible, I thought!

As he stepped down the flight of stairs the Israeli Army Band struck up HAIL TO THE CHIEF. Brother Bartholomew looked up at the sun. It was shining brightly. Not a cloud in the sky.

Shalom Ben-Mayer saw his upward glance and seemed to convey that he knew everything would be all right. The limousine quickly whisked us through the streets of Jerusalem up the winding road to the Mount of Olives. The streets were packed with people. They must have been twenty deep. Only a narrow aisle permitted our car to pass.

As we reached the top of the Mount of Olives I gasped in amazement. Literally every spot of land was covered with people...from the Mount of Olives down the hill to the Kidron Valley, up the other side of the hill to the walls of the Inner City. An aide told me that never before in history had so many people assembled in one place. He estimated that five million people filled the valley and surrounding areas.

I shivered with fear as suddenly I thought...suppose BB's ring is aimed just slightly off course. Millions would die and he would be massacred for his action.

Shalom Ben-Mayer approached the podium specially erected for the occasion. A hush fell over the valley. He spoke.

> For 4000 years Jews have lived in Palestine. The Six Days' War in June, 1967 brought the return of the whole city of Jerusalem to Israel for the first time since A.D. 130-132 during the Bar Kochba rebellion against the Romans. Here Abraham prepared to sacrifice his son Isaac. Here rose the City of David. Here Solomon built his temple in the days of Israel's glory. Here the Queen of Sheba's caravan—a "very great train" of camels bearing "spices and very much gold, and precious stones"—made its soft-footed way into Solomon's resplendent capital.

> Jerusalem knew the heavy tread of conquerors: Nebuchadnezzar, who carried its populace off to Babylon....

As Ben-Mayer continued his introduction I looked out over this vast expanse of people. Pharaohs and emperors, sultans and kings all vied through the ages for these hills of Judea.

Ben-Mayer was finishing his speech.

> Forces from the North since the early 1960's have been seeking to devour us. They have agitated our Arab neighbors, have led them to believe we are their enemy. For years we have fought little wars, skirmishes. But now these evil forces are massed at our borders...massed waiting for the signal to march on Jerusalem. I say they will not conquer Jerusalem. For no matter how large their armies, no matter how big their arms, no matter

how great their leaders, God is on our side and He will prevail. This Goliath will be slain. For they may have their Goliath. But we, the proud nation of Israel, we have our DAVID!

Never before had I heard such a fiery speech. The response was like a roaring thunder, creeping up the valley until it became a deafening roar that seemed to shake the very earth beneath us. Five million Jews all shouting in unison...

WE HAVE OUR DAVID
WE HAVE OUR DAVID
WE HAVE OUR DAVID

BROTHER BARTHOLOMEW stood up, held up his hands. Slowly the crowd quieted, sat down on the verdant ground. He spoke.

My brothers and sisters in the Lord. Since the days of Pharaoh your people have suffered. Ramesses II, who for 67 years ruled Egypt, made the lives of the children of Israel bitter with bondage. Yet from ancient papyri found back in his day...comes a school teacher's message that applies well to those who would seek to invade this beloved country. For years Russia has been the poison whose venom has touched every country surrounding Israel. She has spewed her hate at every opportunity. When your great leaders talked, she would not listen. Let's read the proverb an ancient Egyptian penned thousands of years ago. It reads like this:

The ear of the boy is on his back, and he
listens when he is beaten.

This Promised Land once and for all must teach the intruder his lesson. If he will not listen with the ears on his head, America will stand with you in making sure he listens with the ear on his back. For Russia will be beaten. The United States will form ranks with Israel to bring eternal peace to this sacred land.

The Al Aksa Mosque fire in 1969 was the first step used by Russia to camouflage its dastardly intents. It was then that the Saudi Arabia King called for a holy war with his statement, "We Moslems should call for a day not far away when we will all meet in Jerusalem to save our holy places and our holy land and achieve either victory or death in martyrdom."

Look behind you, 34 acres in the heart of your city. Yet it is not yours. On it is Al Aksa Mosque and the Dome of the Rock Mosque. In all Jerusalem they still remain the focal point of every eye...the bone in the chicken's throat. And right here God will declare his judgment.

I looked up at the sun. It was almost overhead now. I looked at Brother Bartholomew. Unnoticed by anyone I saw Brother Bartholomew quickly slip the protective cap from the laser ring.

In A.D. 73, he went on, the Jewish people sacrified their very lives at Masada. No more will Jews be asked to suffer another Masada. God has given me a special annointing...many years ago in this Holy Land...an annointing that some day I would save His people. Today is that day. Today your nation can once again build your Temple on the site which has been denied you. Today the 34-acre compound dominated by the Dome of the Rock...today that holy ground so precious to every Jew...today that will be yours....

With that Brother Bartholomew raised his right hand high into the sky. The sun was directly overhead. The rays of sunlight seemed to focus on the diamond channel in the center of the onyx ring. To me it seemed that some extraordinary power was surging through his body. When would he take down his arm and point it as the Mosque area. One minute must certainly be up. It seemed like minutes had dragged by. Not a word was said. I am sure the people thought Brother Bartholomew was offering a prayer to God. He looked like Moses...like a prophet of old. Then, slowly, almost unperceptibly, his arm slowly lowered, the fingers on his ring hand curved slowly. The arm stopped.

Like a bolt of lightning there was a rapid flash but no

thunder—just a deadening WOOSH! I looked quickly at that familiar golden dome upon the Dome of the Rock mosque. Then...my eyes darted back and forth...before my very eyes, and the eyes of everyone there...it had VANISHED!

The people went wild. They jumped to their feet screaming "MESSIAH, MESSIAH, MES- SIAH!" Hordes of them were climbing up backs until they formed ladders over the Inner City wall. When they reached the hallowed spot they kissed the ground.

I am come in my Father's name, and ye receive me not: if another shall come in his own name, him ye will receive. (John 5:43)

Shalom Ben-Mayer was elated. He kissed Brother Bartholomew with the kiss of welcome and led him to the waiting limousine. I entered with him.

The car had just started when the red light flashed on the mobile Picturephone. BB picked up the phone, flipped the video screen switch. An Israeli General appeared. He was standing outside a kibbutz on a hill overlooking a Jordanian valley.

He spoke sharply and quickly. "Mr. Prime Minister. THE RUSSIANS ARE COMING!"

And the word of the Lord came unto me, saying,

Son of man, set thy face against Gog, the land of Magog, the chief prince of Mesheck and Tubal, and prophesy against him,

After many days thou shalt be visited: in the latter years thou shalt come into the land that is brought back from the sword, and is gathered out of many people, against the mountains of Israel, which have been always waste: but it is brought forth out of the nations, and they shall dwell safely all of them. (Ezekiel 38:1, 2, 8)

Chapter 7

Triumph and Tragedy

Alexi Bazenoff was more than an armchair general. As Premier of Russia he offered the country new energies and direction. His grandfather Nikita Koschenov, unknown to many, had been in his younger days a Bible scholar. His sudden downfall in the 1960's was to lead to a misguided purpose. For in his day after day of inactivity he would carefully school little Alexi in the ways of man and the tactics of war.

One of Koschenov's favorite portions of the Bible was in Ezekiel. Disheartened because his personal ambitions were thwarted, he wanted to lead Russia on to new heights through his grandson. Alexi Bazenoff, he was sure, was destined for greatness.

Sitting by the hearth with the fire crackling through the logs, Nikita would open up a well-worn Bible, one his mother gave him.

"Alexi, read this," he urged. In halting childish tones Alexi read:

"And thou shalt say, I will go up to the land of the
unwalled villages; I will go to them that are at rest,
that dwell safely, all of them dwelling without walls,
and having neither bars nor gates.

...In that day when my people of Israel dwelleth
safely, shall thou not know it?"

"Good, Alexi, Good, read on. This next verse, Ezekiel
38:15, is very important!"

Alexi continued:

"And thou shalt come from thy place out of the
north parts, thou, and many people with thee,
all of them riding upon horses, a great company,
and a mighty army."

"Now read verse 16, Alexi, read verse 16!"

"And thou shalt come up against my people of
Israel, as a cloud to cover the land..."

"That's enough, Alexi, now listen to me. I am a very old
man but I see my destiny for tomorrow in you. Someday you
will be great. And I want you
to remember what I say. Someday the Russian forces will be
as a cloud so big and so great
that they will cover the land of
Israel. The wealth of the Dead
Sea is without estimate. You
will have for an inheritance all
that is now Israel. Look at her,
dwelling without walls, arro-
gant, gobbling up more and
more land...land that could be better put to use by our beloved country."

> And thou shalt say, I will go up
> to the land of unwalled villages; I
> will go to them that are at rest,
> that dwell safely, all of them
> dwelling without walls, and having
> neither bars nor gates,
> To take a spoil, and to take a
> prey; to turn thine hand upon the
> desolate places that are now in-
> habited, and upon the people that
> are gathered out of the nations,
> which have gotten cattle and
> goods, that dwell in the midst of
> the land. (Ezekiel 38:11, 12)

"But why horses, Pop Pop? I want to shoot them down
with atom bombs and big tanks."

"Listen, Alexi, that's exactly what they would expect and
prepare for. You could almost spit over Israel. And one bomb
would kill everyone, Russians and Jews. There is no God; but

this Bible was written by someone with a clever mind. What could be more deadly than an entire army of galloping horses, winding in and out of the valleys, the roads, and the forests which the Jews so foolishly planted after the Six Day War? They would have to fight us singlehandedly. And there would be more of us than of them. What I wouldn't give to live in that day, Alexi. But alas, I am old. But I will live through you. You must remember this, Alexi. You will lead an army as a cloud to cover the land...all of them riding upon horses."

That had been 30 years ago but Alexi Bazenoff never forgot that conversation. Pop Pop Koschenov had long been dead...but his words were to live on in the plans Bazenoff had laid before his field staff that night.

Bazenoff inherited his grandfather's Bible and he made an exhaustive study of horses and the part they played in warfare. He read in I Chronicles 18:4 where David took from the Philistines a thousand chariots and seven thousand horsemen and their horses.

And he knew Job 39:19-25 by heart, and that night encamped at Maras at the southern portion of Turkey, he recited it to his elite group of generals under a moonlit tent:

"Hast thou given the horse strength?
Hast thou clothed his neck with thunder?
Canst thou make him afraid as a grasshopper?
The glory of his nostrils is terrible.
He paweth in the valley and rejoiceth in his strength:
He goeth on to meet the armed man.
He mocketh at fear, and is not affrighted;
Neither turneth he back from the sword.
The quiver rattleth against him,
The glittering spear and the shield.
He swalloweth the ground with fierceness and rage;
Neither believeth he that it is the sound of the
trumpet. He saith among the trumpets, Ha, ha; and he
smelleth the battle afar off,
The thunder of the captains and the shouting."

Bazenoff reveled in the fact how well he knew Jewish history. They were now so filled with modern modes of transportation, the horse was almost unknown to them. He knew that early in the Israel-

Deuteronomy 17:16
1 Kings 4:26

ites' history that the king was prohibited by Mosaic law from multiplying horses to himself. And while Solomon had ignored this law, yet now horses were only a zoo animal in Israel.

The Russian horses combined Arab and English breeding. They stood over 17 hands, weighed a ton and could pull 27 times their own weight.

Morning came, cool, bright, and glorious. The Turkish Government had sent a guard of honor to meet Premier Bazenoff. Premier Bazenoff knew a little of the language and greeted the guard with, "Merhaba."

"Sağol, sağol," the guard replied.

Turkey was a very hospitable country. Sagol was the greeting meaning long life.

Turkey began her conquest of Asia Minor in the fourteenth century A.D. Then in 1453 Constantinople and the Eastern Roman Empire at last fell at the Turkoman onslaught. In 1516-17, in the reign of Sultan Salim I, the Turkish army captured Palestine. Turkey's seizure of the Mecca and Medina, Islam's holiest cities, earned for the Turkish Sultan the title of Caliph, head of the believers in the Islamic religion.

When Palestine fell to the British in World War I, Turkey longed for the day when this land would again be in her grasp. So, when the opportunity presented itself now in the 1990's, an unholy alliance was formed with Russia, Iran, Iraq and other countries to once and for all wipe the Jews from the face of the earth.

It was because of this desire that Turkey's leaders permitted Premier Alexi Bazenoff to use their country as a step-

ping off point for their impending great invasion of Israel...
an invasion of mounted horsemen.

It was late May. Summer was beginning. The air was dry.
The skies were clear and only in the coastal areas was there
any evidence of water when the nights brought refreshing
dew. During the day the temperature would soar over 100^oF
and at night suddenly drop to 30° F.

The Esdraelon-Jezreel Valley is the largest valley in Israel
and its plains were the scenes of many bitter battles.

Brother Bartholomew and Prime Minister Shalom Ben-
Mayer were now comfortably seated in a specially constructed tower observation post atop the Mount of Olives.

Brother Bartholomew had ridden up the gradually sloping
mount only an hour before. He
had exited from a special car
and he was invited to climb the
hill astride a white horse which

> And I saw, and behold a white
> horse: and he that sat on him had
> a bow; and a crown was given
> unto him: and he went forth
> conquering, and to conquer.
> (Revelation 6:2)

had been readied for the occasion. The throngs nearby
cheered and Brother Bartholomew waved sternly but cor-
dially. I followed with Ben-Mayer behind and on foot. The
crowds obviously looked upon him as a saviour arriving at
the crucial hour. Now from their vantage point atop the
tower they could with binoculars see Tiberias and Nazareth
70 miles to the north. Special television monitors mounted
on roving space satellites were also focused on the northern
border of Israel.

A row of screens faced both men. Brother Bartholomew
was talking. "Tune in Tiberias and angle the screen north."

Some dials turned...soon a picture was coming in to focus
on Screen 2. There appeared to be nothing but a cloud of
dust.

"That's only dust," commented Ben-Mayer.

"Is it important?" Brother Bartholomew questioned.

"Not only important, my dear brother, but very dangerous.
That dust you see is the dust of galloping horses. Turn the

space camera east to west. Now, look at the expanse of dust. It runs the whole gamut of the country. There must be one million horses or perhaps even more!"

"Horses?" Ben-Mayer said in derision. "Those stupid Russians are still fighting a Dark Ages war. Our military arms with nuclear heads will wipe them out in minutes. I'll alert the Generals to begin firing."

"Hold it, Shalom, it is you who are the fool, not they. For, for every thousand horses you kill, they will replace them with two thousand and your indiscriminate nuclear arms will kill more of your people than theirs and horribly contaminate the land...and they know it!"

"What shall we do?" Ben-Mayer shouted in distress.

"Nothing," Brother Bartholomew calmly replied, "Just let them come!"

"Are you mad...just let them come?...surely you must have a plan." With that, the Communications sergeant handed me a report off the picturephone teletype. This new teletype pictorially reported what it saw, combining it with commentary from the general in that specific field.

I handed it to Brother Bartholomew. He read, "The main force has left Maras, they are passing near Damascus." He turned to me and ordered, "George, get me Washington on the picturephone. Get me Science Strategy Division."

I pushed the necessary buttons. Abel Epstein appeared. He was such a mild-mannered man on the surface, it somewhat belied his tremendous intelligence. The laser ring was his discovery as were a few other highly sophisticated methods of destruction. His father was a Jew. His mother a Christian. But Abel was an atheist who believed in nothing, nothing except Brother Bartholomew's power to save the world. And for this he worked day and night to give BB that superior power.

"Abel, looks like an unusual invasion here. The nuclear detonation equipment won't work. Estimate millions of Russians on horseback already near Damascus. What do you suggest?"

"Kill or maim, sir?"

"We can't kill them all, they'd clutter up the countryside. Just stop them...turn them back."

"That rules out CBW sir. That's fatal in 30 seconds and a shift of the wind could prove disastrous. VX would kill them and would react again after six hours. That would get most of the bodies out, sir."

"No," Brother Bartholomew shouted.

"What about Q fever?"

"Epstein, have you lost your senses? You know that six ounces of the Q fever virus would be enough to wipe out 28 million people!" "Not this new mixture, sir, it's a watered down version, mixed with smallpox, typhus and encephalitis."

"Fine, Epstein, but mix in a little of that nerve gas that throws the enemy into a state of confusion, affects their thinking powers. Will three ounces be enough?"

"Yes sir. It will be ready in ten minutes."

"Good," BB replied, "We have no time to waste. Send it over by special Rocket messenger. Land on the Mount of Olives. We must have it here within the hour."

The screen faded.

I punched Screen 3 to get a later battle strategy report for BB. "The horses are near Capernaum at the northern end of the Sea of Galilee and are headed towards Mt. Tabor, sir."

Alexi Bazenoff rode his horse like a king. A most unusual horse it was. A mutation in cross-breeding had made it a fiery red in color. It was the only blood red horse ever bred. Leading his army through the desert paths he held up his banner to hail another army of horses coming from Jordan to join forces.

A cloud to cover the land, he mused as he looked around him. The dust of the horses had cast an ominous cloud over all the land. Pop Pop Nikita

> Thou shalt ascend and come like a storm, thou shalt be like a cloud to cover the land, thou, and all thy bands, and many people with thee. (Ezekiel 38:9)

had been right. He was to be a man of destiny. A saviour!

Alexi Bazenoff knew his history well. Palestine had been the homeland of Arabs for 2000 years. Zionism, the political movement designed to create a Jewish state, was the catalyst that pitted Arab against Jew. Russian policy was to help fan this conflict...fan it to the advantage of the U.S.S.R. Charges and counter-charges arose. The 1967 Six Day War had been a bitter blow for the Russians. Bazenoff was a boy then, but he remembered Nikita telling him of the toll. 15,000 Arabs killed. Only 679 Israeli casualties. $700 million in new Soviet military equipment captured by the Israelis. From that encounter Bazenoff had formulated his own military principle: namely, if you are going to fight a war, fight it — quickly, fiercely, totally, aiming for nothing less than complete victory at the earliest possible moment.

To bolster his hatred for the Jew his grandfather had pointed out President Truman's statement in his memoirs:

> "My efforts to persuade the British to relax
> immigration restrictions in Palestine might
> have fallen on more receptive ears if it had
> not been for the increasing acts of terrorism...
> committed [by Jews] in Palestine...
>
> I do not think I ever had as much pressure and
> propaganda aimed at the White House as I had
> in this instance. The persistence of a few of
> the extreme Zionist leaders — actuated by political
> motives and engaging in political threats —
> disturbed and annoyed me..."

With these thoughts in his mind Bazenoff felt sure of his gamble that the United States would not rush in to rescue the Jew. The thunder of hoofs behind him assured him he was leading an avalanche of power...power no one could stop!

Back in Washington Faye and Bill were trying to collect their thoughts. They huddled in the little bedroom in George's apartment. The room, about the size of a large closet afforded Faye and Bill the privacy they so much needed at this time.

Faye was heartsick. She still had not gotten over the shock

of the last few days since her hospital experience. George had warned them about the PRAYER CHANGES THINGS plaque on the wall.

That's why they huddled in the bedroom and as though they were commiting a criminal offense they furtively pulled out George's Bible from beneath the mattress.

Faye spoke first.

"Bill, I don't remember much Scripture. I never listened to that religious stuff. Now I see things so much more clearer, but some of these passages I still don't understand. Bill, I am sure now there is such a thing as the Rapture. I'm sure Helen and the kids were caught up in

> For then shall be great tribulation, such as was not since the beginning of the world to this time, no, nor ever shall be. (Matthew 24:21)
>
> Alas! for that day is great, so that none is like it: it is even the time of Jacob's trouble, but he shall be saved out of it. (Jeremiah 30:7)

it. And I remember once a preacher speaking about a Great Tribulation and Israel. Then I recall, he said that Russia would in those days come marching down on Israel. Bill, we've got to begin to memorize the book of Revelation today. I don't know how long we will have this Bible."

"Faye," Bill replied, "I know you're upset and I agree something is happening but I'm sure it can all be explained. There's peace in the Middle East. The Jews have never had more freedom. You must be wrong."

A thud on the door brought them to their feet. Faye quickly slipped the Bible under the mattress. Bill went to the door, opened it, just as the newsboy was walking down the hall. Bill picked up the newspaper. His face turned pale. Faye ran to him, looked at the headlines. She fainted.

RUSSIAN HORSEMEN INVADE ISRAEL

Bazenoff's band of horsemen would not be stopped. They were rounding the east side of Galilee. The historian Josephus Flavius, writing in the first century A.D. had related, "For the men of Galilee were warriors from a tender age and great in numbers at all times; their hearts were never ruled by fear, nor did this land ever lack men ready to bear arms."

But northern Galilee with elevations of 3-4000 feet offered a rapid descension for the hordes of Russians. Brave as they were the Israeli forces were no match. The cloud of dust engulfed them and moved on...like a giant steamroller crushing a mustard seed. The Jews had faith but the Russians had power.

The horsemen had traveled over 300 miles since they left the rendevous point of Maras in Turkey. And the million or more horsemen, from their very first mile of the journey had kicked up clouds of dust. Now, some 300 miles later the blue sky had turned to a blanket of dull brown. Everywhere you looked the thick choking dust penetrated the nostrils, blinded the eyes and the flying grit had ground to a halt many an Israeli tank and piece of mobile equipment.

From his observation post on the Mount of Olives Brother Bartholomew was noting this new development as he talked to Shalom Ben-Mayer. "This dust storm is something I hadn't anticipated. It can cause atmospheric hazards and upset nature's delicate balance. Anything can happen now."

The light on Picturephone 4 was blinking. BB flipped on the switch. It was the Mt. Tabor command post but the dust all but obliterated the picture. BB pushed the Atmospheric Clear-

And there went out another horse that was red: and power was given to him that sat thereon to take peace from the earth, and that they should kill one another: and there was given unto him a great sword. (Revelation 6:4)

ing Device. Almost all of the haze disappeared. You could see the horsemen approaching the foot of the 1843 foot Mt. Tabor. The rider on the Red Horse was clearly visible.

"Give me a rundown on Tabor, George."

I pushed the computer search buttons. A screen lit up with the Tabor data.

MOUNT TABOR

Limestone mountain in Galilee,
5 miles east of Nazareth. Isolated.
Scene of Gideon's defeat of Midianite

camel raiders. From Tabor's summit
one looks down on the Plain of Esdraelon.
Nearby river Kishon known to reach flood stage.
Height 1443 feet. Based upon a plain 400 feet
above sea level. Summit 1843 feet above sea level.

Ben-Mayer and BB were not paying attention to my comments. They stared intently at the action on Picturephone 4. Suddenly the screen clouded up again. BB angrily punched the ACD button...but this time the clearing device was not operative. Later we learned the dust had become so thick even the ACD could not penetrate it.

Air view of Mt. Tabor relayed on Picturephone 4.

Picturephone 4 screen was now almost black. Suddenly a brilliant flash of light surged across the screen! For a minute the whole area at Mount Tabor was exposed in raw, brilliant light...light so blinding even over the picturephone that for a moment I couldn't see. A long, rolling thunder could be heard in the far-off plains. It was like standing behind the pins in a bowling alley. First the roll of the ball. The sound builds up and within moments an awful, ear-splitting crash that shook the very mountain from which BB and Ben-Mayer viewed the battle.

Above the din BB was shouting to Ben-Mayer: "There's been an earthquake!" We looked at the screen. Mt. Tabor had split in half. Fire was erupting! What appeared like molten lava was rushing down its sides lapping up men and horses in its wake. From the black clouds above a space ship came hurtling to the ground. I recognized it as ours. It exploded in a fiery flame.

"My God!," BB exclaimed. "The space ship carrying Q fever is down!" The noise on the roof was deafening. "What's that?" BB shouted. "Hailstones, sir, as big as grapefruit." Ben-Mayer turned white. "Hailstones in Israel in 100° heat? Have the gods turned on us?"

With that he slipped to his knees, his head and hands facing heavenward. "Oh God of Jacob, hear us, help us, save us! Thou art one God. There is no other." With that he buried his head in his hands and wept unashamedly. Brother Bartholomew looked at him. I could see disdain and disgust form on his face.

Quickly he turned to the screen. Above the confusion Premier Alexi Bazenoff was still on his Red Horse, urging on what remained of his army of horses. The speaker on Picturephone 4 picked up his voice. In Russian he was shouting

ON TO JERUSALEM
ON TO JERUSALEM
ON TO....

Just then his voice trailed. From the heavens came a bolt of lightning making a direct strike on Bazenoff. There was no telling him from the fallen red horse and the ever widening pool of blood that eddied where he once had commanded. Bazenoff was dead!

The minute the surrounding horsemen saw this, they fled in confusion. A puff of smoke emerged from the fallen space ship. As it passed through the ranks of horsemen they suddenly become disoriented, confused, beginning fiercely to fight each other.

BB pushed the CLOSE-UP button on the Picturephone. The scene he saw was not a pleasant one for tender stomachs. Sores erupting over the skin of the Russian soldiers; running, open sores that generated welts of puffed up flesh. The hot sun combined with the unquenchable fires made the flesh burn. The crazed horses were trampling on man and beast. The crazed army was pitted man against man, dying on their brother's sword, becoming victims to their brother's bullets.

> And it shall come to pass at the same time when Gog shall come against the land of Israel, saith the Lord God, that my fury shall come up in my face.
>
> For in my jealousy and in the fire of my wrath have I spoken, Surely in that day there shall be a great shaking in the land of Israel;
>
> So that the fishes of the sea, and the fowls of the heaven, and the beasts of the field, and all creeping things that creep upon the earth, and all the man that are upon the face of the earth, shall shake at my presence, and the mountains shall be thrown down, and the steep places shall fall, and every wall shall fall to the ground.
>
> And I will call for a sword against him throughout all my mountains, saith the Lord God: every man's sword shall be against his brother.
>
> And I will plead against him with pestilence and with blood; and I will rain upon him, and upon his bands, and upon the many people that are with him, an overflowing rain, and great hailstones, fire, and brimstone. (Ezekiel 38:18-22)

Just a few miles away...the Israeli army was kneeling in prayer. The intense heat and fire of the battle did not touch them. The heavens had opened and flooded the Israeli position with a violent, blessed rain.

The battle was over. The Lord had given His remnant people, the Jews, the victory. No matter what Brother Bartholomew said about the wonders of his Science Strategy Division, this was not a battle won by man. It was a battle won by God.

The Shofar horn sounded. And the Jews rushed to the Western Wall to go offer their grateful prayers. This was a day of rejoicing for them. Almost all of these Jews were attributing this victory to God. One young Israeli soldier—who told me that he had only a day ago become a Christian, a Christian-Jew—told me that Christ

> Thus will I magnify myself, and sanctify myself; and I will be known in the eyes of many nations, and they shall know that I am the Lord. (Ezekiel 38:23)

was the one who had intervened. I had no time to listen, BB was leaving.

Brother Bartholomew said goodbye to Ben-Mayer and promised that he personally would financially sponsor the building of the new Temple on the former site of the Moslem Dome of the Rock. It was going to be, BB assured the Prime Minister, the most magnificent structure in this part of the world.

BB and I boarded the Presidential plane at the Jerusalem airport. The pilot walked back to BB's inner office and handed him a communique. The Common Market states were praising BB's feats in Israel. They urged him to stop immediately in Brussels, Belgium for a most important meeting. The die was cast. BB instructed the pilot to fly to Brussels.

It seemed like every newsman in the world was covering

Common Market Headquarters Building, Brussels, Belgium.

this Brussels event. I met many of my old friends there. Tom Malone, BB's Presidential Secretary, was there also.

"That was some coup BB pulled in Israel," Tom remarked. I added in a half lament, "You'll never believe the destruction. I have never seen such carnage in my entire life. Bodies, blood everywhere. It will probably take a month to bury everyone."

"You must be kidding," Tom replied, "practically the whole Russian army was killed. Israeli officials estimate it will take seven months just to bury the dead. They'll be shoved into one valley. Tourists will know it as the Valley of Russia's Host. The pictures we got back here make the battlefield look like a scene from a Middle Age history book. Bows, arrows, shields, spears everywhere. Crude weaponry but highly sophisticated with nuclear explosives for close-up fighting. Some say it will take seven years to burn the stuff."

> And it shall come to pass in that day, that I will give unto Gog a place there of graves in Israel, the valley of the passengers on the east of the sea: and it shall stop the noses of the passengers: and there shall they bury Gog and all his multitude: and they shall call it The valley of Hamon-gog.
> And seven months shall the house of Israel be burying of them, that they may cleanse the land. (Ezekiel 39:11-12)
> And they that dwell in the cities of Israel shall go forth, and shall set on fire and burn the weapons, both the shields and the bucklers, the bows and the arrows, and the handstaves, and the spears, and they shall burn them with fire seven years. (Ezekiel 39:9)

The long table of delegates was impressive. Heads of every participating state were present from the King of England to the Prime Minister of Sweden. Even a delegate from the United States had been invited in anticipation of its union with the European bloc. England's King was taking an active role in politics now. Quite a switch from the 1970's.

The Table of Power, as I called it, was a circular affair with a slight extension coming out one side. Along this table were ten chairs. The eleventh chair was at the end of the extension. It commanded the view of all ten delegates.

The following countries were represented:
England

France
West Germany
Italy
Canada
Belgium
Norway
Sweden
Finland

The smaller European countries had long ago merged into France and Belgium. With Russia out of the picture, France was once again a free nation. The newly seated United States delegate was in the tenth chair.

The King of England was speaking: "...The armies of the North have been defeated through the brilliant maneuvers of Brother Bartholomew. But while the problems of the North have been solved, at least temporarily, our security is threatened by the forces of the Orient. In today's complex world another war could destroy man himself and make this earth uninhabitable. As spokesman for these ten countries of Europe and America we realize that we must now be as one under one head, under one government, under one leadership. In private meetings already held, each government has unanimously commissioned me, Mr. President, to invite the United States into our Federation—a Federation hereafter to be known as the United States of Europe. Your United States representative, John Marsh, is already seated in your nation's newly set up chair. And we ask you, Brother Bartholomew to be our Leader and President of this newly organized Federation."

With that the delegates of all ten nations stood up. Everyone in the vast rotunda stood up, clapping and looking at Brother Bartholomew. I sensed a look of triumph on his face... yet a triumph that was masked in a godly humility.

And the ten horns out of this kingdom are ten kings that shall arise: and another shall rise after them; and he shall be diverse from the first, and he shall subdue three kings. (Daniel 7:24)

The King of England motioned to the chair at the head of

the table. Brother Bartholomew approached it...sat down. The King removed the Crown of England from his head, knelt slightly, arose and then gently placed the crown on Brother Bartholomew's head.

The audience was hushed into silence. The King was speaking. "Ladies and Gentlemen, The PRESIDENT of the UNITED STATES OF EUROPE."

France was chosen for the Victory Parade...a parade that would convince the world of the solidarity of this new alliance of countries. It had borne the brunt of many wars and this gesture was one to bolster its tarnished pride. The great parade would pass through the famous Arc de Triomphe, the monument commemorating Napoleon's victories, completed in 1836. At the center is the tomb of France's Unknown Soldier, guarded by an eternal flame. The Arc, situated on the Place de l'Étoile (Star Place) is so called because 12 avenues radiate from it. Paris, the City of Light, was to be host to the world's most brilliant light—Brother Bartholomew.

It was a clear day. The sun accented sparkles of beauty as streaks of light played on the highly polished rifles carried by the armies of Europe. Never had so large an assembly of combined military might been witnessed.

The crowds were unbelievable. The crush of the crowds was tremendous. Viewing tiers four stories high had been erected to accommodate all the people who wanted to see the miles-long parade.

In the front limousine, standing up waving, was Brother Bartholomew. In each of the ten cars behind him rode the delegates of the other United States of Europe. THEN...

Just as Brother Bartholomew's car passed under the Arc de Triomphe, a wild-eyed youth broke through the restraining barriers, a pistol in his hand. Those around him said he was hysterically shouting, "ANTI-CHRIST, ANTI-CHRIST!"

A shot rang out. I was walking by the side of the lead car. I looked up at Brother Bartholomew. Blood was pouring from his temple. In a moment his lifeless body had crumpled to the floor of the car.

There was much shouting and confusion. A doctor ran to the car.

"Oh no!" I shouted. "Oh, no...no...it can't be...."

I knew it before he spoke.

"I'm afraid," he said, "Brother Bartholomew is DEAD!"

Chapter 8

Secret Flight to Babylon

The world was stunned.

Brother Bartholomew dead? It was true! Tom Malone quickly got on the intercontinental picturephone to Bishop Arthur. As the second highest officer in the government Bishop Arthur would automatically succeed to the Presidency. His appointment as the President's Consultant on Religion had assured him of this advancement. And as President of the United States he was now also President of the United States of Europe.

The free world looked to him. Times were desperate. And Bishop Arthur had to pull the world out of the fire.

Tom was speaking, "Sir, what shall we do with Brother Bartholomew's body?"

"Where is the wound?"

"In the temple, sir. The bullet is in the brain."

"Keep the body cold," Bishop Arthur replied. "This must be done at all costs. Dr. Curter will fly to Paris within the hour to prepare the body for the deep freeze. He'll bring a cryo-capsule with him."

In the morgue the still, lifeless body of Brother Bartholomew seemed godly even in death. A surgeon from the Rejuvenation Division of the President's experimental health department was already working.

This Division was rather new. Most people did not know it existed. Only the President's close aides were aware of the purpose of the RD department. The doctor worked skillfully and without wasted motion, carefully removing the spent bullet and cosmetically stitching the wound in BB's temple.

As he finished, Dr. Curter walked in. Behind him two men were wheeling the cryo-capsule.

From Dr. Curter's briefcase came foil sheets in roll form. Brother Bartholomew's body was sprayed with a special solution. From a pocket in his case Dr. Curter pulled out a plastic hood. It was placed over BB's head. There was an opening at one end...like the nozzle on a tire tube. Dr. Curter screwed a metal capsule on to it, pulled a release switch. Liquid swished into the plastic hood, enveloped Brother Bartholomew's face. Then the slow process of enveloping the

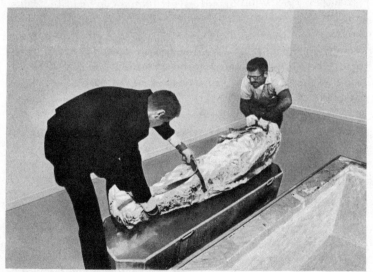

The body was carefully placed in cryo-capsule.

entire body in foil began. The body was then lifted, and carefully placed in the now very cold cryo-capsule.

Everything went like clockwork...as though it had all been planned beforehand. And somehow I sensed that it had.

The gold market had collapsed. The financial stability of the entire world was jeopardized. What little gold that was left was kept behind sturdy protective bars in an underground, secret room. But it gave the international business world no hope. Money was worthless. Governments could not control their own people. The population of each country was out of hand.

The ominous cloud of dust generated by drying and treeless regions had in recent years triggered disaster around the world. Much of the United States had not seen the sun for months. Only 25% of the sun's rays were filtering through. Now with the recent dust storm in the Middle East caused by a million galloping horses this was cut down even more. The now aggravated usual dust blanket over the cities created a form of carbon-dioxide pollution. It kept sunlight from hitting the ground. Blanketing the cities in the middle of summer, the weather was freezing. A simple virus, that in the past could have been shaken off with a few aspirin, now meant death in many cases. Burial was out of the question. There was no room for those 1970 niceties. Bodies were carted to disposal centers, treated to remove harmful bacteria, ground into special protein cakes. To me at first it sounded gruesome. Soon everyone accepted it. It was the only real meat anyone knew. And it made it possible for each one of us to exist just a little bit better off.

Bishop Arthur had alerted the international television network to be ready for his emergency Presidential address to the United States of Europe.

I knew that the transition had been made when I saw an aide slip a red mantle over the Bishop's shoulders.

Bodies were carted to disposal centers, ground into special protein cakes.

The address began.

Fellow citizens of the United States of Europe, brothers of the world. This is a solemn occasion. This is a sad occasion. Yet I accept this new office with a degree of humbleness and responsibility.

The events of the last few days have shocked all of us. Brother Bartholomew has given his life for us all. He died while serving us. Oh what love! He has also, in this case, given his life especially for the Jew. He and he alone stopped the hordes of Russian horsemen from swallowing up the little state of Israel. Not content to direct activities from Washington, this great soul without regard for his own safety, personally directed the battle from the Mount of Olives. And for this zeal and dedication what was his reward? The Jews, even Prime Minister Shalom Ben-Mayer rushed to the Western Wall thanking God for their victory. But it was not God who had promised to rebuild their Temple. Brother Bartholomew promised this. And the Temple will be built! How sad that as Brother Bartholomew humbly took part in the Victory Parade his yet young life was to be cut down by an assassin's bullet—the bullet, ladies and gentlemen, fired by a fanatical Jew! Their so-called Messiah, Jesus Christ, who they have yet to acknowledge, was crucified only between two thieves. Brother Bartholomew, however, in the prime of his youth, 33 1/2 short years, gave his life between millions of adoring followers.

But I promise this, while no one has seen or heard since of this fabled Christ who supposedly rose again... you will see...you will hear BROTHER BARTHOLO-MEW...for he WILL YET RISE AGAIN! RISE TO BE THE SAVIOUR OF THIS SICK AND DYING WORLD!

The papers that day emblazoned the news:

BROTHER BARTHOLOMEW TO RISE AGAIN
Bishop Arthur Blames Jews For Growing Famine

In school I remember reading about the 1969-1970 famine in Biafra. I can still remember being appalled at those photos of starving children. The death of some 3 million Ibos seemed a great tragedy.

...lo a black horse; and he that sat on him had a pair of balances in his hand. And I heard a voice in the midst of the four beasts say, A measure of wheat for a penny... (Revelation 6:5, 6)

But the world today was experiencing far greater tragedy. Food was never very plentiful, but because I was in the inner circle I managed to obtain artificial orange juice and a protein cake for breakfast, a spaghetti-like crude-oil concoction for lunch and a slice of DC protein meat at night. The Disposal Center protein meat, while only 8 ounces, was a life saver.

Now my food allotment had been reduced to the artificial orange juice and half a protein cake for breakfast...no lunch... the other half of the protein cake for dinner. Once a week, 6 ounces of DC protein meat.

Faye and Bill had the same fare. But somehow we made out. We knew we had to endure. More and more we delved into the Scriptures. And more and more we were discovering a hope worth living for. Our only fear was that Bishop Arthur's new rage against God might spell our doom.

Tom Malone and I were becoming very loyal friends. I couldn't tell him to his face, but somehow I felt he wanted the same hope of living that Faye, Bill and I possessed. But Tom had to be careful and I didn't want to place him on the spot.

I was afraid that out of his fight for mere existence, he would then have to terminate our friendship.

The whole country was a death camp. Tom filled me in on the reports that were coming in on the Picturephone. He was always careful to talk to me in a private office which not even BB seemed to have known about. This office had no PRAYER CHANGES THINGS spy plaque.

"George," he said, "I am sure we are on the brink of disaster. Refugees from all over the world are swarming to

America. Our one protein cake a day is heaven to them. What **And there shall be famines and pestilences...(Matthew 24:7)** meager possessions they have they carry on their heads. The sight of the children is pitiful. Wrinkled faces, haunted staring eyes, the utter apathy of aged men and women. In many cases I have seen the skin stretched so tight that every rib, hip and shoulder bone protruded. When they are given a protein cake the food won't stay in them. Mostly they are dying of diarrhea and malaria, a vicious strain our doctors can't control. When they die there's hardly any flesh left... so they can't even be put in the DC units. George, we are entrapped in a cruel web of circumstances. There is no way out."

"Tom, can't people be sensible about this? Stay where they are until a solution is worked out?"

"People will fight their own grandmother to live, George. Yesterday, walking through those muddy pools we call streets a girl accidentally dropped just a small piece of her protein cake. You would have thought that the inferno had broken loose. Immediately a band of girls were grovelling in the mud to claim the food. Two of them didn't come up alive."

"Tom, I remember reading predictions years ago about a day when there would be wholesale famine...but I didn't believe it."

"I have an old newspaper clipping here, George. It's yellowed with age. Sunday, July 6, 1969, Philadelphia Sunday Bulletin. Let me read these paragraphs my father had circled:

> A child born today, (that's 1969)
> living on into his seventies would know a world
> of 15 billion. His grandson would share the
> planet with 60 billion.
>
> In 6 1/2 centuries there would be one human being
> standing on every square foot of land on earth.

I feel fortunate to have a 12 foot square room all to myself."

"Tom, give me the facts straight, how critical is this famine?" "Far more critical than any of us can imagine. Even Bishop Arthur doesn't comprehend its magnitude. Health experts already are agreeing that at least one-fourth of the population of the world will be dead within the year!"

And when he had opened the fourth seal, I heard the voice of the fourth beast say, Come and see.

And I looked, and behold a pale horse: and his name that sat on him was Death, and Hell followed with him. And power was given unto them over the fourth part of the earth, to kill with a sword, and with hunger, and with death, and with the beasts of the earth. (Revelation 6:7, 8)

I was shocked beyond words. I slipped to my knees, right in front of Tom and uttered a simple prayer...

> Dear God, if we ever needed you, we need you
> now. Watch over Faye and Bill and Tom and
> me. Give us the crumbs from the Master's table
> to sustain us until the answer comes. Thank
> you Jesus.

Tom wiped the corner of his eye and walked out.

I ran all the way home to tell Faye and Bill the bad news that had just been revealed to me. I was surprised how calmly they accepted it. In the last few days their faith had grown stronger. Faye beckoned me to sit on the stool near the bed. She pulled out the well-worn Bible from beneath the mattress...then spoke.

"Dad, Bill and I have found some wonderful comfort in the Scriptures and today both of us discovered Psalm 91. Bill, you read the words we underlined."

In a soft voice, Bill read:

> He that dwelleth in the secret place of
> the most High shall abide under the shadow
> of the Almighty....

> Thou shalt not be afraid for the terror by
> night; nor for the arrow that flieth by day...

> A thousand shall fall at thy side, and ten
> thousand at thy right hand; but it shall not
> come nigh thee.

I, George Omega spoke, "Isn't it odd how things come back to us now that we have re-discovered God's Word. As Bill was reading from the Psalms I remember the Bible story that was taught to me in Sunday School about Elijah...how he multiplied that handful of meal. Faye, look up Elijah in the Proper Names Index in the back of the Bible."

Quickly she turned to the index.

"Here it is, Elijah raises the widow's son. I Kings 17...and here's another reference about Elijah taken up by a chariot of fire. II Kings 2."

"Read that I Kings reference first," Bill urged.

She turned the pages and read:

> And she said [the widow], As the Lord thy God
> liveth, I have not a cake, but an handful of meal
> in a barrel, and a little oil in a cruse: and
> behold, I am gathering two sticks, that I may go
> in and dress it for me and my son, that we may
> eat it, and die.

> And Elijah said unto her, Fear not; go and do as
> thou hast said: but make me thereof a little cake
> first, and bring it unto me, and after make for

thee and for thy son....

For thus saith the Lord God of Israel, The barrel
of meal shall not waste, neither shall the cruse
of oil fail, until the day that the Lord sendeth
rain upon the earth.

"God's promises are wonderful," I responded. "And I've
noticed something here that slipped me in the past. Here the
widow had but one meal left between her and death and yet
she shared that meal with God's prophet...and because of
her faithfulness God multiplied the little that she had.

You know, Faye and Bill, I realize that this proposal may
seem most unusual. But starting tonight let's share our
protein cake with God...he will be our unseen guest and
King."

Tears welled up in Faye's eyes. She put her arms around
my neck and hugged me as she exclaimed, "Oh, Dad I love
you so much."

For a moment she sat quietly, just dabbing her eyes with
her handkerchief. "Oh, I almost forgot," she exclaimed, "II
Kings 2, that's when Elijah rode a chariot to heaven. He did
not die. He was translated. Here it is...verse 11...

And it came to pass, as they still went on
[that's Elijah and Elisha], and talked, that,
behold, there appeared a chariot of fire,
and horses of fire, and parted them both asunder;
and Elijah went up by a whirlwind into heaven.

Isn't that wonderful, Bill?"

"Seems almost too fantastic to be true," Bill replied. "If
Elijah didn't die, whatever happened to him? How I wish
that all of us could right now ride in a chariot of fire right
up to heaven. It would be an answer to prayer."

I added, "Come to think of it Bill, somewhere in Revelation
there's reference to two witnesses. Somehow I wonder if we
might get to meet Elijah. I remember at one of Helen's
prayer circles overhearing the women talking about the day
Elijah and Moses would come back to earth. I wasn't inter-

ested then. I wish I had listened more closely."

"Well, I know one thing," Bill added, "I certainly would hate to be a Jew today. Bishop Arthur, in fact most of the world, has built up a real hatred for the problems they have caused all of us. But in my heart I can't condemn them. None of us is without sin...and the Jews are God's chosen...

Alas! for that day is great, so that none is like it: it is even the time of Jacob's trouble, but he shall be saved out of it. (Jeremiah 30:7)

After a while the subject changed. Faye inquired of me, "Dad, how did Brother Bartholomew ever reach such a high pinnacle of power?"

"Well, basically the people put him there," I replied. "The previous Presidents were spending taxpayer's money in areas which the people believed to be very foolish. Take the mid-1960's of President Johnson's era. $89,000 was awarded the University of Texas to study the sea breeze. The Department of Agriculture spent five years revising pickle standards in order to describe the difference between curved and crooked pickles. A grant of $33,101 was given to the Israel Institute of Applied Social Research to study a 'test of husband-wife relationship.' Among the $1 billion allocated in one year by the Food for Freedom program was a grant to study the behavior of elephants in Ceylon. And all this while a world was slowly starving."

"Then to top it off, the 1968 Presidential election set the trend for expensive politicking. Total bills then for all offices reached over 250 million dollars. Presidential timber to have any chance for success needed two things...a good advertising agency and $25 million dollars. The first they could do without...the second was a necessity. After several elections like this, people said it's time for a change. That's when Brother Bartholomew came into the picture. He had temporarily settled the Arab-Israeli cold war, eased the China picture and the Pope had made him honorary leader of the Church of the World."

"Where did he come from, dad?" Faye questioned.

"Faye, that's it!" I exclaimed. "I had never given that much thought. Oh yes, I interviewed him once in the Mideast before he came to America. That's when he began to like me. But I never researched his origins. They seem to be somewhere in Iraq. Was it Baghdad or Babylon? Say I remember that at the time there were some strange rumors about his birth and early life—almost like Christ's angelic announced birth. Faye, you've hit the nail on the head! I'm going to fly to Iraq tomorrow and get to the bottom of this. Tom will find some excuse to send me. I can depend on him."

When I arrived at Tom Malone's office he was busy poring over the latest Picturephone reports on world conditions. Disgustingly he flipped a sheet in my direction.

"Here, look at this," he said.

Young people using brooms and insecticide were trying to knock down the doors of a religious library in Rome. The insecticide was to symbolically disinfect the poison the clergy had spread about Brother Bartholomew.

I put the report down and put my hand on Tom's shoulder. "Tom," I said, "I've got to go to Iraq. Get me clearance, please to get the next space shuttle to the Mideast. Send me on an investigative mission...give any excuse."

Tom could see the earnestness of my face. And I knew he would make all the arrangements.

I took a slower shuttle to Iraq because I wanted some time to catch up on research on the country. Tom had slipped an old history book into my attache case. It filled me in on the facts.

Rumor had it that Brother Bartholomew came from Babylon. This was just a small town about 65 miles south of Baghdad in Iraq.

Ancient Babylon was once the rich and powerful capital of a civilization that almost created astronomy, added richly to the progress of medicine, and which taught the Greeks the rudiments of physics and philosophy.

Young people were trying to knock down the doors.

When Nebuchadrezzar II took over the second Babylonian kingdom he spent the tolls of his trade and the taxes of his people in beautifying his capital. "Is not this the great Babylon that I built?" he had asked.

Babylon a mysterious word! I always had known that the word *Babel* in the Hebrew meant "confusion." My further

> Therefore is the name of it called Babel; because the Lord did there confound the language of all the earth...(Genesis 11:9)

research, however, revealed that *Babylon* also meant the *Gate of God.* Nebuchadrezzar, as other ancient kings, was not very humble. For all the bricks archeologists recovered from the site of the original Babylon bear the proud inscription: "I am Nebuchadrezzar, King of Babylon."

Just north of the Tower of Babel were the famous Hanging Gardens, which the Greeks included among the Seven Wonders of the World.

What would I find in this little town of Babylon? I did not know. The space shuttle landed in Baghdad. The streets were bustling with people. They were rushing to the city square.

I asked why but no one seemed to respond. Quickly I followed the crowd. Soon I was to see the reason for all the excitement. There in the square were scaffolds. And uncontrollingly jerking back and forth were the spasmodic bodies of Jews...stars of David painted on their foreheads.

> And at that time shall Michael stand up, the great prince which standeth for the children of thy people: and there shall be a time of trouble, such as never was since there was a nation even to that same time: and at that time thy people shall be delivered, every one that shall be found written in the book. (Daniel 12:1)

I turned my head and walked away.

The purge had already begun.

I managed to get an official car to drive me to Babylon. We passed Al Mahmudiyah and Al Musayyib. Knife-edged mountains of shifting sand scallop the barren countryside. The plains suffer extreme heat and strong northeasterly

Uncontrollingly jerking back and forth were the spasmodic bodies of Jews hanging in the city square.

winds. Arabs comprise about 75 per cent of the population of Iraq. The largest minority (15 per cent of the people) is the fiercely independent, nomadic Kurds.

I started a conversation with my driver-guide. I knew he could be of inestimable help to me. Tahir Arif had a kind face. I was sure he would be cooperative.

"Tahir, you know we all mourn the loss of Brother Bartholomew. It is my understanding that Iraq is his homeland and that Babylon is his birth place."

"Honored sir," Tahir replied, "I hear only rumors that a great one was born in Babylon some 33 years ago. But no one seems to know the facts. It's as if they are hiding something. Please sir, I want no trouble."

"No trouble, Tahir, I assure you. I come representing the United States of Europe."

With that Tahir appeared to tense up even more. As we drove into Babylon I began to interrogate him again. In answer to my question he replied..."Sir, some say that the one you call Brother Bartholomew had no father. His mother swears to this day it is so. But, sir...I am only telling you what *they* say. I want no trouble."

"One who I call Brother Bartholomew? What do you mean one who I call 'Brother Bartholomew,' Tahir? Don't people in Babylon know him as such?"

It was amazing. I as a reporter had been so sloppy in my early reporting days. I had accepted the fact that this was his name; I had never investigated his origins closely.

Tahir Arif stopped the car in front of a very small makeshift house. We got out, went to the door of this rock-hewn dwelling. Inside was a surprisingly beautiful Persian faced woman of about 50. She beckoned us to sit down. Tahir acted as my interpreter. He explained why I journeyed here.

I interrupted. "What is your name?"

Through the interpreter she replied. Tahir turned to me and said, "In our language you would not understand the name. In English you say it; Mary.'"

"Was Brother Bartholomew her son and if so, who is his father?"

As the interpreter asked her my question I could see her get highly excited. She waved her arms as she spoke.

She says, "My son have no father. My son miraculously born. No father. Over there. Over there!"

> For false Christs and false prophets shall rise, and shall shew signs and wonders, to seduce, if it were possible, even the elect. (Mark 13:22)

I looked in the direction she was pointing. It was a manger! "What is his name," I asked.

The interpreter repeated the question in her language.

The reply confused him.

He asked her again.

She repeated slowly gesturing with her fingers and pointing to a well-worn calendar as she spoke.

He understood.

She says, "My son was born in June, the 6th of June at 6 o'clock in the evening. He was born without father. So I cannot name him after father. June is 6th month. Day is 6. Time is

> Here is wisdom. Let him that hath understanding count the number of the beast: for it is the number of a man; and his number is Six hundred three score and six. (Revelation 13:18)

6. His birth is miraculous. I give him no man name. He is above sinful man's name. I give him number name. No one has number name but my son. You are the first one I tell this to. His real name is Six hundred sixty-six!"

I shuddered. Could it be true? Born in a manger. Miraculous birth. No name but a number. And the number 666? Quickly I thanked the woman and beckoned for Tahir to drive me back to Baghdad.

Upon my arrival back in Washington, Bishop Arthur called me into his office. To me it looked more like a throne room. I could see he was angry. He had discovered the real reason I flew to Iraq. He warned me that I would be dealt with harshly as would Faye and Bill if my loyalty to his service bordered on disunity.

I assured him this was not the case. I was merely following through in investigative reporting procedures to help him in resolving Brother Bartholomew's death.

Faye and Bill were overjoyed that I had returned home safely. In the short time that I was away conditions had become even more critical. Food allotments were cut down further. There was talk of more drastic action: elimination of the weak, the elderly over 55 and those not useful for the progress of society.

I was in a stupor as I quickly told Faye and Bill in our little bedroom corner what I had learned in Babylon. All the pieces were now fitting together. We could see it clearly. Faye had been doing some intensive studying of Revelation and Daniel. Bill would read some verses, then they would tell each other what they thought they meant. After much repeating, soon the truth of the verses became plain. Much time had been spent on their knees, pleading and pleading to God for wisdom. "Dad," Faye cried, "God must be answering our prayers for the Scriptures are becoming clear to me now."

With that came a knock on the door. As though it was well rehearsed, Faye quickly slipped the Bible underneath the mattress. I walked to the door. Bill sat down in the tiny living room.

"Open up, George, it's me, Tom."

I opened the door.

"George, I just had to see you as fast as possible. I have some bad news. Bishop Arthur is going to make a strange pronouncement tomorrow in his telecast. In commemoration of Brother Bartholomew everyone must honor him as God. This homage must be so indicated by a mark either in the right hand or on the forehead."

> And he causeth all, both small and great, rich and poor, free and bond, to receive a mark in their right hand, or in their foreheads.
> (Revelation 13:16)

"What kind of mark," I exclaimed?

"The mark of 666!"

Chapter 9

Startling Pronouncement

Bishop Arthur insisted that I fly to China with him. I felt he was beginning to doubt my loyalty and wanted to make sure of my every movement. I had to be careful, not for my sake only, but for Faye and Bill.

Bishop Arthur had promised that Brother Bartholomew would rise again. I was hoping his promise would not come true for I felt that anything Bishop Arthur had a hand in would not be for the good. And yet I longed to see Brother Bartholomew again. He had been so kind to me and in spite of my findings in Babylon I felt that perhaps he might have the answer.

But I couldn't reconcile Brother Bartholomew with the Scriptures. In fact the more I studied the Scriptures the more I doubted. If it were not for Faye, I am afraid I would have become more confused and simply thrown in the sponge.

It was apparent to me that Bishop Arthur never glorified himself. But he was like a catalyst, generating respect and then directing praise and homage to Brother Bartholomew.

And I beheld another beast coming up out of the earth; and he had two horns like a lamb, and he spake as a dragon.

And he exerciseth all the power of the first beast before him, and causeth the earth and them which dwell therein to worship the first beast...(Revelation 13:11, 12)

But Brother Bartholomew was dead. Or was he? Of course, he was! I had seen his lifeless body with my own eyes. I had seen Dr. Curter wrap his body in a protective foil. Come to think of it, in all that hysteria of that day I don't remember any burial. The last I heard was that his body lay in a special room in the Rejuvenation Division of Capitol Hospital.

Bishop Arthur could have taken the fast one-half hour shuttle to Peking, but he later decided to take the slower 2 hour flight. The rapid change of time zones always gave him a severe headache. Dr. Curter had made sure that I was loaded down with anti-disorientation capsules. One day, shortly after Brother Bartholomew had died, Dr. Curter confided to me that with one slight change this powdered substance could become a lethal disorientation mix. When spread by spray such a mix would affect the nervous system, make one confused, disoriented, and ready to follow any command or directive.

Our space ship took off. Bishop Arthur patted me on the head like one would do to a good little boy.

"George," he said, "Things are moving very smoothly. I have a few surprises in store for you, in fact for the world. This quick trip to China should unlock the final door to my plan. By the way, did you catch my speech yesterday in my worldwide address?"

"No, I didn't sir, I was..."

"No need to tell me, George, I know exactly what you were doing. Our Central Intelligence knows every step you take. Not that we don't trust you. It's simply a matter of maintaining your loyalty Our CI division is very efficient...no botched up mess like that Green Beret episode in the late 1960's or the My Lai massacre in Quang Ngai Province that we once discussed. We have checks and double checks. Since the 60's our people have accepted very well the fact that their government has a right to lie...and does lie."

"You mean your statement about Brother Bartholomew rising again is a lie, sir?"

"No, George, that will become a reality."

And with that he punched a button on the work table in front of him. A television screen emerged.

"There, George, thought you'd like to see an excerpt of yesterday's address."

As the picture came into focus, I could see the Capitol Building. Everywhere I looked there were people, raising their hands in a victory salute.

...and in closing may I say this. At no time has this administration questioned the loyalty of its peoples. But we

And the ten horns which thou sawest are ten kings, which have received no kingdom as yet; but receive power as kings one hour with the beast. (Revelation 17:12)

are no longer a nation. We are many nations merged into one...ten nations all giving their allegiance to the new unit of power...the unit called The United States of Europe.

In these days of distress and famine, we must not be discouraged. We must lift up our eyes. We must become the Master of our Ship. Those who would betray this sacred trust can no longer hide under the cloak of respectability.

I have declared, in honor and in homage of our late Brother Bartholomew, each citizen shall from now on bear proudly the mark 666. For convenience of our ladies, it may be placed either in the right hand or on the forehead.

What greater way is there to show respect and loyalty than by this external evidence of our pride in being a responsible citizen of the world?

Those who refuse to bear this mark will automatically show their disloyalty to each of us

> And he causeth all, both small and great, rich and poor, free and bond, to receive a mark in their right hand, or in their foreheads:
> And that no man might buy or sell, save he that had the mark, or the name of the beast, or the number of his name. (Revelation 13: 16-17)

and to the honored soul of Brother Bartholomew.

It would not be right for them to pluck the morsels of bread from faithful families whose children may die for lack of nourishment.

The already restricted allocations of food must not be wasted on those who will not make a sacrifice of love and obedience.

No one may buy or sell without this mark. Such a decision needs time. A grace period of 30 days, starting today will be allowed. At the end of that 30 days, everyone must bear the mark of 666.

Remember, we have nothing to fear but fear itself. Let us lift our hearts to God and give thanks, for God

told us in His Word, *'in everything give thanks.'*
May our faithfulness bring an Elijah, an Elijah
who will take our barrel of meal and cruse of oil and
multiply this finite substance dedicated to God..."

Now I knew Bishop Arthur was aware of my every step.
Elijah! Faye and Bill and I had just discussed this miracle
ourselves. Life seemed so unreal.

The screen went blank and the unit returned to its original
position.

As we prepared to land in China I could see the venerable
Great Wall. Built 22 centuries ago as a defense against invaders, the wall still was a wonder of the world. Serpent-like,
it winds from east to west across more than 1500 miles of
China.

Leader Chou, Chairman of the Chinese Communist Party
greeted us quite warmly. We drove to the Gate of Supreme
Harmony, a magnificent structure of typical chinese archi-
tecture. Chou told us that here the first Manchu emperor
took his throne in 1644. The Gate of Heavenly Peace provided the entrance to the Imperial Palaces.

I wasn't sure why Bishop Arthur was coming to China but
I knew, as I smelled the aroma coming from the palace
kitchen, that here was one of the last places on earth where
food, real food, still existed. But only on very special oc-
casions could even Leader Chou enjoy such a feast. Once or
twice a year, the vaults would be open where these frozen
delicacies were stored. A bowing Chinesewaiter told me that
most of the delicacies were put in those vaults 25 years ago
in 1975 when Chinese leaders became aware of emerging
famine symptoms.

Chinese, standing in line, were shoving and pushing hoping
to retrieve just a scrap of left-over food.

The large round table was extremely glossy from a million
rubbings. In Chinese letters burnished in gold and lacquered
red were the words Hou Te Fu — meaning "Unbounded
Virtue and Happiness."

I had never seen so much real food in over twenty years. While my taste buds had become accustomed to the protein cakes I knew it would not take long for them to relish food that was not artificially made.

The first course brought what Leader Chou considered his favorite, "Fire pot eggs" — a fluffy souffle with thinly sliced lily bulbs suspended in its golden interior. Bear claws were also on the menu, but I never got around to trying them.

The main course was duck. It was a thing of beauty. First thin crisp slices of skin, dipped in sauce and wrapped with a small spring onion in a thin unleavened pancake, then the juicy meat, finally a fragrant soup.

The meal was topped with a dessert called Peking Dust. I could see Bishop Arthur's mouth water when this was mentioned. It was a puree of chestnuts, slathered with whipped cream and dotted with preserved fruit.

Imagine not having eaten real food in twenty years and then suddenly feasting on this table. Of the billions of people on earth, I was part of a very select few...eating real food. What a privilege! And yet I felt guilty. After the first burst of enthusiasm my heart sank. For I could see Faye and Bill, kneeling at the bed in our apartment, carefully breaking half a protein cake into two quarters...then each gently breaking the quarter into an eighth...setting aside one tenth as a tithe for Jesus in a little offering box we had made...slowly eating what remained...and then giving thanks to the Lord.

Right now they had so little. I had so much. Yet I was unhappy. I was sure they were rejoicing at their precious banquet and praising God.

After the meal both Bishop Arthur and I excused ourselves, walked quickly to the restroom. The meal had been too much for us. Like starving men we had eaten ravenously. Our stomachs could not contain such wholesome fare. As I bent over the washbasin I realized that real food had lost its meaning to me. No longer would I desire it. Such a lesson was preparing me for the months ahead.

Chinese, standing in line, were shoving and pushing hoping to retrieve just a scrap of left-over food.

Bishop Arthur was anxious to make sure the Chinese were sympathetic with the aims of the United States of Europe. Previous frequent border clashes with Russia had come almost to a standstill since Russia's defeat in Israel. And Bishop Arthur was fearful that this Asian Giant would start flexing her muscles in our direction. He seemed to fear this especially now because of BB's being assassinated and not on the scene to control things.

China's influence had grown in the last twenty years. She had swallowed up Japan, India, Pakistan, Vietnam, Laos, Thailand, all the little islands, Taiwan, and the Philippines. Finally even Australia was now yielding.

Leader Chou assured Bishop Arthur that the nations would live at peace. Each country, he said, had too many internal problems to solve. And Chou had remembered America's sincere humbleness in the late 1970's when she recognized China and shared her nuclear advances with China. Leader Chou had respected Brother Bartholomew and thus he had invited Bishop Arthur to make this trip to discuss the possible rejuvenation of this great man through the administration of the Chinese miracle-drug herbs. Both China and the United States of Europe were working for many years to bring a dead man back to life. Both were so near to the solution, yet so very far away.

Chinese Herb Doctors were still plying their trade in spite of what Americans called advance medical techniques. China had 24,000 pharmacies, 8700 licensed herbal doctors.

Leader Chou snapped his fingers. A door opened. An elderly gentlemen with the traditional long grey-white beard entered.

"This," leader Chou proudly introduced, "is Dr. Wu Hai-feng. Were it not for him I would have been dead long ago."

Bishop Arthur spoke: "Dr. Hai-feng, I am sure you have read of the modern advances which we have made in medicine. Do you feel your herbal remedies are better than our most recent discoveries?"

"Begging humble pardon, Great One," Dr. Hai-feng replied, "but the very fact that you are here is evidence enough that perhaps we have something you are seeking."

Bishop Arthur blushed. "Yes, Dr. Hai-feng, Brother Bartholomew is dead. A bullet through the brain. Dr. Curter of our Rejuvenation Division has developed a formula that should bring him back to life. But there is a missing link. For a brief second the body comes to life, the eyelids flutter...and then total collapse...dead again." Bishop Arthur then asked, "Why don't you use our Western techniques?"

"Easy to explain, Great One," Dr. Hai-feng continued, "We shun such so-called advanced Western practices as X-rays and blood tests. Chinese medicine is 5000 years old. Chinese herb medicine cures your disease fundamentally, even if it takes time. Western medicine — it cures quickly, but the disease may come back. Your ingredient brings life... but the disease...death...comes back. In this case...very quickly."

Bishop Arthur queried: "But the body is a most complex instrument, one must have a knowledge of the inter-actions of muscle, nerve and blood vessels. Am I not correct?"

"Not so, Great One. Herbs control the balance of yin and yang, the opposing forces that dwell in every person. Yin is passive and dark; yang is active and light. When a person has a cold, the yang dominates. Therefore I prescribe a herb to redress the balance of yin and yang."

"But there is more to the science than that," Dr. Hai-feng continued, "Traditional Chinese medicine says the body is composed of five elements — wood, fire, earth metal and air — and each of these elements has yin and yang. In a complicated illness, the balance of yin and yang in the five elements varies. That's why treatment varies from person to person. Because of the greatness of such a one as Brother Bartholomew and what we here in Asia hear of his supernatural birth, treatment of yin and yang may prove most difficult."

As I listened I wondered silently, "Was Dr. Hai-feng speaking of yin and yang to keep the Chinese discoveries secret—or did he believe this?"

With that Dr. Wu Hai-feng placed a flask on the table. In it were what appeared to be brown and green slushes bubbling. He explained that this was a herb mixture which included chin pu hun, a pulverized twig called ma huang and a few other exotic names which I could not remember.

"Leader Chou," Dr. Hai-feng continued, "has told me in detail of your mission. Perhaps our old customs of medicine combined with yours may bring back Brother Bartholomew. One catalytic ingredient — Formula 6 — is still missing to make this flask potent. Years ago Leader Chou had it flown to the moon and deposited in a crevice called China Crevice. There in underground vaults it is held. Place one cubic centimeter of Formula 6 in with this flask. Complete instructions are in this envelope. Give it to Dr. Curter. We wish you success."

I had never been to the moon. This was to be a real adventure. Leader Chou had made his spacecraft available for our use. Our own space craft was to rendevous above the moon and wait for us.

At the airfield the space craft prepared for lift-off. I had never seen such a vehicle. We were advised that it was a utility aircraft, a flying, crawling vehicle for lunar exploration. It looked like two large tubes connected with two center posts. Each of the tubes had landing gear resembling wheels ordinarily seen on tanks. On lift-off these tractor-type wheels receded into the spacecraft.

As we approached the moon Bishop Arthur pushed a button that revealed the floor viewing screen. There below us was Tranquility Base...the original landing sight of man on the moon back in July, 1969 some 31 years ago.

"We've made much progress since then, George," Bishop Arthur commented. That landing site is now an international shrine. The bubble enclosure makes it habitable. Millions of people since 1981 have taken the Earth-Moon shuttle to view this accomplishment. The first 240,000 mile journey was a big project then. Apollo-Saturn V which launched those first space men was 363 feet tall, the height of a 36-story building. Since then we modified the height and weight through miniaturization of materials and use of nuclear energy."

"Wasn't it one of our astronauts that said after that first landing, 'I've always believed that nothing is impossible and now I'm convinced of it.'"

"That's right," Bishop Arthur replied. "And it was the President at the time who replied, 'This is the greatest week in the history of the world since the Creation.' You have a Bible, George. It's a King James Version...rather outdated... but our new Revised Standard Version spells this feat out quite clearly in Genesis 11:6...

> And the Lord said, "Behold, they are one people, and they have all one language; And this is only the beginning of what they will do and nothing that they propose to do will now be impossible for them.

"That's why, George, Man is the Master of his fate. The Jews recognized this when they forced back the Arabs in that Six Day War. Many said it was God...the Jews were returning to Israel. Others were much wiser, however. It was their might, their energies. Now they have softened. I fear they are returning to that imposter God of the Bible. You will see, George, Man will bring Brother Bartholomew back to life. It will be a miracle. I promise that you will see this with your very eyes."

The grayish-tan surface of the moon came into focus as we prepared to land. It reminded me of the Sahara desert. A fine grain dust covered the surface. When we walked on it, it had the cohesiveness of wet beach sand. Every step we took left footprints. But our footprints were hard to distinguish. So many people had walked here that one footprint simply was superimposed upon another. The area we were walking on was restricted territory. Originally the then United States had hoped that the moon would be a neutral territory. The U.S. had thus made an agreement with Russia. But as with all agreements with Russia, this too was broken.

And once it was broken, the other nations rushed in to claim their territories on the moon.

What was commonly called by us "The Chinese Crevice" was located near the 2-mile-deep, 56-mile-wide Crater Copernicus, whose flat but rubble-strewn floor was broken by a chain of 1,000-foot high hills.

A Chinese astronaut was lowered by crane down into the crevice. We were told that at its base was an underground vault, guarded with special electronic spy-gear to prevent others from entering. China's top classified secrets were kept here.

Within a few minutes the astronaut returned to our space ship. In his hand was a vial. It was labeled, "Formula 6."

The talk in Washington was all about The Mark 666. How would it be administered? Was it a large mark? Women buzzed about the cosmetic significance. Most women were inclined to have their mark placed on their hand. Some felt it would show a greater sense of loyalty to have the mark on the forehead where all could see. Rumor had it that those with the mark on their forehead would be allocated a greater ratio of food, receive the better jobs. Earth's population had grown so out of control and resources were so limited that those who were able to find jobs were restricted to only two hours per week. It was the only way to somehow, ineffective as it seemed, spread the work opportunity. Many learned the trick of not notifying an employer that their brother or sister had died. The unemployed in the family would then take on that two hours of work as though nothing had occurred. Strange alliances among employees kept such shady dealings, for the most part, secret.

Faye, prior to the announcement of The Mark, had already been reduced to the one hour per week work category. Bill could find no work...not even in the disposal centers.

Bill walked in the apartment that night discouraged. Over 6000 people had lined up that day at the disposal center... eager to apply for the one job opening that had been posted. Bodies were coming in at a faster rate...thus the opening.

Faye could see the disappointment on his face.

"Bill, come over here honey. I know how you feel. Life today seemed hopeless for me, too. The girls at work were all talking about The Mark. I said nothing. I sensed that they knew I could not wear the brand. At the end of my work hour my supervisor came over. He said my work privilege had been cancelled. We'll starve to death with no protein cakes... but we must not lose our faith in God."

"I know Faye," said Bill, "my mother used to tell me it's darkest right before the dawn."

Bill then sat down on the floor in the bedroom next to Faye. They looked out the window. Of course they could not see the stars. The murky haze of thick brown dust clouded the view.

"Bill, let's pretend this is our little honeymoon cottage. The fireplace is over there. You've just put a log on the fire. The wood is crackling a sweet song of peace and contentment. Outside the snow is gently falling blanketing the tiny shoots of grass and the tall stately trees in a brand new white winter coat. And you and I are alone together. The night is still. Not a sound. And we're all alone with our dreams. Up above the stars are twinkling a canopy of light. And the baby stars nestle in the velvety blanket of midnight blue."

Bill dreamily responded, "Then, Faye, the moon will majestically make its way across the Heavens and the stars will play tag happily following. Watch, I'll find the big dipper for you!"

"No you won't, Bill, honey. I'll find it first. And look there's Pleiades. Oh, how I remember how much fun we used to have in naming those six sisters."

And with that tears formed in Faye's eyes. Her sobbing broke Bill's heart.

"Oh, Bill, Bill, Bill, why does life have to be this way? What has happened to the simple freedoms of life? Why has man's advances cursed man's living? Why did I turn my back on God for so many years? Helen, little Sue and Tommy. They're in Heaven now enjoying the blessings of God. But we're here on this miserable, sophisticated, progressive, godless, everything-goes earth. Bill, I have faith. I believe God...but I can't go on. I can't go on. I can't go on!"

Bill was crying.

"Faye, just lean your head on my shoulder...remember that honeymoon cottage now. Careful, honey, your tears will put the fire out. Then I'll have to go out and get some more dry logs. And it's awfully cold outside. Remember Faye, that night we watched the sun rise. It was very dark. Then just a slight hint of red peaked across the horizon. A little hue of yellow. A few impatient streaks fanned out. The dark sky became a mirror reflecting that precious light, bringing a lighter cast over the earth. Soon just the tip of that bright red sun appeared. The velvety shadows began to disappear. The warmth of the sun began to fill our room. Soon the darkness vanished...vanished so quickly that it seemed it had never appeared. Faye, right now the dark sky is above us day and night. But beyond it, waiting for God's holy signal is the sun, God's Son. We've read the Book of Revelation and

For then shall be great tribulation, such as was not since the beginning of the world to this time, no, nor ever shall be. (Matthew 24:21)

Daniel together. We have seen the signs God has told us... the Great Tribulation, the last half of Daniel's Seventieth Week, is about to come. It will be dark, Faye, very dark. But it's in God's timetable. And we should be rejoicing...for beyond this brief time of Tribulation the sun will bring back to the world its love, its warmth.

And Faye, when you and I look back, basking under His light in the New Heavens and New Earth, why it will be as though the darkness of Satan never

And when these things begin to come to pass, then look up, and lift up your heads; for your redemption draweth nigh. (Luke 21: 28)

appeared. God in speaking about His nation Israel, told us in Isaiah 48:10:

> Behold, I have refind thee, but not with silver;
> I have chosen thee in the furnace of affliction.

And that is our promise too. Then in II Corinthians 4:17...

> For our light affliction, which is but for a moment, worketh for us a far more exceeding and eternal weight of glory.

Faye, you're smiling now."

His head bent down to hers.

Their tears mingled as they kissed, tenderly, not in passion, but in understanding.

Faye jumped up...like a little girl with a toy.

"Bill, I've a little surprise for you...and for daddy."

The sound of a key was heard at the door. It was George. "Daddy," Faye shouted, "you came just in time." Then realizing she was in the room with the PRAYER CHANGES THINGS plaque, she whispered in George's ear to come to the bedroom.

Startling Pronouncement • 173

George entered, shook Bill's hand, and then sat down wearily on the floor. Quickly he briefed them on his trip to China and to the Moon. His face betrayed his emotions. He was afraid something drastic would happen soon.

"But let's not talk about me, what's the surprise?" Bill questioned.

Faye held a compact, small rectangular box in her hand. "It's that pocket record player you and mom gave me one Christmas, Daddy," Faye replied. "And remember that little plastic record mom's church used to pass out on visitation nights. I still have the one she gave to me. It was one of the

few things I threw in the overnight bag that night we fled New York. And I had forgotten about it until just a few moments before Bill came home from job hunting. Let me put the record on and play it. I have never yet played it so it will be a surprise to all of us."

Faye hurridly placed the record on the spindle. Flipped the ON switch. Nothing happened.

Disappointment shone on her face.

George picked up the record player...then spoke. "Faye, this won't play. The batteries have long since lost their power. I remember Helen giving that to you over three years ago. The batteries are dead. How cruel can life be to us?"

Bill's face lit up. "Wait a minute. I wasn't a Boy Scout for nothing. As a kid I remember how we made record players play. I'll just put my finger on the turntable and turn it around manually at the speed where the record makes sense." And with that he started the turntable spinning. At first it sounded like a Model T Ford being cranked up with all sorts of sounds emanating from the machine.

Then when Bill found the right speed, he maintained it and words of a song sung in a beautiful contralto voice filled the little room....

> It's not the first mile
> that's so important;
> It's the last mile
> when day is done.

> Then you'll see Jesus
> in all His Splendor;
> And He will have for you
> the Crown you've won.

Over and over again they played it like little children. Then George spoke. "You know, I had forgotten it until now but I can remember Grandmother singing to me while she put me to sleep. In her rocking chair besides the bed...she would sing the hymn 'Blessed Quietness' over and over again. She sang it so often, I could repeat it by heart — all five verses."

And with that he broke into song...

> Joys are flowing like a river
> Since the Comforter has come
> He abides with us forever
> Makes the trusting heart His home.

> Blessed quietness, holy quietness

What assurance in my soul!
On the stormy sea, He speaks peace to me,
How the billows cease to roll!

Bill spoke. I could tell his heart was touched. "George, Faye, I have had perhaps greater opportunity to study God's Word because I have had no job. And it just dawned on me. We've been talking about God...about how we know He will care for us, how we understand His prophecies. But I can't recall that any of us have ever asked Christ to come into our hearts...accept Him as our personal Saviour. John 6:37 tells us that

...him that cometh to me I will in no wise cast out.

and John 6:47 says

Verily, verily I say unto you, He that believeth on me hath everlasting life.

And Romans 10:9

That if thou shalt confess with thy mouth the Lord Jesus, and shalt believe in thine heart that God hath raised him from the dead, thou shalt be saved."

"How true, how very true, we have forgotten the most important thing of all," Faye replied. Let's right now make a pact with ourselves and with God. Let's kneel and hold hands and pray asking Christ to come into our hearts. Dad, you've heard mother pray so many times. You lead...please."

George, Faye and Bill knelt in the tiny room, each holding the other's hands. George began:

"Dear Lord, we don't know the right words to say. In fact we don't understand much of thy Word. But Helen told me there's a verse about 'Lean not to thy own understanding.' And we don't understand.

But I know this and so does Faye and Bill. We are sinners. Lost sinners. The world has gone mad...and we're headed straight for Judgment and Hell.

Lord Jesus, we want to right now confess
our sins. I want to confess my sins. I
believe you died and rose again from the
dead. I know that I cannot save myself.

Save me dear Jesus according to the promise
in your Word. I want Christ to come into
my heart, be my Saviour and my Lord.
                    Amen"

Bill continued the prayer...

"Precious Lord, we claim Romans 10:9
as a promise for our lives, for my life.
I, too, want Christ to come into my
heart right now."

Then Faye prayed...

"Thank you Lord for keeping us together
as a family. Thank you for Helen's
testimony to us. Thank you for dying
on the cross of Calvary for my sins
and the sins of the world.

Save me now, Lord. Forgive me for turning
my back on you. Save me and keep me.
Make our reunion with Helen and Sue and
Tommy soon, dear Lord.

I, too, accept Christ as my Saviour and
my Lord.

                    Amen"

As Faye finished a loud buzzer sounded. It came from the
wall near their heads. Startled the trio stood up quickly.

"What's that, Dad?" Faye asked.

"Sounds like its coming from behind the drapery," George
replied. Quickly he pulled back the drapery.

There like a symbol of death hung a plaque. On it the
words

PRAYER CHANGES THINGS

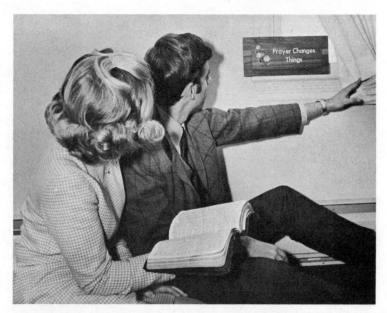

A voice then spoke from the very plaque itself. It was the voice of Bishop Arthur.

"George, you have betrayed me. And more important you have betrayed the soul of Brother Bartholomew. You and your daughter and your son-in-law will pay for this decision you made to your God. Then let's see if He can save you. The first payment will be in blood...the day after tomorrow. Bill will be the first to meet the convincer. And what a most appropriate place we have for that spectacle to occur! The day after tomorrow Bill will die. He will die by guillotine!"

And when he had opened the fifth seal, I saw under the altar the souls of them that were slain for the word of God, and for the testimony which they held. (Revelation 6:9)

...and I saw the souls of them that were beheaded for the witness of Jesus...(Revelation 20:4)

Chapter 10

Search for Safety

Dr. Curter was pleased with his progress.

"Those Chinese are clever, Bishop Arthur, their age-old medicine appears to be the missing link we desperately needed. I believe we are going to have success."

Bishop Arthur smiled. His diabolical plan must succeed. Brother Bartholomew must be brought back to life.

The damage to the nerve cells of the brain worried Dr. Curter. His remarks conveyed this fear: "I feel sure of success in restoring life, Bishop Arthur, but we have no way of telling what mind will evolve...a genius, an evil or benevolent mind, or a mentally slow person."

Bishop Arthur interrupted, "Don't even suggest such a thing, you idiot."

"Now, now, Bishop," reassured Dr. Curter, "we mean no disrespect to Brother Bartholomew. We are just evaluating the situation realistically. You see the 10 billion nerve cells of the brain make a bumpy knot of gray and white matter inside the skull. The brain is an integrated unit. I'm particularly worried about the cerebral cortex. This is the brain's most elaborate center, where voluntary actions are initiated. It has been called 'the seat of all which is exclusively human in the mind,' for here decisions are made, higher thought processes occur, and memories are stored."

"What about brain transplant?" Bishop Arthur queried.

"I don't think it's indicated here, sir," Dr. Curter continued. "And besides it is Brother Bartholomew's head — not his body—that we want to bring back. Besides, while medical science has advanced we haven't perfected the technique yet. Complete head transplant is no problem. In the early 1960's we were transplanting heads on dogs. And here's how advanced we have become..."

With that Dr. Curter pressed a button, a door slid open from the wall. There in a glass viewing enclosure was a dog... but not an ordinary dog. This one had a human head!

Momentarily even Bishop Arthur was shocked. He stepped back and motioned with his hand to Dr. Curter to close the viewing door.

"A head transplant would be out of the question. We must maintain the same head, the same features Brother Bartholomew had before he was shot," Bishop Arthur now affirmed.

"For the most part," Dr. Curter continued, "the brain controls the 600-odd muscles of the body. And damage to the brain may affect the 60,000 miles of tubing which carried blood to every part of the body. But in this particular case it's the nerve cells that worry us. Nerve cells in the brain alone use up as much as 20 per cent of all the oxygen available in the adult body, for they are working at a frantic speed 24 hours a day. Sleeping does not, as some would believe, give the brain much of a rest. Quite aside from maintaining breathing and the rate of heartbeat, the brain may function during these sleep periods to try to search out answers to particularly difficult problems and to reconsider experiences of the day that were flowing in too fast to be dealt with carefully at the time. Normally, during the course of every 24 hours, we lose some neurons. They wear out and die. Fortunately great numbers would have to die to produce any noticeable effect, but the small losses inevitably accumulate. Once a neuron is destroyed—it is destroyed. No new nerve cell will ever take its place; a year-old baby has all the neurons it will ever have. If we can find the answer to this we can slow down mental old age, eliminate senility."

"Enough of these medical explanations, Dr. Curter, what are you trying to tell me?" Bishop Arthur asked impatiently.

"Just this, sir, with the special solutions we injected into Brother Bartholomew's body and his prompt placement into the cyro-capsule...we were able to forestall complete death and deterioration and place him in what medical science might term a death-sleep. During this death-sleep the brain still remains active...just as active as when you and I sleep. But with no physical activity, brain activity increases, and in this case the neurons may or may not die. Once brought back to life we have no way of knowing the direction Brother Bartholomew will go. Will this intense brain activity explode into a man-created monster who may kill half the world with plans which, in his pre-dead condition, would have never occurred to him? And the neurons...will they be effected in some way so they direct him to evil? It could even be that he may upon awakening see himself as a god!"

"Stop, stop," interjected Bishop Arthur. "I should have had you replaced..."

* * * * *

The heads of state from all over the world were invited. It was to be the most historic occasion the world had ever witnessed. Even greater than man's landing on the moon.

Looking at the new structure from the air, it resembled a cross. In physical beauty it was stupendous. Pure white marble steps led up to the main entrance. This was the building Bishop Arthur had talked so much about. The building to house a memorial for BROTHER BARTHOLOMEW. Three stately columns were on each side of the entrance door. On these columns were recorded the accomplishments of Brother Bartholomew.

Six large oval screens appeared over the building's door. A special black light made the area between the pillars and the building wall completely dark — so as you looked at the structure from the front you were met by a mass of darkness broken by the light emitting from the open door. Then there was in color, the six television-like screens portraying activities and events that Brother Bartholomew took part in before his assassination. One screen would light up at a time and as the picture of Brother Bartholomew walked across the panorama of screens his voice filled the square. Similar television screens were mounted throughout the city of Washington and were awaiting the press of a button that would make all of them relay stations showing Brother Bartholomew. They were as plentiful as street lights. Plans were made to install them throughout the United States of Europe. Wherever you looked one would see Brother Bartholomew.

What was not known at this time was that these relay video-lights had a dual purpose. They could not only send pictures over the screen but act as a very effective spy system to weed out dissenters. No one noticed the receiving units located at the bottom of each screen.

Bishop Arthur insisted that I and Faye and Bill accompany him to the ribbon-cutting ceremonies.

A special elevator brought the dignitaries and Bishop Arthur to the main floor. We were made to walk up what seemed endless steps. There were six landings before one reached the main floor. On each set of landings were 66 steps. I know because I counted them!

Upon entering the long hall it was difficult at first for us to see. Darkness seemed to envelop us until our eyes became used to the conditions. An usher with a small flashlight guided us to our seats. We were ushered right to the very front.

It seemed like a church, yet the front appeared devoid of anything. A long black drape from ceiling to floor blocked the area where a pulpit normally would have stood many years ago.

Bishop Arthur was now talking...

Friends of the world. How significant it is that leaders from every country of the world have gathered here...gathered for one purpose only...that singular purpose of paying homage to the greatest of men...so great we in honor refer to him as god-like.

I will not take the time to recount even his recent exploits: His single-handed victory over Russia and his bringing of peace to the land of Israel.

The video-lamps installed on every street corner in the western world will convey that message far better than I.

Today I press two buttons. One to light these video messengers of God's will...the other to light both the outside and the inside of this building, illuminating forever the name of this hallowed structure.

He pressed the first button. A large screen above lit up showing a panorama of the city of Washington, and in the darkness little dots of light formed. The video screens were telling their message.

Then the large screen disappeared.

He pressed the next button. On each side of the wall, as though they appeared from nothing, words glowed in a brilliant gold:

BROTHER BARTHOLOMEW
THE SON OF GOD

Then as quickly as they appeared, they disappeared.

Bill, Faye and I stared in horror and in disbelief. We held each other's hands tightly as a way of giving each of us inner strength.

In the very dim light I glanced at Bishop Arthur. Something big was about to happen. I knew not what. But his face no longer resembled that of a Bishop of the Lord. Some-

how, in my heart, I knew him to be a Prophet of Satan himself. And whatever his surprise, it would be Satanically
inspired.

Suddenly the lights went out. The long hall was pitch
black. I could tell that even the honored delegates were ill
at ease.

Slowly a pale light played on the velvet-like drape in the
front of the vast structure. It was not a flood light, but more
like a spot light that only lit one small portion at a time.

It started at the very bottom. It looked like a rough-hewn
piece of wood. As the light went up it appeared that this was
a vertical standing piece of wood...then some feet appeared...
a spike piercing them. You could see what seemed to be real
blood gushing down the black velvet in rivulets of stain.
Then legs, a body. Suddenly a cross piece of wood appeared.
The light played on one hand. Then went out. Then played
on the other hand.

Both hands were pierced with a spike and from those
hands blood oozed.

It was all clear now. It was a cross. The cross of Calvary.
But why would this godless man display the Cross of Christ?

Then it became all too clear. The light in a burst of dramatic drum roll shone on the face. Faye sobbed.

The face was not the face of Christ. It was the face of
Brother Bartholomew!

It was all too clear now...too sickening clear! The apostasy
of the early days in the 1930's, 1960's, 1970's had borne its
fruit. First it was the liberal churches. Then it was the evangelicals watering down the Gospel with their introduction of
the beat Gospel music...the Christian Rock groups...the
relevant Christianity that played down the prophetic Word
of God...stressed only the need for social concern. Now I
saw how subtly the forces of evil had worked to turn the
zealousness of the Church away from winning souls towards
a more material, business-like type of Christianity.

The wine of apostasy had been emptied fully. And Faye,

Bill and I were to inherit its bitter dregs.

Bishop Arthur continued:

> Brother Bartholomew sacrificed his life so that we might have life. He bore his cross to make our burdens lighter.
>
> This painting was suggested by the Bishop-delegates at the last United World Church Union. What a fitting memorial from such an auspicious religious body. To them we owe our deepfelt gratitude.
>
> The fabled Christ of the Scriptures of the New Testament has not met our needs...has not saved the world. God is still on the Throne. He has sent his son. My own discovery of scrolls near the Dead Sea shed light on this revelation. There is no evidence that the Christ of the heretical New Testament rose from the Dead. Not even the records of Josephus can confirm this. And if he rose...I ask you this... WHERE IS HE? Our scientists in their might have built spacecraft. We have searched the heavens. We have scoured Venus and Mars. Inch by inch we combed the moon. It was obvious that this Christ was not walking with us on earth. And our astronauts have not located him walking even in the heavens! So called Christians have quoted John 14:2,3
>
> "In my Father's house are many mansions: if it were not so, I would have told you. I go to prepare a place for you.
>
> And if I go and prepare a place for you, I will come again, and receive you unto myself; that where I am, there ye may be also."
>
> But the scrolls that I have found near Mezad-Zohar at the Dead Sea reflect a picture that will revolutionize the world.

With a flick of the wrist, Bishop Arthur unrolled a long scroll, obviously a duplicate of what he claimed was an original. Tom Malone had told me some ancient bits of hide were photographed and printed into scroll form for this occasion. He had believed them to have been made into reproductions of some of the missing Dead Sea Scrolls.

Bishop Arthur continued:

This scroll contains the complete book of BAR-THOLOMEW, a book which previous church historians have chosen to ignore.

Let me read you verse 6 of chapter 66.

"If I should die, I will come again and prepare a place for you, a place for you on earth.

And those who would seal their devotion with a mark shall live again in newness of life. Old things shall pass away...behold all things shall become new.

Beware of false prophets and continue in steadfastness until my soon coming again."

Let us now pause in silence to meditate upon these words.

With this again the lights in the building went out. A minute passed in complete darkness. Not a sound. It seemed like an eternity. At first the silence was broken by hushed whispers. Then silence.

Then as if on cue, what appeared to be a roll of thunder shattered the silence. A bolt of lightening in a blinding flash rent the veil-like drape in two.

And, behold, the veil of the temple was rent in twain from the top to the bottom; and the earth did quake, and the rocks rent. (Matthew 27:51)

The audience gasped. Behind the drape stood a life-like statue of Brother Bartholomew in gleaming gold. The way the lightening had struck seemed almost Elijah-like.

Bishop Arthur went on to describe the statue...that it was 90 feet or 60 cubits high and 9 feet or 6 cubits wide. constructed from elements found in

Nebuchadnezzar the king made an image of gold, whose height was threescore cubits, and the breadth thereof six cubits: he set it up in the plain of Dura, in the province of Babylon. (Daniel 3:1)

the Dead Sea.

Then he continued:

"What you are viewing is more than a statue of refined gold. For it is symbolic of life...the life of Brother Bartholomew." And then raising his voice, he shouted:

"Brother Bartholomew will you LIVE AGAIN?"

Slowly the mouth of the statue started to move. The lips opened ever so slightly, the cheekbones rose, the eyes appeared to twinkle, the tongue came slightly forward.

SUDDENLY THE VERY STATUE WAS SPEAKING! It was Brother Bartholomew's voice!

YES, I WILL LIVE AGAIN.

I AM HE THAT LIVETH, AND WAS DEAD; AND BE-

And he had power to give life unto the image of the beast, that the image of the beast should both speak...(Revelation 13:15)

HOLD, I AM ALIVE FOR EVERMORE, Amen; AND HAVE THE KEYS OF HELL AND DEATH. [Revelation 1:18]

There was a stirring in the audience yet no one moved. Photographers suddenly leaped from all parts of the hall and lit the room with the flashing bulbs.

Suddenly the room darkened. From high on the ceiling a youthful sound of angelic-like voices came. First the chord of an organ...the words seemed so familiar...

Hallelujah! Hallelujah!
Hallelujah! Hallelujah!
....

And He shall reign for ever and ever
....

King of Kings and Lord of Lords....

Now I remembered.

It was the Hallelujah Chorus!

Then a spotlight was directed to the ceiling. It seemed as

though a platform broke through the ceiling...and it now was descending. Soon a man's figure was apparent standing on what appeared to be nothing. It must have been a square block of glass.

The light shone on his face. The audience gasped as one voice

IT'S BROTHER BARTHOLOMEW!

Women fainted. Faye collapsed in Bill's arms. Photographers were fighting for space to get a picture.

He descended slowly and came to a stop on top of a podium I had not noticed before.

A woman's shriek pierced the hall...

HE'S ALIVE! HE'S ALIVE!

Bishop Bartholomew was alive. He had come back from the dead! Bishop Arthur had performed a real miracle. This man, Brother Bartholomew, could hold the world in his hands now. They would follow him like lost sheep!

And I saw one of his heads as it were wounded to death; and his deadly wound was healed: and all the world wondered after the beast. (Revelation 13:3)

Then a strange thing happened.

Slowly Bishop Arthur approached Brother Bartholomew... looked up at him...then knelt down as though he were a knight paying homage to a king.

Brother Bartholomew smiled benevolently at Bishop Arthur, then extended his arm as if in blessing...then spoke.
"Well done, thou good and faithful servant:
thou hast been faithful over a few things,
I will make thee ruler over many things."

Then Brother Bartholomew turned to the audience and spoke:

I have risen again and my ministry is to build my kingdom here on earth...for all those

Let no man deceive you by any means: for that day shall not come, except there come a falling away first, and that man of sin be revealed, the son of perdition;

deemed faithful...who bear my Mark...and by so doing die again, bury their selfish pride... and rise to walk with me in newness of life.

Who opposeth and exalteth himself above all that is called God, or that is worshipped; so that he as God sitteth in the temple of God, shewing himself that he is God. (2 Thessalonians 2:3-4)

I am a God of love but I hate sin. Tomorrow the punishment of sin will be shown throughout the world. One will die. I have spoken.

Then, looking at Bishop Arthur he continued:

For your faithfulness, I pronounce you Prophet Arthur...for you have been a worthy prophet of the Messiah.

The Marking Stations were doing a land-office business. After the news had been published of the MIRACLE of the Shrine...it seemed that everyone was convinced Brother Bar-

And he exerciseth all the power of the first beast before him, and causeth the earth and them which dwell therein to worship the first beast, whose deadly wound was healed. (Revelation 13:12)

tholomew was God. Marking Deputies worked throughout the night applying the identification numbers 666 on foreheads and right hands. The deputies were quite surprised that most people wanted the marking on their forehead. They felt this a greater show of loyalty. Very few asked for the mark on their right hand.

Police stations and schools served as Marking Stations as did Churches. With the population growth schools had long been closed. I recall, the first day that schools closed, seeing the pathetic picture of a teen-age girl coming to school and finding it empty. It did not happen overnight. In the late 60's and early 1970's riots and demands by students were very effective. They soon had the courses they wanted...lovemaking, bar tending, mystic meditations, sex and family re-education. Soon the system had degenerated to such a state that, combined with the over-populated masses, school closing was made mandatory. Schools now became living quarters. As many as 30 families lived in each classroom.

I recall seeing a teen-age girl coming to school and finding it empty.

The Marking Stations were quite efficient, Tom Malone had told me. Everyone was now a number anyway. A small IBM-like card which resembled a credit card had various holes punched in different positions. It became your identification number throughout life. Upon entering a Marking Station you indicated where you wanted the Mark 666 placed and whether you wished a cosmetically branded or a bold visually branded number. A cosmetically branded number was applied by laser-beam and appeared invisible. However, as one walked on the streets and passed the video-lamposts, a special ultra violet light emitted from the base of the video unit made the invisible number very visible. Wherever one walked other "check lights" would verify whether the citizen was loyal and bore the Mark 666.

And yet, surprisingly, most everyone wanted a visual 666 and most chose red as their color preference. This was applied by an instant-heat radio beam branding iron. To them it became both a beauty mark and a mark of sacrificial loyalty as it involved some pain at the moment of application.

For application of The Mark, the laser or the branding iron method could be selected. The branding iron method further combined its flash heat with application of a red flourescent dye. There was the pain but it soon departed. Scar tissue in a few weeks made the Mark impression irreversible. No plastic surgery could conceivably correct it should one change his or her mind.

Again, most chose the branding iron method.

It was necessary to keep perfectly still. A slight movement could cause the Mark of the instant-heat radio beam to miss its mark and blind the citizen for life. Therefore recipients were asked to lay on a special stretcher. A mild sedative was administered. Hundreds of stretchers lined the halls and spilled out onto the street. The line moved fast. Out the rear of the building those who had received the Mark were dismissed. A mirror at the back door was installed so they could view their new badge of identification.

Children were given a light anesthesia, and strapped down tightly to the stretcher. From our apartment Faye, Bill and I could hear the muffled screams of what appeared to be an endless stream of children—bewildered, frightened...suddenly drowning into the soft anesthesia of sleep.

Only one stretcher moved into the Marking Room at a time. The Identification Badge of each individual was removed from the card holder at the foot of the stretcher. The Badge was run through a computer. The identity was automatically transmitted to Central Intelligence and the so numbered person became an acknowledged disciple. While this was being done, the patient's head was carefully positioned in a firm, but cushioned brace. Above was a bright light and a plate about 2" x 4" which automatically molded itself to the curvature of each individual forehead. It was as though one's head was looking up at the stamping mechanism of a printing press.

Most patients were relatively calm. But under these circumstances even the loyal would develop doubts. But not for long. As they looked up at the branding iron...they failed to notice the quick spray of an air needle on their leg. Within a second they were asleep...dead to the activity that surrounded them.

Everything worked like clockwork. A button was pushed. Quickly the branding iron came down, molded itself around the forehead. Another button was pushed...a special red dye came coursing downward through a transparent plastic tube that terminated at the head of the branding mechanism.

There was a short burst of steam as instant heat met dye and iron met forehead. Then it was all over. The branding iron returned to its original position. The stretcher was whisked out through the swinging doors.

Another air needle was sprayed — this time on the arm. The patient instantly awakened as though nothing had happened. The injection not only awakened him but erased the memory of the last hour. It was a relatively new medical discovery called the Sleep and Memory Fader.

The patient climbed to his feet, was given a pill to swallow, then directed to the door. It was then and only then that reality hit him full blast. On his forehead, still slightly puffed, was emblazoned in brilliant red his mark of identity and loyalty...

666

George knew he must do something to save Bill. He persuaded Tom to give them passes for flight to Asia. George was surprised how quickly and anxiously Tom consented.

George's Dad had fought in Vietnam and before his death, had many times recounted how cleverly the Viet Cong built underground hide-aways, stocked with food and ammunition. He remembers his dad saying that the discovery he had made of one such unit made it very evident that the enemy could hole-away for years unnoticed.

Little foilage was left in Vietnam now, but George remembered one incident of an underground home that dad said was never destroyed. Some GI's used it at the end of the war. It was located not too far from Saigon at Xuan-loc.

After three days of searching Faye and Bill discovered the air vents that were hidden in the bushes...but these vents were too small for one to enter. It was then that George remembered that sometimes these underground quarters were entered by a pond passageway. Soon they found the pond, swam underwater towards the shore and after passing under earth for about five feet finally hit an air pocket. Then there was a mound of earth walled with a passageway that brought them entrance into their underground hide-away. Besides the small supply of man-made food provisions which they had managed to collect, they had only brought one thing with them...their Bible. It was to serve them well through the long weary days and nights. Here they also fortunately found real food, old C-ration cans abandoned over 30 years ago.

And to the woman were given two wings of a great eagle, that she might fly into the wilderness, into her place, where she is nourished for a time, and times, and half a time, from the face of the serpent.

And the earth helped the woman, and the earth opened her mouth, and swallowed up the flood which the dragon cast out of his mouth. (Revelation 12: 14, 16)

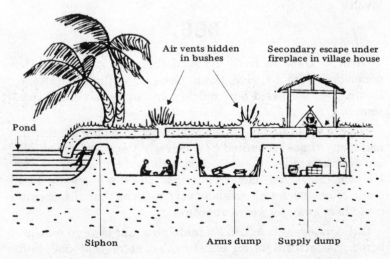

Air vents hidden in bushes

Secondary escape under fireplace in village house

Pond

Siphon   Arms dump   Supply dump

One night as they were praying a song formed on George's lips. And as he began singing, Faye and Bill joined in....

It will be worth it all
When we see Jesus
Life's trials will seem so small
When we see Him.

One glimpse of His dear face
All sorrows will erase
So bravely run the race
Till we see Christ!

That night if Helen and Sue and Tom were looking down from Heaven they must have surely been rejoicing. I wonder if the Lord Jesus Christ wasn't gently whispering to them? Just a short while longer and their song would become a glorious reality.

Suddenly their worshipping was broken by the sound of heavy equipment moving down a road somewhere above their bunker. The sound of one vehicle breaking rank was apparent as the sound of its motors came clearer. Then it appeared to stop directly overhead above their underground hideaway. Voices could be heard.

George held his finger to his mouth to warn Faye and Bill to keep still and quiet.

Then a penetrating sound and a WHOOSH as though a vacuum bottle had been opened. The entire dirt ceiling above them was suddenly sucked up as though someone had cut out a neat little circle.

A floodlight cruelly exposed their hideaway.

Faye, Bill and George stood up, temporarily blinded by the sudden light. But there's was no mistaking the voices.

One was that of Brother Bartholomew speaking:

"Congratulations, you did a fine job of discovering them."

The other voice replied,

Then shall they deliver you up to be afflicted, and shall kill you: and ye shall be hated of all nations for my name's sake.

And then shall many be offended, and shall betray one another, and shall hate one another.
Matthew 24:9-10.

"I knew they were there, sir. Since they refuse to bear The Mark. I wanted to be the first to expose theo , sir."

Blindfolded, we could have spotted that voice with ease. No longer our friend, we had been betrayed by a Judas. For the voice was the voice of TOM MALONE!

Chapter 11

The Shocking Spectacle

Brother Bartholomew had Faye, Bill and I returned to Washington. We were quite surprised that we were allowed to return to our apartment. Brother Bartholomew warned us there was no use trying to escape. Dr. Curter had implanted micro-detector units into the muscle of our arm. We were told Central Intelligence had us tuned in. These detector units would relay our every move...but not only that, our every thought. With some pride Dr. Curter told us of his devious discovery that enabled BB to partially read one's mind. Our brain waves would register on a computer-indicator which would monitor us. It would show when we were tense and when we were relaxing; when we were thinking hard and when we were passively listening and learning. Now even our thoughts were no longer private.

One day left for living for Bill. And BB had allowed us to have a picture phone in our room, much as one would give a sumptious meal to a person ready for execution. We could tune in on any part of the world and as BB put it, "See how my influence has spread over the entire earth."

Before Tom's betrayal of us he had told me of strange happenings in Jerusalem. Two men had appeared as though from nowhere and were going through the land like the old time preachers of judgment of the 1800's and early 1900's.

Laughingly Tom had called them the "modern-day Dwight L. Moody and Billy Sunday."

But then his face took on a troubled look as he told me how these two men were seeing flocks of Jews becoming converted to their message. He had said that there was talk of these two performing miracles, even striking some down to their death simply by a vocal command.

And I will give power unto my two witnesses, and they shall prophecy a thousand two hundred and threescore days (1260 days), clothed in sackcloth.
And if any man will hurt them, fire proceedeth out of their mouth, and devoureth their enemies: and if any man will hurt them, he must in this manner be killed (Revelation 11:3, 5)

I picked up the picture phone, dialed Jerusalem, a direct dial that tied me in with local television lines. Faye, Bill and I crowded around the screen. There suddenly were two men, near the Damascus Gate. They wore harsh appearing sackcloth garments. They were surrounded by people. Voices were shouting..."IT'S MOSES and ELIJAH!"

An announcer appeared on the screen...

"Ladies and gentlemen,
recent disturbances in Jerusalem have
caught the attention of Brother Bartholomew.
He is sending Prophet Arthur to inspect the
area and make his recommendations.

Jews are flocking to the Temple given by
Brother Bartholomew to offer thanks to God."

The earth suddenly shook. The screen darkened. There was a low, long rumble. Bill and Faye looked out the window. Faye screamed...

"Look, Dad, it's like a long row of dominoes falling. One building after another is falling. Earth is splitting open. Whole buildings are disappearing. Dad, it seems like it's headed this way!"

Not since the San Francisco earthquake of April 18, 1906 had such devastation been seen.

The first quick burst of disaster was soon over...but the low, continuing rumble was a constant reminder that more was to come.

...and earthquakes in divers places. (Matthew 24:7)

Brother Bartholomew nervously fidgeted in his office. He called in Tom Malone.

"Malone, what's the latest report on these earthquakes?"

"The San Francisco suburb of Los Angeles has been completely devastated, sir. Much of it has disappeared. The entire city of Los Angeles shows danger of sinking. Dallas reports dangerous crevices with some chasms dropping as much as 1000 or more feet. Other reports from around the country are the same. In fact Europe, Asia and the Middle East report similar earth disturbances."

"Malone, we've got to move our headquarters temporarily. Earthquakes, disturbances in the sun, meteor showers, cloud formations such as have never been seen...and this infernal rumbling is still continuing! We're bound to have another quake, perhaps more deadly. What's the safest place you know?"

And I beheld when he had opened the sixth seal, and, lo, there was a great earthquake; and the sun became black as sackcloth of hair, and the moon became as blood;
And the stars of heaven fell unto the earth, even as a fig tree casteth her untimely figs, when she is shaken of a mighty wind. (Revelation 6:12-13)

Malone thought for a moment. His eye lit up as though he had made a discovery. Then he spoke: "My grandfather, sir, was a member of the Church of Jesus Christ of Latter-Day Saints. They were known as Mormons. I understand they kept perpetual storage vaults deep within a granite mountain in what was then called Utah. Salt Lake City, I believe."

Brother Bartholomew pushed some Memory Bank buttons behind his desk. In front of him a card slowly emerged from a slot in his desk. He read it:

GRANITE MOUNTAIN RECORDS VAULT

Little Cottonwood Canyon
25 miles from Salt Lake City

Average temperature 58° F
Electrostatic air filters
Protective Vault Door — 14 tons
Inner Protective Doors — 9 tons
Natural water supply provides 8000 gallons a day
700 feet below surface

He turned to Tom Malone, then spoke: "Malone, alert Air Force 1. We're flying to Little Cottonwood Canyon in two days."

Meanwhile Faye and Bill and George were praying, hoping against hope, that somehow God would rescue them from what seemed certain death.

There was no food to eat. Their protein cake allotment had been cut off. Hunger pangs began to become evident. One guard, however, had left on a chair some oil base purple grapes. Faye picked them up and spoke, as though something had suddenly occurred to her.

"Dad, Bill, we've never done it before. But we should. Let's together take communion, just as the Lord Jesus Christ did before He went to the cross."

Bill questioned: "How can we take communion? We have no bread. We have nothing to eat. All we have is a little water and these few grapes."

"That's it, Bill," Faye replied, "we DO have bread. Don't you remember how each day as we broke our protein cakes, how we placed a portion away in this drawer as the Lord's share?"

Pulling out the drawer she exclaimed, "Look! It's still here." "But if its the Lord's, we can't eat it." George reminded.

"But Dad, today I was reading the 12th chapter of Matthew and how David when he was hungry ate the shewbread, holy bread. We will be eating only a portion to represent the body of Christ and drink just a little purple grape water to represent his saving blood shed for us."

George nodded his agreement and smiled, "Reminds me of that verse in Ecclesiates 11:1 which I memorized just a few days ago. Funny, how, in the midst of hunger we each day set aside a portion of our protein cake to the Lord and now in the midst of need that verse becomes a reality...

Cast thy bread upon the waters:
for thou shalt find it after many days.

George broke one protein cake into three small pieces. With heads bowed they placed it on their lips and prayed. Then George give Faye and Bill each a teaspoon of the juice. And with them he drank the precious drops and prayed. Faye's joyous voice began to sing...to sing a song I never realized she knew. It was such an old hymn. I could remember my grandparents singing it in church. The entire congregation, after communion, without the benefit of any musical instruments would sing their praise in glorious harmony... Faye began this very song and soon all three of us were singing.

From ev'ry stormy wind that blows
From ev'ry swelling tide of woes
There is a calm, a sure retreat:
'Tis found beneath the mercy-seat.

Ah! wither could we flee for aid,
When tempted, desolate, dismayed;
Or how the hosts of hell defeat,
Had suff'ring saints no mercy-seat.

After their communion, George turned on the picture phone to see if he could once again get Jerusalem. The rumbling had eased up a bit and the picture was once again coming on clear. The camera was showing areas of destruction. Prophet Arthur had diverted his space craft to Petra. The reporter was announcing that many high-ranking officials had fled to the natural mountainous refuge of Petra...many were hiding in the rocks and caves near the Dead Sea.

And said to the mountains and rocks, Fall on us, and hide us from the face of him that sitteth on the throne, and from the wrath of the Lamb:

For the great day of his wrath is come; and who shall be able to stand? (Revelation 6:16-17)

It was as though an eclipse had occurred, the announcer reported. The sun had turned black, the moon blood-red. Meteors began to fall.

Then he continued:

"The surprising thing is that in the midst of all this havoc and destruction many Jews were like Daniels in the fiery furnace. They were not touched... not a hair was singed, and not a bone broken.

From all over the world Jews have been flocking to Jerusalem. They bear a strange seal on their foreheads...not the customary Mark of 666 that is beginning to appear all over the world.

We have 12 representatives with us at this telecasting studio. They have agreed to brief us on their mission."

With that the announcer turned to one who appeared to

be the spokesman: "Sir, our on-location television cameras have been photographing the catastrophes as they occurred —the earthquakes, the fires, and in each case where masses of people have disappeared or been crushed to death...those with this seal on their forehead seem to have some guardian angel over them...they come through unscratched."

"Yes, sir, that is true. The living God, the Lord Jesus Christ, has annointed us from above to become witnesses for Him in these last days of tribulation. From each of the 12 tribes of Israel 12,000 Jews have been elected to bear His seal and bear a testimony to all that Christ is coming again. Working with our two prophets, the modern Moses and Elijah, we are ministering throughout the world. Already many thousands, yes even great multitudes from every nation, kindred and tongue are coming to Christ, their Saviour, their Risen Lord, their soon coming King."

> Saying, Hurt not the earth, neither the sea, nor the trees, till we have sealed the servants of our God in their foreheads.
>
> And I heard the number of them which were sealed: and there were sealed an hundred and forty and four thousand of all the tribes of the children of Israel. (Revelation 7:3-4)

> ...These are they which came out of great tribulation, and have washed their robes, and made them white in the blood of the Lamb. (Revelation 7:14)

The low-pitched rumbling increased...the picture phone screen went black. The earth shook violently as though it were heaving its last breath. George, Bill and Faye placed their hands on the Bible, held it firmly, bowed their heads and prayed.

And outside the terrifying screams of men, women and children penetrated the still air as they stumbled down what seemed to be bottomless chasms of judgment.

Just as quickly as it came...the earthquake ceased. Outside the window George could see dust and smoke rising everywhere. Silence prevailed. It seemed as though the whole earth was one big funeral pyre...for as far as the eye could see not an inkling of movement could be detected.

Never had the trio experienced such quietness. Deadly silence. Just deadly silence.

Slowly the darkened sky gave evidence that dawn was coming.

There was a knock at the door.

George opened it.

There stood their Judas...Tom Malone.

He was rather apologetic.

"George, I'm sorry, but when it comes down to brass tacks, my loyalty must be to Brother Bartholomew. I've come because I have bad news that could be good news. In a few minutes the guards will come to take Bill to the Guillotine site. Brother Bartholomew has asked me to come and talk to you. He promises that if Faye will accept The Mark—not the cosmetic invisible Mark but the visual-branded Mark of 666...he will be merciful and spare Bill from the guillotine."

For a moment Faye, Bill and George stood in silence. Then Faye shouted, "I will, I will. If it will save Bill, I'll give my life!" Bill pulled Faye closely to him, "No, darling, never. If it's my time to die it means that it will be that much quicker that I **And I stood upon the sand of the sea, and saw a beast rise up out of the sea...(Revelation 13:1)** will meet my Lord and Saviour. I know your love for me, darling, but your taking that mark would be like kneeling in obedience to antichrist. It's a trick. He will kill me anyway. He and his world government are a Beast!"

"No," Tom replied, "Brother Bartholomew will keep his word."

Just then six guards entered. Two positioned themselves at Bill's sides and held his arms, one stood behind him, another in front of him. Two more led the way. They jerked him away so quickly he had no time to kiss Faye goodbye. He turned as he was let down the long hall, his voice echoing against the sides of the wall...

"Faye, don't take the Mark...Faye, don't take the Mark! Faye, don't take the Mark!"

Faye was crying hysterically. George held her firmly in his arms. His arms slackened as he broke out in uncontrollable sobbing.

The glass cubicle was mounted on a high pole thirty feet in the air. Its base was only two feet square...allowing little room for movement. Imprisoned inside was Bill. Execution was set for twelve noon. It was now 8:30 in the morning. Already crowds were forming. Special tiered seats had been erected to accommodate those who were fortunate enough to receive special passes. All could look up in the sky and see the glass cubicle. The crowd was getting frantic. Bill looked down in both disgust and horror. It seemed like a bad dream...a nightmare. Down there wherever he looked...up-turned faces, sneering, scoffing, all bearing the brilliant red 666 on their foreheads. "What has happened to humanity?" he thought. "Have they all turned into a pack of wild animals?"

Bill felt calm in spite of his trials. Now he knew what dying grace meant. For his heart was at peace. Soon he would have victory...complete victory.

Tom ushered George and Faye down to the waiting limousine. Faye was already reconciled to the fact that in spite of Bill's pleading she would accept The Mark. In her heart, she thought to herself, her alliegance will always be to God. Christ was her Saviour and Lord. He always would be. This outward mark would, in her mind, stand only as her symbol of contempt for antichrist and his sin. George had whispered a plan...a plan of escape to Jerusalem. All three would go. The last thing George had told her was:

"Faye, the ones they call Moses and Elijah will save us!"

As they entered the limousine, Faye stepped back in aston-ishment. In the back seat waiting for them was Brother Bartholomew. He motioned for them to enter.

"Well, what is your decision? "Brother Bartholomew questioned, "as if I didn't know already." With that he broke into a laugh.

Faye spoke, "You're a son of the devil. Enjoy yourself now while you can for the day will soon come when God's judg-ment will be poured out against you. Then we'll see who has the last laugh!"

"So you think your God will save you? What a fairy story. Who arose from the dead...your Jesus? Of course not. But with your own eyes you witnessed my resurrection."

He thrust his hands in George's face. "Here," he continued, look at my hands. What do you see?"

George looked on in shock, but said nothing.

"What do you see? you fool. Speak!" Brother Bartholomew commanded.

"Nailprints, sir."

Faye spoke, quietly and firmly,

> "II Thessalonians 2:11
> And for this cause God shall send them strong
> delusion, that they should believe a lie..."

Brother Bartholomew was visibly angered. "Don't quote your fabled Scriptures to me. What is your decision? Right now your husband is imprisoned in a glass cubicle at the execution site. Shall I give the command to proceed with the execution?"

"No," Faye replied, "I will accept The Mark."

Faye and I fully expected to be taken to the Marking Station. But the car approached a huge crowd of thousands. Above the crowd could be seen a tall pole. Atop the pole, a glass cubicle. And in the cubicle, a man.

Faye's heart sank as she caught a glimpse of Bill. George tried to give her reassuring comfort by putting his arm around her.

The crowd parted to make way for the limousine. There in front of them was a sight that looked as though it had come out of the Middle Ages...there in its grisly horror was the guillotine. Much more polished and refined than those of antiquity, this one had a special electronic triggering device, and a large numerical counter that registered each time the heavy-bladed knife went swishing to its mark.

At the base, where the knife came to a halt, was a transparent box. A liquid swirled about in it...like a washing machine display in a store that had a cutaway transparent section to make visible the swishing action. When the head was severed, it would drop into this purification tank, jet streams would wash blood and dust away...it then would move up a conveyor that would diabolically project it into a display stand the same height as the glass cubicle. It was to be a dramatically staged gesture to show the people that the penalty had been paid.

The heavy blade slid easily between the two grooved posts. Up and down, up and down, the executioner was testing his equipment to see that all was in order.

This was to be the first execution by guillotine. The numerical counter was turned to 0.

The car drove slowly passed the guillotine site. Faye had thought the execution was scheduled in a public square. But as she looked up she saw a cross...then a steeple. How cruel, she thought. The execution site was on the front lawn of a church...a church that once was a center for the preaching of the Gospel. Because of its testimony, this church had been wrecked inside.

"What blasphemy!" George exclaimed.

"Why are you taking us here?" Faye demanded. "This is not the Marking Center."

"You are a very special person," Brother Bartholomew chuckled. "And for very special people we have a most unusual Marking Center."

They entered the church parking lot. Guards met them at the door. George and Faye were ushered up the long aisle. The familiar picture of Christ knocking at the door had been changed. Brother Bartholomew's face was substituted.

As they came to the pulpit area, two husky guards stood at each side of the communion table. On the table in a special unit lay the Instant Heat Branding Iron. Special portable equipment was plugged in. A transparent tube from a unit on the floor was surging red flourescent dye to the branding head. The mold on the die was clearly visible....666.

Brother Bartholomew quickly motioned to two guards. They grabbed Faye...dragged her to the communion table...the branding iron released a small whisp of smoke.

Faye looked at the front of the communion table. The carved inscription read:

THIS DO IN REMEMBRANCE OF ME

Then, as though she received an extra measure of faith... she stopped dead in her tracks, looked directly into the eyes of Brother Bartholomew. Her own reflection seemed to come back. She could see the guards dragging Bill down the hall. She could hear the voice of Bill calling back: "FAYE, DON'T TAKE THE MARK; FAYE, DON'T TAKE THE MARK."

With determination she spoke, "I will not take The Mark. 'Fear not them which kill the body, but are not able to kill the soul: but rather fear him which is able to destroy both soul and body in hell.' This is my testimony from Matthew 10:28. And it is the testimony of Bill and my father. Do what you may...but I will not take The Mark!"

Brother Bartholomew was enraged. Tom Malone pleaded with her, assuring her that no harm would come to Bill if she accepted The Mark.

> ...If any man worship the beast and his image, and receive his mark in his forehead, or in his hand,
> The same shall drink of the wine of the wrath of God...(Revelation 14: 9-10)

Faye remained firm.

With that Brother Bartholomew quickly motioned to the guards. They grabbed Faye by each arm, dragged her to the communion table. Two guards forcibly held her back, pressing it down against the table. Another held her hair, forcing her chin on the table, her face looking upward.

Brother Bartholomew directed Tom Malone to activate the branding unit. The limp tube of dye stiffened. The branding iron released a small whisp of smoke.

George tried to rush forward. Two burly guards held him back. "ANTICHRIST! ANTICHRIST!" George shouted. "YOU DIABOLICAL DEVIL. Is there no mercy in your heart? Give me The Mark. Let me take The Mark in place of Faye!"

Faye squirmed, kicked, but to no avail. The guards held all

the tighter. Above her The Mark slowly came closer. The moist red numbers glistened with crackling heat. It was all a bad dream, she thought. Yes, a bad dream. I'll wake up and find I was dreaming. But those ugly numbers came closer. She screamed. That's all she remembered.

The next sound she heard was Brother Bartholomew laughing. He directed Tom Malone to bring a mirror.

"Now Holy Queen," Brother Bartholomew shouted, "look at your beauty mark! Kneel and pay homage to your God!"

She turned her back on him, her head drooped in despair as George put his arm around her and together they prayed for strength.

Tom Malone rushed over, tears in his eyes. "Don't feel bad George and Faye. I know it's a shock to both of you. But you've saved Bill, and that's what's important."

"Malone, you foolish one," Brother Bartholomew reprimanded. "Did you think for one minute that Bill would escape the guillotine? Why you are more foolish than these two. Dr. Curter, come over here."

Dr. Curter walked over carrying a little black box.

"You seem to forget, Dr. Curter has implanted micro-detector units in all of you," Brother Bartholomew reminded. When your nervous tension goes above a certain level the micro detector begins to record your every movement and whisper."

"Play a portion of the recording from Faye's unit, Dr. Curter."

Dr. Curter flipped a switch, turned a dial...from this black magic box what were Faye's whispered thoughts suddenly came forth.

My allegiance will always be to God.
Christ is my Saviour and Lord.
He always will be.

The ones who are being called
Moses and Elijah will save us.

The recording stopped. Tom Malone now joined the ranks of the saddened and shocked.

They walked out of the church stunned, Bill, who had already been removed from the glass cubicle, was standing head bowed at the base of the guillotine.

The guards quickly placed Faye and George on a special hoist, and squeezed them into the small cubicle above the hysterical mob. Faye and George looked down. On the front row sat all those whom Brother Bartholomew considered his distinguished and faithful clergy. On every forehead was The Mark—666.

Faye was sobbing hysterically. The confines were so tight the whole unit shook with each sob.

His hands tied behind him, Bill was led up the six steps to the guillotine. Prophet Arthur was reading the death sentence:

> Bill Sanders, being of sound body and mind,
> refused to bear The Mark of our God and our
> King either on his forehead or on his right hand.
> In accordance with the laws of the New Earth
> death shall be awarded by guillotine. May
> Brother Bartholomew have mercy on your soul.

With that, a guard assisted Bill in kneeling at the guillotine. His head was placed in the molded receiving block. The top semi-circle restraining block was clamped down. His head was secure.

As though to say, don't mourn for me Faye...his pleading eyes looked upward at the two forms in the glass cubicle.

The executioner's hand went up to the electronic release switch.

Faye screamed.

SWOOSH!

The severed head of Bill dropped in the swirling bath.

The maddened crowd surged forward. The pressing weight bent the pole on which the cubicle was suspended.

...and I saw the souls of them that were beheaded for the witness of Jesus, and for the word of God, and which had not worshipped the beast, neither his image, neither had received his mark upon their foreheads, or in their hands, and they lived and reigned with Christ a thousand years. (Revelation 20:4)

Suddenly the pole snapped.
The cubicle came hurtling down on the crowd!

Chapter 12

The Strange Destroyer

George and Faye were momentarily stunned as they lay on the ground. The glass cubicle had shattered as it fell. The mobs in their frenzy to reach the guillotine all but ignored the two.

George quickly lifted Faye up to avoid being trampled upon. The glass cubicle apparently had been made from safety-breaking glass which shattered upon impact into tiny safe round-edged smooth bits. Had it been the old time glass of the 1960's they would have surely been severely cut or killed on the jagged pieces.

Just as they came to their feet, Tom Malone was by their side. Without trying to explain he grabbed George's arm and motioned for George and Faye to follow him.

Somehow I felt it was for our own safety and we obeyed without hesitation. Tom urged us to run while the interest of the crowd was still on the guillotine scene and on Bill's now beheaded body.

About two hundred yards down the main highway he diverted us down a small country road to a waiting compact car.

We jumped in. It was a Press car. Press cars had special driving privileges since the Press was controlled by Brother Bartholomew. Tom Malone knew this.

"What's happening?" George asked.

"No time to talk now, George, wait till we get to the dock."

Since only government officials had cars and most of them were at the execution site...the roads were almost empty.

Arriving at the airport, Tom advised the control tower that we had been cleared for take-off to New York harbor. The city of New York had long since been destroyed...but the harbor was already an active port again.

Within a matter of five minutes we were landing at the port airstrip. Faye and I both turned to Tom and almost in one voice asked, "WHY?"

Tom spoke, half apologetically. "At first I had been a fool ...a sincere fool...who was so sincere, sincerely wrong. My allegiance had been to Brother Bartholomew. I was sure he would solve all the world problems. This would call for drastic action. In the last three years he accomplished so much. He brought peace to Israel. He built them the Temple which for two thousand years they sought after. Major conflicts have ended. But at that Temple scene I realized that the face of Brother Bartholomew was not one of God...it seemed like one of the devil reborn. But I was afraid...secretly I accepted The Mark—but made from a special fade-out dye... I was afraid...And Bill..." Tom's head dropped. For the first time I saw Tom actually weep. Quickly he regained his composure.

"When they killed Bill, I knew I had to stand up and be counted for Christ. This fade-out Mark on my forehead may have for a time identified me with Brother Bartholomew...but inside...in my heart, I now know I am a child of God. I don't know what the future holds for me...for my acceptance of Christ now may be too late. I am still a marked man in more ways than one."

Faye cautioned, "You were at the beginning deceived just

as we were...you didn't know."

George spoke up: "Tom, Faye, we can't go on talking like this. Don't you realize we have micro-detector units implanted in us. Brother Bartholomew's men will be here in minutes."

Tom smiled and spoke: "No they won't, George."

With that he reached into his pocket, pulled out a small pill box. He held it gingerly as if its contents were the most precious things on earth. Four tiny red pills.

"Here," Tom urged, "quickly swallow one of these pills." Without asking they followed Tom's initiative and each swallowed a pill. "Now what was that all about?" Faye asked.

Tom replied. "For some time now I have become very close to Dr. Curter. He may be a diabolical man...but he's a man with a heavy burden of guilt on his heart. There are two faces to him. He must under all conditions show complete loyalty to Brother Bartholomew. But one day in his weaker moments he confessed to me his doubts. He deeply admires you, Faye, and George. He knew Bill would be killed regardless of your acceptance of The Mark. That's when he unloaded his inner feelings on me. Somehow he had compassion on me. He gave me these four red pills. Since we three have each taken one, there's only one left now. But just as Dr. Curter cleverly used his medical and scientific knowledge to bring back Brother Bartholomew from the dead...to create the sinister micro-detector units that read both thought impulses and relay location...he also developed an antidote that renders powerless the micro-detector unit."

"That antidote was the red pill each of us just swallowed. And now, from this port, as far as BB is concerned, we could be heading to anywhere in the world. He won't find us."

Faye, joy on her face, reached up and gently kissed Tom on the cheek. "Tom, you're simply wonderful. I thought you were a Judas...but God has provided a way...and used you as a channel."

Tom blushed and then became serious again.

"Let's get to the dock quick. We're going to board one of the new inventions that Brother Bartholomew has instituted to help answer the problem of the population explosion."

At the dock we boarded a small AVC water-surface transfer ship. Suddenly, over the horizon we saw a most unusual sight. Two ships, as if at anchor in the middle of the ocean. Between them an odd-looking object...very, very large. A

circular steel dome-like building with a funnel projecting from the center.

"That," Tom told us, "is a Sea House."

"But does it just stay there?" Faye questioned.

Tom replied, "Normally it stays anchored in one position. You are only looking at the roof of the Sea House. It extends down to the ocean floor once it is anchored at its final location. Until then, the bottom telescopes up to within 50 feet of the surface of the water. This particular Sea House is destined for use in the Mediterranean Sea, just off the coast of Cyprus."

"Are we going to board it now?" George asked.

"Yes, George. It's our safest way to escape. Brother Bartholomew may have all the other modes of transportation covered in search for us. He will least expect that we will board an empty Sea House."

"But what about the crew? Surely they will suspect something and turn us in," Faye said fearfully.

"Normally yes," Tom replied, "but this is a most unusual crew. Everyone is a Jew for these are Israeli ships. The Sea House is a gift from our government to theirs...probably the last gift they will ever receive from BB."

Now it was all clear. We settled back for the uneventful ten day cruise.

Brother Bartholomew was in a rage. Nothing Prophet Arthur could do seemed to calm him down. The console in front of him was blinking lights...but the message wasn't getting through.

He flipped a switch...an intercom. "Dr. Curter, come into my office immediately."

Within a few moments Dr. Curter appeared. He thrust his hands into his long white coat so Brother Bartholomew would not see that he was visibly shaken.

"Curter," Brother Bartholomew bellowed, "I punched every button on this console and still cannot locate Faye, George or Tom Malone. What's gone wrong? When I find them I'll have a triple guillotine execution. The people will go wild! What's wrong with this unit?"

Dr. Curter walked over to it, pretended he was trying to make some adjustment...pushed a few buttons...the machine buzzed defiantly indicating that the Locate Numbers and Thought Numbers were not operative.

He turned to Brother Bartholomew, "I'm sorry sir, I don't know what is going wrong."

Prophet Arthur chimed in, "Have you pushed the right identification numbers? Perhaps we have the wrong numbers?"

"No Arthur," Brother Bartholomew said, "here they are right here." He held up the identification cards:

FAYE SANDERS	777 02 583 11
GEORGE OMEGA	777 11 624 38
TOM MALONE	777 32 395 00

"Strange," Prophet Arthur thought out loud, "each one begins with 777!"

The Sea House trip was quite smooth despite the bulky bottom. The accompanying host ships anchored the Sea House at Lido di Ostia, about 25 miles from Rome. There they were to pick up a group of people that witnessing Jews had led to Christ. It was an unscheduled stop...one which would not have gone unnoticed if Brother Bartholomew hadn't been so pre-occupied with finding Faye and George.

Faye accompanied Tom into Rome as both of their Marks looked genuine. George could not go, for without the Mark it might prove rather dangerous. Faye had never been to Rome and Tom briefly showed her what was now considered the most fabulous city in the world. It was the center of trade. Activity among the merchants was so voluminous that Lido di Ostia had become a major seaport. Gold, silver, pearls, the finest in fabrics...all this and more made Rome a world center for business. Noted for its wines, its convivialty, it was like a magnet attracting trade from around the world. When Brother Bartholomew was first installed as President of the United States of Europe one of the congratulatory telegrams he treasured most was signed...

...Alas, alas that great city, that was clothed in fine linen, and purple, and scarlet, and decked with gold, and precious stones, and pearls!

The merchandise of gold, and silver, and precious stones, and of pearls, and fine linen, and purple, and silk, and scarlet, and all thyine (perfumed) wood, and all manner vessels of ivory, and all manner vessels of most precious wood, and of brass, and iron, and marble,

And cinnamon, and odours (perfumes), and ointments, and frankincense, and wine, and oil, and fine flour, and wheat, and beasts, and sheep, and horses, and chariots, and slaves, and souls of men. (Revelation 18:16, 12, 13)

And here is the mind which hath wisdom. The seven heads are seven mountains, on which the woman sitteth. (Revelation 17:9)

Best wishes from the City of the Seven Hills.

Rome, a city of two faces: One reflecting its past history, the other glassy skyscrapers that towered over medieval palaces. Powerful floodlights illuminated centuries-old cathedrals while loud speakers blared rock tunes amid Renaissance treasures.

The Colosseum, symbol of ancient Rome, still attracted a constant stream of modern-day visitors. Dedicated A.D. 80 by Emperor Titus, the amphitheater witnessed 200 years of bloody games, games in which many Christians may have been brutally martyred while thousands cheered.

Now the sound of hammers was being heard again. As Faye peeked in between the columns she asked Tom, "What's that going up in the center of the Colosseum?"

"Faye, apparently they are following Bishop Bartholomew's plans to the letter. They are erecting six guillotines in each of three locations...in the center of the Colosseum floor and on the two sides...almost like a circus with a center ring and two side rings. Six...six and six."

Tom went on to give Faye a background of Rome...a background he knew well for Brother Bartholomew, who had expressed a great interest in this city, urged Tom to do as much research as possible on it and give him a report.

"Rome, once an imperial capital and still a focus for world-wide religious loyalties, has been a tourist attraction for over 2000 years. Tourism ranks high among industries earning foreign money. In the first 7 months of 1969 almost 3 million outsiders swarmed into Rome as tourists. That was small. This year, 2000, almost 50 million have come in a comparable time period. There are many ways the leaders of Rome make money. As an example, for many years Michelangelo's masterpiece statue of Moses stood in the Church of San Pietro in Vincoli. The statue was shrouded in shadows. But by inserting a coin in a nearby coin machine and electric bulb would light permitting the photographer-tourist 30 seconds to snap his picture."

Tom Malone continued: "Every summer night the Roman Forum revives the drama of Caesar's triumphant return from Gaul and Mark Antony's funeral oration."

"But what about Vatican City?" Faye questioned.

"One of the most magnificant sites is St. Peter's Square," Tom continued. "The Basilica of St. Peter utilized the genius of Italy's finest artist-architects — Bramante, Raphael and Michelangelo."

"Tell me about the Pope," Faye urged.

"Faye, until recent years the Pope had executive as well as legislative and judiciary powers. He could be judged by no man. There was no appeal from his decisions. Besides being the ultimate word, speaking infallibly on religious matters, he could also:

1. Approve or sanction or supress religious orders
2. Grant indulgences
3. Beautify or canonize saints
4. Appoint bishops
5. Erect, administer, alter or suppress bishoprics
6. Assign an auxiliary bishop for one who is incapacitated
7. Found and legislate for papal universities
8. Issue liturgical books

and a host of other powers."

"How much does the Vatican own?"

"No one really knows, Faye. But Brother Bartholomew has shown a keen interest in this. It is known that they own one of the largest corporations in the world that deals in mining, metallurgical products, fertilizers, and pharmaceuticals as well as electric power. While not owning outright, it controls 70 per cent of Italy's artificial and synthetic textile fibers. One fully owned Vatican company with capital into the millions controls gas companies in at least 36 Italian cities. They are heavily involved in banking and own and control hundreds of banks. A large number of insurance companies are Vatican owned. As early as 1970 it was estimated that one-third of Rome was owned by the Holy See. Estimates of wealth are in the billions."

"Incredible," Faye remarked.

"Yes it is, but one must remember that even in the 1960's the then Protestant arm of the church was also very much in big business...the real estate business, as an example. They had invested $80 billion in real estate, mostly in Church structures...structures that were used less than 1% of the time. No wonder BB turned them into museums and living quarters. They placed money in apartment buildings, electronics firms, shopping centers, plastic companies, and even in a girdle company! All this, when their time and attention should have gone to preaching Christ and reaching the seeking men with the message of eternal life."

"There's been quite a change since then," Faye commented.

"Quite a change. Slowly the Pope lost respect. Even Catholics questioned his authority. This paved the way for Protestants to effect a merger into one great religion just a few years ago. Leadership in the UNITED WORLD CHURCH changes every 4 years by election now.

The present Pope is a pretty shrewd man, too. And I am of the impression that BB is a little on edge about this whole situation."

Back in Washington Brother Bartholomew was more than edgy...he was furious. Not only could he not locate the "troublesome trio" as he called them, but he sensed that the United World Church was taking on too much power. It had once been fanatically loyal to him; they both in a sense had helped each other — Brother Bartholomew and the United World Church — to rise in power. Now, however, the World Church was becoming too independent!

> So he carried me away in the spirit into the wilderness: and I saw a woman (World Church) sit upon a scarlet coloured beast (Antichrist), full of names of blasphemy, having seven heads and ten horns. (Revelation 17:3)

He summoned Prophet Arthur into his office. Prophet

Arthur, once a dissident religionist, had been thrust into office with surprising rapidity. Brother Bartholomew was very fond of Prophet Arthur. He served him faithfully without question. He never directed glory to himself...always gave the glory to Brother Bartholomew. BB never forgot this humbleness on Prophet Arthur's part. And he was to be amply rewarded.

"Prophet Arthur, it's time we make our next move. I have great plans for both you and me. This United States of Europe is only but a fourth of the world. The whole world must be placed under our wise dominion. And you will have a part in my glories. Tonight we fly to Rome. Tomorrow I will install you as permanent leader of the United World Church. The others will be banished for, shall we call it, 'lack of dedication to the cause?'"

After some further talk, BB continued, "...Good idea. You clean up the mess in Rome. Proclaim me as the one and true God. Install my pictures and statues in place of Jesus or Mary where these appear. Use the guillotine as frequently as necessary to keep the populace in line. Make a spectacle of each occasion right in the Colosseum. There are three rows of 6. Have the trip levers go off in sequence. For a change, let a little child push the electronic release button. Stage the whole thing like a big Hollywood production."

"If necessary, offer an extra ration of water. Only have it spiked with Dr. Curter's new mind-influencing drug...the drug that lulls the senses, makes people obey one central voice."

Prophet Arthur beamed. "Fantastic sir, with the lack of any rainfall the past 3 years they'll rush to drink that extra water ration like flies around honey."

"As good as done, Arthur. Let's get ready to go. I'll drop you off at Rome, see that you are officially installed, then fly to Jerusalem. I have a most unusual job to accomplish there. One I will most certainly relish!"

George was relieved when Faye and Tom returned to the Sea House accompanied by a group of believers.

"Am I glad to see you. I've been getting worried. Picture phone reports indicate that Prophet Arthur and Brother Bartholomew will be flying tonight to Rome. Nothing was said of the purpose of their mission. I was afraid that they may have found our hiding place."

The Captain of the Sea House spoke: "Your brave testimony for Christ has meant a great deal to us. When our time comes, we will also suffer gladly, for Christ has promised to gather us under his wings like a hen gathereth her chickens. But right now, it's time for quick action. Each Sea House is equipped with a small shuttle heliojet. Doesn't fly very fast; only 700 miles per hour but it can land anywhere because it lands vertically. Nuclear powered, too, so your available fuel should last quite some time. Tom, you know how to fly these. Take ours and take Faye and George with you. Don't tell us where you are going. That way our thought processes will not reveal your location. But you must leave within the hour."

> O Jerusalem, Jerusalem, thou that killest the prophets, and stonest them which are sent unto thee, how often would I have gathered thy children together, even as a hen gathereth her chickens under her wings, and ye would not! (Matthew 23:37)

We thanked the captain for his courtesies to us, boarded the heliojet, and took off. Down below the Sea House looked like a bobbing ball...but it was a happy first step in an escape that would hold terrifying moments for all of us.

Tom first intended to fly straight to Jerusalem. All of us wanted to go there to see the two prophets who were being called Moses and Elijah. We had heard they were clothed in sackcloth. That didn't matter to us. We just wanted to touch the hem of their garment. Somehow we dreamed that in so doing we might be translated like Elijah in a chariot of fire — directly to Heaven to see our loved ones again.

But our hopes were soon crushed.

Tom looked at his water-coolant indicator, then shook his head. While there was sufficient fuel, the water level was low. The 3 years of no rain made water very precious. Someone had siphoned off most of the water...just to survive.

"What are we going to do?" Faye cried.

"How long will this thing stay up?" George asked.

"Not too long, George, but long enough to get us to a land area. Let me check out my flight map. Looks like we have about two hours of flying time in water-coolant left. We could go about 1400 miles. But we're not going to find much water in Jerusalem."

"Let me see that map," George asked.

Tom handed him the flight map.

George rested his hand on his chin as if in deep thought. Suddenly it came to him. "I have the answer, Tom!"

"What is it?" Faye exclaimed.

"Remember in late 1969 when some scientists announced they thought they had discovered the remains of Noah's Ark? It was buried deep in a frozen lake near the ice-capped summit of Mount Ararat."

"Where is Mount Ararat?" Faye chimed in.

"Mount Ararat is the high northern twin-peaked cap of an entire elevated range. This range—once called Mount Ararat—the Bible says was the resting place of Noah's Ark after the Flood is in the eastern part of Turkey," George replied. "And they found pieces of timber preserved by ice. I recall reading that pieces of timber were showing near the surface of the ice pack. And underneath this spot was reported to be a small lake covered by an ice and debris cap, varying in thickness from 20 to 30 feet. Ararat is 16,946 high. There must be some small flat surface near there where we can land."

"But I don't get it," Tom queried, "what are we going to do, build another ark? Is there going to be another flood?"

"No, Tom," George smiled. "Let's land our heliojet there. People have forgotten about this spot. And yet it probably is one of the few places in the Middle East where a fresh water supply still exists. You can replenish your water-coolant tank and we can take off again. That same water may help us survive in the days ahead. Who knows?"

It was an excellent idea. And after refueling at Mount Ararat we took off again.

From the air we could see that Jerusalem was covered with a mass of people. They seemed to converge around the Temple area. Tom directed the heliojet to land in the vicinity of nearby Bethlehem. The town was almost empty. Everyone was in Jerusalem. He was able to store the heliojet in one of the many large caves of this region.

The cool water of Mount Ararat had refreshed us. We took long drinks while there and stored sufficient water in our heliojet. We were going to need it.

George wanted so much to go with Tom and Faye into Jerusalem. He, however, had no Mark and Tom was afraid he would be discovered. While many in Jerusalem did not bear The Mark, it was risky. George had another idea.

"There's a tent down there," he said pointing down near a ravine. "See if you can buy some native dress. Get an abayeh and that headcloth that's worn like a turban. It will cover my forehead and help avoid suspicion."

Soon all three were dressed like natives of the country. They melted into the crowd at Jerusalem. Tom remarked how the woman who sold them the clothes looked strangely familiar, but the remark was soon forgotten. By shoving and pushing they were able to make their way near the entrance of the Temple. Tom explained to George and Faye that the Temple was considered most holy by the Jews. The High priest only entered its holiest chamber the Day of Atonement. The Temple was built as closely as possible to look like Solomon's Temple. Long and narrow, the entrance was at one end, the Holy of Holies at the other. Fifteen broad steps led up to the entrance. Two landings in the flight provided dramatic space for ceremonial processions of singers. To enter the priests passed through tall, narrow cypress doors carved with symbolic cherubim, palm trees and open flowers inlaid with gold.

The Temple layout comprised three elements: (a) the Ulam, vestible porch from which the priest walked into (b) the main chamber, called the Hekal, or Holy Place and (c) the Debir, the innermost Holy of Holies or Oracle, the special abode of the Lord. Here in Solomon's Temple in times past rested the Ark of the Covenant. Here is where dwelt the invisible presence of the Lord.

It was the Day of Atonement. There on the steps walking ahead of the priest was Brother Bartholomew. A man in front of him was carrying a small statue, a statue of Brother Bartholomew. The priestly procession walked into the Temple. We were later told that Brother Bartholomew went into the Holy of Holies, and revealed himself to the High Priest as the one containing the very Spirit of very God returned to earth in flesh to save his people.

> Let no man deceive you by any means: for that day shall not come, except there come a falling away first, and that man of sin be revealed, the son of perdition;
>
> Who opposeth and exalteth himself above all that is called God, or that is worshipped; so that he as God sitteth in the temple of God, shewing himself that he is God. (2 Thessalonians 3-4)

In a short time, the priest, his aides and Brother Bartholomew emerged. The priest approached the bank of microphones at the top of the Temple steps. He spoke:

> "Children of the Lord. For years, yea, many thousands of years, we have been waiting for our Messiah.
>
> Today is the Day of Atonement. Today is the day we can have complete communion with God.
>
> For today our Messiah has returned. Brother Bartholomew is our Messiah...."

Brother Bartholomew was smiling, bowing to the multitude. Everything was going as he had planned.

Then suddenly the High

> When ye therefore shall see the abomination of desolation, spoken of by Daniel the prophet, stand in the holy place,
>
> Then let them which be in Judea flee into the mountains. (Matthew 24:15-16)

Priest paused, then spoke rapidly, shrieking as he spoke:

"THIS IS NOT YOUR MESSIAH. HE IS AN IMPOSTER. HE IS NOT GOD. HE HAS DESECRATED THE TEMPLE OF THE MOST HIGH. HIS BLAMPHEMOUS STATUE NOW STANDS OVER THE ARK OF THE COVENANT IN THE HOLY OF HOLIES. OBEY HIM NOT. FLEE FOR YOUR LIVES!"

That's the furtherest he went in his warning.

For Brother Bartholomew held up his hand. Within a twinkling of an eye, the High Priest simply disappeared, disintegrated.

Brother Bartholomew patted his ruby laser ring, replaced the protective cap, went to the stirring multitude, assured them that he and he alone was their God...and ended with:

Before your very eyes you have seen that the hand of the Lord has spoken. His judgment is swift.

Suddenly the skies opened. The dull, grey, air polluted skies seemed to part in one vast explosion that seemed to split the heavens. It was like being in semi-darkness for three years and then have a brilliant light shine on your face. The sudden heat of the sun was terrifying.

The first angel sounded, and there followed hail and fire mingled with blood, and they were cast upon the earth: and the third part of trees was burnt up, and all green grass was burnt up. (Revelation 8:7)

Grass, browned by lack of rain, suddenly crackled into flames all around us. Hail came down. A large fleet of jumbo jets overhead were crumbling, disintegrating with the forces of wind and hail. It seemed as though hail mixed with the blood of thousands of air passengers was falling all over us. It was a ghastly sight.

Then a pause.

Suddenly from the sky a huge red object looked as though it was hurtling straight for the earth.

The people were shouting...

IT'S EROS! IT'S EROS!

"What's Eros?" I shouted to George.

"Faye, Eros was discovered in 1969. It's a brick shaped chunk of debris. At that time it was about 15 miles by 5 miles in size. It last passed earth in 1975...about 17 million miles away. From the looks of it, apparently it has picked up other debris and has changed its orbit. It looks as though it will strike earth itself," George shouted.

"How prophetic," Tom yelled so we could hear him. "Eros, the god of love that sent the United States down the sewer of servitude to sin and Satan!! What a cruel hoax. From this angle it looks like Eros' main force will strike the United States itself!"

And the second angel sounded, and as it were a great mountain burning with fire was cast into the sea: and the third part of the sea became blood. (Revelation 8:8)

Brother Bartholomew was whisked to his new headquarters atop the Mount of Olives. From this command post he listened to reports filtering in from around the world. Chaos was king. The news everywhere was bad. His picture phone consoles showed nothing but devastation, death, confusion.

Prophet Arthur had flown to Headquarters immediately on hearing the news of the Eros meteor.

"What's the report from Oceanography?" Brother Bartholomew asked Prophet Arthur.

"Not too good, sir. Early reports show one-third of all of our ships have been destroyed, estimates are that one-third of all the fish have been killed and the seas are rapidly having much of their surface covered with blood."

And the third part of the creatures which were in the sea, and had life, died; and the third part of the ships were destroyed. (Revelation 8:9)

Just then an aide interrupted their conversation shouting, "Sir, another giant meteor has been sighted. It is falling toward earth in flaming fire because of the atmospheric friction generated as it passes through our air...Meteorology

Department has just informed us that its density is..."

Brother Bartholomew quickly flipped the HORIZON switch. An oval screen lit up and a view of the earth could be seen from a hovering satellite. A flaming star, large, brilliantly red, was streaking down through the atmosphere towards earth.

"Can it be Icarus?" Prophet Arthur cried out in terror.

"I don't know...but it's bound to hit earth. We're on a collision course!"

As it hit the atmosphere of earth, the flaming tail intensified in brillance...suddenly a blinding flash filled the screen.

Oceanography was back on the picturephone reporting. "Sir, quick checks around the world have indicated that about one-third of all the available water, rivers, seas, springs.... are POISONED. Apparently that meteor hit an underground water source that reaches many of the tributaries. Some people have already died from drinking the stuff. A few before they gasped their last breath complained about the extreme bitterness, sir."

> And the third angel sounded, and there fell a great star from heaven, burning as it were a lamp, and it fell upon the third part of the rivers, and upon the fountains of waters.
> And the name of the star is called Wormwood: and the third part of the waters became wormwood: and many men died of the waters, because they were made bitter. (Revelation 8:10-11)

"Prophet Arthur," Brother Bartholomew commanded, "get my heliojet. I'll show the people who is Lord. If we don't do something they'll be in a state of uncontrollable panic. To the Underground Complex!"

Just then a long roll of thunder shook the earth. In an odd occurrence the sun, moon and stars were visible. But even more strange a third of each surface was darkened on the sun and moon and suddenly even the flickering stars dimmed.

> And the fourth angel sounded, and the third part of the sun was smitten, and the third part of the moon, and the third part of the stars; so as the third part of them was darkened, and the day shone not for a third part of it, and the night likewise. (Revelation 8:12)

The panic had started. This latest phenomenon had triggered the population into an uncontrollable madness.

The heliojet arrived at the Underground Complex location. From outward appearances it seemed like the flat scrub plains of a typical Judean desert. But it wasn't. A small shed stood at one side. It was surrounded by guards. For many days people had speculated why guards would stand around a small shed in the middle of nowhere. They were soon to find out.

Brother Bartholomew entered the shed. A special elevator whisked him down deep within the earth. Satisfied with what he saw, he returned to the surface.

"They are ready, Prophet Arthur. Stand back."

In the small shack was a small panel on the wall. A series of switches and locks appeared when the door was removed. Brother Bartholomew pulled a series of switches in sequence, and then he inserted one key. Prophet Arthur inserted the other key...turned it to the left. Brother Bartholomew turned his key to the right...Suddenly a red light lit above Brother Bartholomew's key. On it were the words ABADDON IGNITION. Quickly he pressed the red button.

There was a slow steady roar, a roar as though it were coming from the very depths of the earth. Suddenly the earth in front of them began to rise, like two portions of a drawbridge, leaving a large gaping hole in the center. A blast of acrid black smoke funneled its way out the hole, cast a pale of death over the countryside.

And the fifth angel sounded, and I saw a star fall from heaven unto the earth: and to him was given the key of the bottomless pit.

And he opened the bottomless pit; and there arose a smoke out of the pit, as the smoke of a great furnace; and the sun and the air were darkened by reason of the smoke of the pit. (Revelation 9:1-2)

Faye, Tom and George had just reached a small knoll overlooking the area just as the smoke cloud rose.

And there came out of the smoke locusts upon the earth: and unto them was given power, as the scorpions of the earth have power. (Revelation 9:3)

Tom shouted. "Look, in the

From the depths of the earth flying men suddenly appeared!

smoke clouds. It looks like thousands...even millions of flying men."

The roar of jet noises was almost deafening.

"Flying men?...Tom. How can man fly without a plane?"

"That's it, George. It's a relatively new discovery, the jet belt. Look, they're covered with a special armor to protect them against projectiles...or against flying bits of meteorities. That gold dome on their heads is their directional device. Brother Bartholomew can automatically change their course, zero them in on any target he wishes."

> And the shapes of the locusts were like unto horses prepared unto battle; and on their heads were as it were crowns like gold, and their faces were as the faces of men. (Revelation 9:7)

"What's that long tail-like effect that flutters behind them?" Faye asked yelling in Tom's ear?

"It's a special virus spray. The liquid is stored in that long tubular section on their back. A switch on the jet belt works the release lever and it dispenses a fine spray over a 150 square yard area. BB calls them ABADDON...that's Hebrew for THE DESTROYER."

> And they had tails like unto scorpions, and there were stings in their tails: and their power was to hurt men five months.
> And they had a king over them, which is the angel of the bottomless pit, whose name in the Hebrew tongue is Abaddon, but in the Greek tongue hath his name Apollyon. (Revelation 9:10-11)

"Does it kill?" Faye asked.

"No, but it would be better if it did...just to end the suffering. Two years ago I saw it tested on some prisoners. It was an awful sight.

The spray feels like a vicious sting...like the sting of a scorpion and the pain lasts for months. After a few weeks, people try to kill themselves... the pain is so unbearable.

They were so close to the take-off point that the army of

> And to them it was given that they should not kill them, but that they should be tormented five months: and their torment was as the torment of a scorpion, when he striketh a man.
> And in those days shall men seek death, and shall not find it; and shall desire to die, and death shall flee from them. (Revelation 9:5-6)

flying men flew over them... headed for Jerusalem.

As they passed overhead George shouted, "They look almost like a plague...a plague of LOCUSTS!"

"Hurry," Tom motioned, "let's get to that heliojet before it's too late." Tom spoke as we ran, "That woman who sold us the clothes. I can't get it out of my mind how familiar she looked...and yet I can't recall ever seeing her."

"Maybe your mind is playing tricks on you, Tom," George suggested. "I don't know, George, there was something evil, something sinister. I just can't put my finger on it. We better be careful...just in case. Let me approach the heliojet first. You and Faye stay about 500 yards behind."

Tom walked on ahead. Coming over the crest of a slight hill he ran towards the heliojet. Not too far away the tent, where he had purchased the clothes, seemed still and quiet.

Faye and George lay behind a clump of bushes watching Tom's every move, waiting for him to signal the OK.

Suddenly out of the tent emerged a man and that woman. She pointed to Tom and shouted...

"He's the man! He's the man that came in that flying machine." For a moment, Tom stopped, dazed, then made a dash for the heliojet. Brother Bartholomew laughed derisively...held up his hand, removed the cover from his ring...the ruby laser beam did its work swiftly, like the cruel snap of a whip.

In a moment, Tom, the heliojet and the cave had disappeared! They disintegrated into scattered dust that in a few seconds settled back down upon the quiet Judean desert.

Faye and George were shocked. They dare not move. They could see Brother Bartholomew bend down and kiss the woman on the cheek. In the dead stillness they could hear his voice.

"You have been wonderful...just wonderful...my dear mother. Poof...there went Tom Malone, there goes George Omega, there goes Faye Sanders and their escape heliojet. Thank you, mother. Thank you."

Chapter 13

The Sound of Death

Leader Chou was getting impatient. Moves by Brother Bartholomew disturbed him. With Brother Bartholomew moving into the Middle East, Leader Chou was sure the next target would be Asia.

As Chairman of the Chinese Communist Party Leader Chou felt a responsibility to his country. And he and his leaders believed that the Middle East belonged to them, and not only the Middle East but all of Africa.

It was amazing the striking resemblance of Leader Chou to the earlier Chinese leader Chairman Mao. Mao had long since died but his goals had been expanded.

China's military might had increased. She had perfected nuclear weaponry. At last the long road to leadership had been accomplished. China was recognized as a power to be feared. Up to now relations with the United States of Europe had been half-way cordial...at least each allowed the other to exist. But that relationship was soon to cease. For Leader Chou had his own worldly ambitions.

From the sights and sounds that filled the night, a visitor may have thought it was a Chinese New Year's celebration.

Blazing lights outlined the buildings around Peking's vast Tien An Men Square and poles on the street corners were laced with strings of multicolored bulbs. Hundreds of thousands of chanting citizens pressed towards the already jammed square, raising great clouds of dust over the center of the city. Everywhere were 30-foot-high papier-mache busts of Leader Chou. Loudspeakers, drums, cymbals and gongs produced a never-ending, nerve-shattering cacophony of sound.

The festivities had been ordered to celebrate the announcement of a historic major political event.

Suddenly, with a flurry of trumpets, Leader Chou stepped to the microphones and addressed the people:

Workers for Tomorrow,

It was our late leader Chairman Mao who said, "The outstanding thing about China's people is that they are poor and blank. On a blank sheet of paper, free from any mark, the freshest and most beautiful characters can be written."

The East wind now prevails over the West. Our country will never again be an insulted nation.

Tomorrow our armies begin the March of Victory. And with us to march as Brothers and allies will be our Russian neighbors who have suffered greatly.

Like Antiochus IV Epiphanes we will march wherever the River Euphrates runs its course. But where Antiochus failed, we will not fail. We will conquer all of Asia, we will conquer the Middle East, we will conquer Africa.

Tomorrow 200 MILLION warriors will march. We will not be stopped until the whole world kneels at our feet. We will be victorious.

The ovation was spontaneous and tremendous as the citizens raised their familiar Red Book and shouted...VICTORY, VICTORY, VICTORY!

Saying to the sixth angel which had the trumpet, Loose the four angels which are bound in the great river Euphrates...And the number of the army of the horsemen were two hundred thousand thousand (200 million): and I heard the number of them. (Revelation 9: 14, 16)

The plan was clear. Euphrates, the longest river of southwest Asia was to be the focal point of conquest. It follows a circuitous course of 1780 miles beginning at two headstreams in Turkey, passes near Babylon, merges with the Tigris River and together they empty into the Persian Gulf.

Leader Chou met with Russian leaders to map out the conquest that would begin the next day. He pointed to a map of the world as he directed the plan of attack:

Most of the Chinese and Russian forces will follow the flow of The Euphrates down through Turkey and head towards Jerusalem.

Another group of our forces will move down into Greece, cross the Mediterranean into Libya and come across the continent, and up to meet us at Jerusalem into a pincer movement.

Russia's previous defeat had made her weak and conciliatory. China controlled her territory and this control made it quite convenient to swarm directly south to the Holy Land.

It was a route somewhat planned after the exploits of Antiochus IV. Leader Chou had read his adventures of conquest with interest. One thing both had in common. Both had a hatred for the Jews. When Antiochus IV was expelled from Egypt by Popilius (168 B.C.) the news reached Jerusalem in the form of a report that he had been killed. The rejoicing Jews deposed his appointees, massacred the leaders of his party and cleansed the Temple of what they felt to be pagan abominations.

Antiochus, not dead, and convinced that the Jews had obstructed his victory for African conquest, marched to Jerusalem, slaughtered Jews of either sex by the thousands, desecrated and looted the Temple and commanded the Temple be rededicated as a shrine to Zeus. He forbade the keeping of the Sabbath, and made circumcision a capital crime. Every Jew who refused to eat pork was to be jailed or killed and the Holy Book was to be burned.

Leader Chou was determined that his reign of destruction would far outshine that of his idol, Antiochus. Leader Chou well knew the devastating power of his arsenal of destruction.

Like a surging flood the march began. Across the Mediterranean Sea millions of Chinese made their way on specially constructed space shuttles that carried 2000 troops at a time. Landing at Tripoli in Libya in early dawn they caught the populace by surprise.

Traveling on individual tracked motorcycles and wearing bullet proof vests and modern gas masks the invaders appeared to be a type of horror horsemen from the Middle Ages. Short snub-nosed nuclear

And this I saw the horses in the vision, and them that sat on them, having breastplates of fire, and of jacinth, and brimstone: and the heads of the horses were as the heads of lions: and out of their mouths issued fire and smoke and brimstone. (Revelation 9:17)

rifles laid down a lethal spray of death wherever resistance appeared. These new weapons were very effective, being able to kill anything ahead in a path from 5 feet fanning out to 100 feet in width in an area one mile long. Soon the Chinese Army was rampaging far south in Africa, and in Kenya killing that country's leader. It had made a half circle route and was now inching north to the Sudan.

The Sudan with 12 million blacks and 18 million Arabs savagely fought the invader in Juba, in Wau and at Malakai. Using bullets filled with Anya'Nya, a slow but fatal poison made by grinding the dried head of the cobra into a fine powder, they successfully killed many Chinese in the forward advance columns. But for every one that fell there seemed to be a thousand to replace him. It was an impossible fight. The White Nile became filled with the blood of the Sudanese.

Nothing would stop them now. They continued past the Sudan and up into Egypt.

From the North, the upper half of the pincer movement of the Chinese-Russian army crossed the Black Sea, crossed Turkey and was headed down through Syria.

In their path, both on land and in the air, their nuclear striking force left a wake of dead almost impossible to imagine. Two nuclear strikes had almost wiped out all of Europe. By these three was the third part of men killed, by the fire, and by the smoke, and by the brimstone (flaming sulphur), which issued out of their mouths. (Revelation 9:18) Most of Africa was reeling under the blow of the Chinese heel of death.

Most of the 200 million army had come through these earlier conflicts unscathed. Now the real kill awaited them... Jerusalem...Brother Bartholomew and Prophet Arthur... then Leader Chou would be ruler of all the earth!

Brother Bartholomew was pacing the floor in his hideaway headquarters on the Mount of Olives.

The news reports were bad. The Chinese were no longer

Soon the Chinese Army was rampaging far south in Africa, and in Kenya killing that country's leader.

It was an impossible flight. The White Nile became filled with the blood of the Sudanese.

Dr. Curter's
SOUND SYNDROME
Decibels Chart

A decibel is an arbitrary unit based on the faintest sound that a man can hear. The scale is logarithmic, so that an increase of 10 db means a tenfold increase in sound intensity; a 20 db rise a hundredfold increase, and 30 db a thousandfold increase.

Since 1950 the noise level in the United States alone has doubled every ten years.

140 — **JET PLANE**
100 ft. away

130 — **PNEUMATIC RIVETER**

120 — **ROCK MUSIC WITH AMPLIFIERS**
4 to 6 ft. away
One trillion times greater than least audible sound
Human pain threshold

110
107 — **POWER MOWER**

100 — **NOISY KITCHEN**

SUBWAY
inside

90

85 — **CITY TRAFFIC**
inside car
Hearing damage occurs if noise prolonged
80

70 — **FORTISSIMO SINGER**
3 ft. away

60 — **ORDINARY CONVERSATION**

DECIBEL SCALE

meeting with any resistance. Something had to be done and done quickly.

He called in Dr. Curter.

"Curter, look at those video screens. Everywhere the Chinese are like a horde of ants, overrunning everything... dead everywhere. We've got to come up with a plan that will stop them dead in their tracks."

Curter thought for a moment. Then spoke. "I have a plan, sir. It's been worked in experimentation only. But it may be the answer. We can inflict them with the SOUND SYN-DROME."

"The sound WHAT?" Brother Bartholomew questioned.

"Sound Syndrome, sir. Since the early 1960's man has been concerned with the increasing noise level. We measure noise by decibels. A decibel is an arbitrary unit based on the faintest sound that a man can hear. As an example the rustle of leaves has a decibel rating of 20. Conversational speech a decibel rating of 60. Now at the decibel range of 85, if it is prolonged, hearing damage can occur. A Jet airliner 500 feet overhead has a decibel rating of 115. And coincidentally, rock music with amplifiers is rated at 120 decibels which is also the noise level of human pain threshold."

"What are you trying to tell me, Curter?"

"Just this, noise above 120 decibels, controlled noise, can be deadly. Since 1950 the noise level in the United States alone has doubled every ten years. Noise can work on humans two ways. One, of course, is to cause deafness."

"But the second effect of noise upon humans is psycho-logical. Excessive exposure to noise constricts the arteries, increases the heartbeat, dilates the pupils of the eye. In tests on animals we found that continued excessive noise made them turn against each other, eat their young and eventually die of heart failure."

"But how can we use this against the Chinese without killing our own people?" Brother Bartholomew questioned.

"There will be some sacrifice, sir. Noise is not selective. But if we act now our Noise Amplifiers can be directed from space platforms in the direction of Syria and Turkey and in the south, towards Egypt and Ethiopia...in other words, we can still reach them before their troops intermingle with ours in the Jerusalem region."

"Excellent idea, Curter, at the same time we'll kill off some of our excess population. Solve two problems at one time. Advise the Noise Amplifier Division to proceed immediately with the plan."

The rapidly advancing Chinese never knew what hit them. At first the slowly developing shrill sound had them looking around wondering where the noise was coming from. They could not locate the source. Soon they became irritated with one another. After a few hours, fights erupted, their nuclear guns were aimed at their own ranks and they became disoriented and confused.

Leader Chou, from his palace in Peking, watched the progress of the war on his video screen. It was not a pleasant sight. Suddenly his marauding army was falling to pieces... but from what? The enemy was no where in sight. In fact innocent bystanders were dropping over like flies as well.

Piles of human flesh marked the trail of the marching Chinese Army. For a while some existed by covering their ears. But the deep penetrating noise level rose to higher decibel ratings and soon even this protection was pierced by the deadly sound.

Leader Chou hurridly called Brother Bartholomew via Picturephone. "Good to hear from you Leader Chou," Brother Bartholomew answered. "If you will surrender I will advise our Noise Amplifier Division to cease operation."

Leader Chou quickly conceded.

"Good," Brother Bartholomew continued, "you have made a wise decision. Besides we should not be fighting each other. A greater war lies ahead, one that will take our combined efforts to wipe out those who think God still exists...those who fail to honor me as the world leader...as the God of this world."

The war had been won. Brother Bartholomew, more sure of himself than ever before, ordered more statues of himself, statues in gold, brass and stone to be placed in every major city in the world. And wherever these statues appeared, people flocked to worship them.

Both Faye and George were covered with bruises and scratches. They had not yet gotten over the fact that their friend Tom Malone was dead— disintegrated right before their eyes. Yet while they mourned

And I heard a voice from heaven saying unto me, Write, Blessed are the dead which die in the Lord from henceforth: Yea, saith the Spirit, that they may rest from their labours; and their works do follow them. (Revelation 14:13)

his death they praised God that his soul was now safe in heaven with Christ. And as George said, "Not a slow chariot ride like Elijah...but in a blinding flash."

Slowly and dejectedly they walked together down a lonely path that at one time was a road.

"Where are we, Dad?" Faye questioned.

"I'm not sure, Honey, but I believe a little past the village of Emmaus. We should be about seven miles from Jerusalem."

Suddenly, as if from nowhere, they heard the footsteps of two strangers behind them. Fearfully they turned and looked. It was too late to run. And even if they could, they did not have the strength.

"Don't be afraid of us," one man called out. "We are your friends."

"Who are you?" Faye asked.

"If we told you, would it matter? You have been walking this road long. You look weary, thirsty. Have you journeyed from afar?"

"You would never believe us if we told you," George replied. "It seems too impossible to be true. We have not had a drink of water for what seems to be ages. No protein cakes...

nothing. We have just about given up hope."

"Where are you going?" the other man inquired.

"We are headed for Jerusalem," Faye answered. "We want to see the two prophets who are called by many Moses and Elijah. Somehow we hope that by our touching their garment, we might be saved from any more tribulation."

"I see the Mark on your forehead," the stranger replied, looking at Faye. Faye quickly sobbed, "But...oh...they forced it upon me. I screamed...I didn't want it...."

"You have gone through much tribulation," one of the two men responded.

The other one spoke. "I am afraid your journey is in vain. The two prophets or witnesses of which you speak were killed by Brother Bartholomew. For 3½ days their bodies lay exposed in the streets of Jerusalem. Many mourned, but far more people spat on them, sneered, and then went into the Temple to worship the idol of Brother Bartholomew."

And when they shall have finished their testimony, the beast that ascendeth out of the bottomless pit shall make war against them, and shall overcome them, and kill them.

And they of the people and kindreds and tongues and nations shall see their dead bodies three days and an half, and shall not suffer their dead bodies to be put in graves.   (Revelation 11:7, 9)

"Then what happened?" George questioned.

The stranger spoke. "The two witnesses disappeared. Some say they ascended to heaven."

The other stranger continued, "While your journey to reach the prophets may not be successful, we can tell you where you will find a stream of pure, crystal water...a place where you will be safe from your persecutors."

And after three days and an half the spirit of life from God entered into them, and they stood upon their feet: and great fear fell upon them which saw them.

And they heard a great voice from heaven saying unto them, Come up hither. And they ascended up to heaven in a cloud; and their enemies beheld them. (Revelation 11:11-12)

"Where, where?" Faye anxiously cried.

"Hezekiah's Tunnel."

And with that the two strangers suddenly stepped behind some rocks and disappeared.

Faye and George looked at each other in astonishment... then collecting their thoughts, both exclaimed together: "MOSES and ELIJAH?"

Could it have been...that the two called Moses and Elijah before ascending from the streets of Jerusalem to heaven paused just briefly on the Emmaus road??? They didn't know. But both Faye and George stopped to praise God and give thanks.

Hezekiah's Tunnel. George had heard of it before. Helen in her tour of Jerusalem had mentioned it...but George had only listened half-heartedly as then he was not interested in Bible history. How he wished he had been more attentive.

"There's only one way to find out where this tunnel is, Faye...and that's to go into the city of Jerusalem, find some faithful Jews who do not bear the Mark. Perhaps, they may have old books which reveal the location of Hezekiah's Tunnel. Maybe a Hasidic Jew?"

"What's a Hasidic Jew?" Faye inquired.

"They are the very orthodox Jews, often disliked by the conservative and liberal Jew...but in past ages they have been learned men, doing much reading. They may provide the clue. And yet we must be careful."

Brother Bartholomew was facing unexpected problems. The recent war with China had resulted in the death of 1/3rd of mankind in the Afro-Asian world. This helped ease the population crisis but the use of nuclear weapons had affected the genes of many women. The next generation would be pitifully sick it was feared.

He presented the problem to Dr. Curter.

Dr. Curter as always had an answer.

"Sir," he explained, "in 1968 experiments began on a way of making babies outside of natural means. Since then we have made great strides and can now determine what IQ we want in a child, whether we want a boy or girl, whether we want all Einsteins or automatons that will follow every order. We call it Cloning."

"CLONING? That's an odd name. What does it mean?" Brother Bartholomew inquired.

"Cloning is the most bizarre development to come along in the field of biology to date. Cloning will make it possible to duplicate any type of man or beast. And each WILL BE A PRECISE DUPLICATE, A CARBON COPY OF THE ORIGINAL."

"Fantastic!" Brother Bartholomew gasped as his mind began thinking of ways he could use such a discovery for his own devious means. "Tell me more."

"Well, if one Einstein could lay down the whole foundation of modern-day physics, what might a dozen Einsteins — or 1,000 — either together or individually accomplish? Cloning can make it possible for a man to achieve in some sense immortality. For as soon as he dies, his family can simply make a whole new copy of him."

"Why the word CLONING?" Brother Bartholomew asked.

"Cloning is a word which comes from a Greek root meaning 'cutting' and is sometimes defined as 'asexual propagation.' This simply means reproduction-without-sex or, put another way, reproduction-without-fertilization."

"What are you saying, Dr. Curter?" interruped Prophet Arthur who had been standing quietly by.

"Just this, sir. We now can produce children of any specific intelligence pattern, boy or girl, to lead or to follow, from long-dead parents, or even from only one parent."

Brother Bartholomew spoke. "Well done, Dr. Curter. You have the problem well in hand." He paused, quickly scribbled some notes on a piece of paper and handed them to Dr. Curter, saying: "Here are my specifications, get that Cloning department working. Money is no object. I'll appropriate whatever is necessary. I want followers, not leaders, and see if you can make them immune from nuclear radiation. And oh, by the way, Curter, I'm giving you a heliojet. My compliments for your fine work."

Suddenly the ground shook. The long, low rumble was a familiar one. They had heard it before. It was an earthquake.

As George and Faye were walking into Jerusalem they were met by thousands of shouting, screaming people fleeing the city, running towards the mountains.

Those who ran all bore The Mark 666. Their faces shone with fear. Boils and sores had erupted on their faces and hands. The Mark 666 seemed to stand out in puffiness, oozing a sickly white pus that streaked their face.

And the first went, and poured out his vial upon the earth; and there fell a noisome and grievous sore upon the men which had the mark of the beast, and upon them which worshipped his image. (Revelation 16:2)

And the second angel poured out his vial upon the sea; and it became as the blood of a dead man: and every living soul died in the sea. (Revelation 16:3)

George stopped one man, asked him why he was running.

"Earthquake in Jerusalem. We have been told that even the ocean has turned to a sea of blood. Everything is dying. The rivers and springs are turning to blood. We are fleeing to the mountains. Come, it is our only hope!"

Each will be a PRECISE DUPLICATE, a CARBON COPY of the Original. We can make 1000 Ministers identical and patterned to obey Prophet Arthur."

"Thank you, friend, but we're headed for Jerusalem!"

"Don't go to Jerusalem," the old man pleaded. "Already there are 7000 dead there lying in the streets!"

And the same hour was there a great earthquake, and the tenth part of the city fell, and in the earthquake were slain of men seven thousand: and the remnant were affrighted, and gave glory to the God of heaven. (Revelation 11:13)

George and Faye continued walking towards Jerusalem on the old Nablus Road. They had seen too much to turn back now. Soon, George remarked, they should reach the Jericho Road bordering the inner city wall.

For the first time in a long time Faye seemed calm and relaxed as she spoke. "Dad, when did religion start falling apart? I mean when did people start turning away from Christ and developing their own theology?"

"That's a hard question to answer, Faye," George replied. "Some say it started in the late 1800's and in the early 1900's. Perhaps the most marked change occurred way back in 1968-69 almost coinciding with the then famous campus revolts. Students were seeking what they called a new religion, one that was mystical, symbolic. One Roman Catholic theologian of that day said,

> 'Almost everybody tends to think of religion
> as an institutional structure. That's really
> not true. What's really religious is an
> ultimate view of self and community and doesn't
> necessarily have anything to do with God.'

Another Professor of religion at a well-known college said,

> 'I call drug-induced experiences, as well as
> the whole ethos built around drugs in the
> youth counter-culture, religious.'

Some well-meaning but misdirected people tried to bring Christ down to the level of the people instead of lifting the level of the people up to the standards of Christ. Part of a musical work I remember had phrases such as this running through it,

'Cause this is real, man. This Person died for me.'
And Wham!!!! That really rocks me!!!!

Then there were the Rock Communions, and the flaunting of sex in the church. Fundamentalists became unpopular. There was more social concern and less soul concern. Slowly but surely, it watered down to a watered down religion...a religion that eventually paved the way for Brother Bartholomew. After all they had experienced everything else. Their appetites had become jaded. Life had lost its kicks. And that's when we entered into the scene. And, Faye, Honey, that's why you and I are walking down this road... searching for tomorrow, a tomorrow when Christ rules the world as King of Kings and Lord of Lords...a tomorrow where every man and woman is safe lying beneath his own vine and fig tree. How much grief you and I could have eliminated if only we had accepted Christ before the Rapture took place!"

"*If,* Dad, *if only.* How often I've heard it said, 'experience may be a good teacher, but some people never graduate from kindergarten.' I guess that's me."

George and Faye reached the end of Nablus road. It deadended into the Jericho Road.

"Which way shall we turn, Dad, right or left?"

George looked both ways. The high walls of the city were an impressive sight. Somehow the earthquakes had not affected them. Then George remembered the tour with Helen. He looked to the left and pointed. Look up there!"

"I don't see anything," Faye replied.

"Look closely, Faye, in the rock. Those indentations that resemble a face. That's Golgotha! The Skull. The place of our Lord's crucifixion."

"Then the Garden Tomb must not be far away," Faye replied, hopefully. "It isn't, Faye. It's close by and so is Gethsemane...the place where Jesus prayed before he was crucified."

"Dad, I have a wonderful idea. Somehow I feel right now

we should go to Gethsemane and pray. God will be there. He will answer our prayers. I've never been to Gethsemane, Dad. Take me there now."

"Praise God, Faye, a wonderful plan...both of us praying in the Garden of Gethsemane, just as Christ did some 2000 years ago. The power of Christ's love has not diminished. How I love that verse...

> 'That I may know him, and the POWER of
> His resurrection, and the fellowship of
> His sufferings, being made conformable
> unto His death.'

That's Philippians 3:10 and then in verse 14 it continues...

> 'I press toward the mark for the prize of
> the high calling of God in Christ Jesus.'

You know, Faye, that's exactly what we're doing, pressing toward the mark...."

Faye and George opened the gate of the old churchyard. And there, there was Gethsemane. Somehow grass was still growing here, the gnarled olive trees still stood as they have through the centuries. The flowers were blooming as if this tiny garden stood still through the ages while the rest of the world deteriorated in sin.

It was dusk, the shades of night were rapidly falling. At the other end of the Garden they saw a movement. A man had been standing, and now he knelt as if to pray.

Faye and George knelt to pray near him.

Suddenly the man stood up. It was hard to see him in the darkness for he wore a cloak around his head and his robe reached to the ground.

He came nearer, touched both of us on the shoulder as we knelt. We turned.

"Faye and George, I thought that if I waited long enough I might find you here at this silly shrine. Brother Bartholomew will be most elated!"

There was no mistaking the voice or the face — it was that of Prophet Arthur!

Chapter 14

March on Megiddo

"A great job, Prophet Arthur! A great job. I thought I had dispensed with those two when I lasered that heliojet near Bethlehem."

Brother Bartholomew was speaking. Prophet Arthur smiled a smile of smug satisfaction.

Surrounded by guards both Faye and George looked dejected as they stood in what some referred to as the "Master's throne room."

It was some time since Faye and George had been in this spacious nerve control center of Brother Bartholomew's. Some changes had been made. In one section of the room was what appeared to be a mechanical monster, a frightening machine with a tall pillar as a base and a revolving circular platform above it, topped with what appeared to be some type of radar receiving device. The entire unit was covered with switches, buttons and screens and it stood some 30 feet high.

Brother Bartholomew noting George and Faye engrossed

251

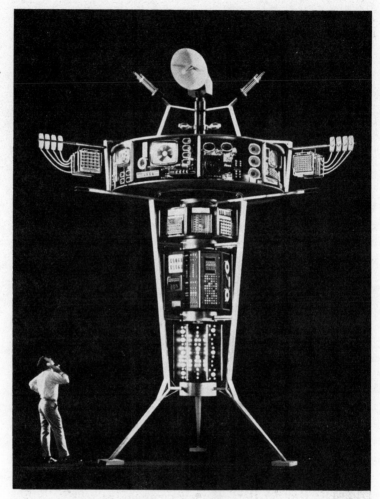

"That's my Christ. It does everything I tell it to do."

in this large mysterious unit, spoke: "What fools you are. You pray to a God who does not hear you, not even in the Garden of Gethsemane!"

Pointing to the mechanical spy he boasted, "That's my Christ. It does everything I tell it to do. It follows my orders without question. I am God and Robo-X is my miracle worker

...keeps me advised on all the movements of my enemies... instantly relays defections within my rank."

Faye and George stared in disbelief. The computer and electronic gadgetry which once was supposed to have been a blessing was now a curse.

"And this time," Prophet Arthur proudly beamed, "this time Brother Bartholomew has great plans for you...plans from which you will not escape."

"Not my plans, Prophet Arthur, your plans," BB replied. "After all it was your idea originally and you should get the credit for it. Tell them what great destiny awaits them!"

"Very well, sir," Bishop Arthur continued. "You two prayed so fervently at the Garden of Gethsemane where this fabled Jesus was supposed to have spent his last night. And yet your prayers were not answered. Perhaps you did not pray hard enough...or, perhaps...at the wrong location? Perhaps you should have been praying at that heretical GARDEN TOMB where your Jesus was supposedly raised from the dead."

"Excellent idea! Excellent!" added Brother Bartholomew. "And what better way to pray, Prophet Arthur, what better way to pray!"

"Yes," Prophet Arthur continued, "what better way to pray than by kneeling, kneeling at the Garden Tomb...and what more comfortable way to kneel and enter into Christ's Kingdom quickly...than to kneel at a dual GUILLOTINE, set up right at the Garden Tomb!"

"Excellent! Excellent! Prophet Arthur you are indeed a wise man!" Brother Bartholomew commended.

"There's more, sir. We have electronically set our release mechanisms so that both heads will roll at the same time... in unison! And for your convenience, we'll place your bodies in the Garden Tomb...just in case your Master should come."

Faye's heart sank. Her eyelids dropped. George was furious and was ready to unleash a tongue lashing at both Prophet Arthur and Brother Bartholomew. Just as he was ready to speak before these confirmed monsters of iniquity the words of Scripture came to his mind...

"He was oppressed, and he was afflicted,
yet he opened not his mouth: he is brought
as a lamb to the slaughter, and as a sheep
before her shearers is dumb, so he openeth
not his mouth."

(Isaiah 53:7)

And George said nothing.

They were told that the execution day would be tomorrow. This would give BB sufficient time to summon a large crowd, and put on a great show.

Quickly they were led to an elevator which went down into a shaft that seemed endless, hundreds of feet below the Mount of Olives.

Faye spoke first. The room was cold and damp. There was no light except for the little light that seeped through the peep hole in their door.

"Daddy, I've been thinking..." and with that she burst into tears.

"Why are you crying, Faye? This is no time to cry. We must have faith. Paul was imprisoned just like we are...in Rome...and yet he asked Timothy to bring him the parchments...God's Word, that he might feed upon them. We still have that little Bible, Faye. It's in my pocket. Do you want me to read to you?"

"No, Dad, it wouldn't do any good. There's no way I can go to Heaven now. All this time I've been running, hiding with you, not realizing that you can go to Heaven...but not I. Never, daddy, never!" Faye screamed hysterically.

"I don't understand, Faye. Why do you say that?"

With tears running down her face and in a choked, half crying voice she sobbed, "LOOK AT MY FOREHEAD, DADDY! LOOK AT MY FOREHEAD! DO YOU SEE THE MARK? EVERYONE CAN SEE IT. 6...6...6 EVEN GOD

CAN SEE IT! MARKED FOREVER FOR DESTRUC-
TION."

George placed his arm around Faye, gently put her head
on his shoulder as he had done many times when she was a
little girl. At first he didn't know what to say...but he spoke:
"Faye, remember when you were just a little girl, 8 years
old, you tripped and fell in the school playground. There was
a slight scratch on your forehead. Do you remember what
you did?"

"Yes, Dad, I came running home after school crying my
heart out saying, 'I'll have a scar for life. I'll be an ugly lady.
No one will love me.'"

"That's right, Faye, but remember how I reassured you
that God would heal that wound. And within a few weeks it
disappeared."

"I know daddy, you're trying to be kind and understanding, but it won't work. That was a physical scar. This is a
spiritual scar. By taking the Mark 666 I am marked as one
rejecting Christ, giving my allegiance to antichrist."

"Symbolically, yes, but it was done under coercion and
somehow I feel this Mark will disappear. You had rejected
antichrist. You were forcibly led to the communion table and
against your will branded with his evil brand. I cannot understand all of God's Word...but I accept it. Since our initial
escape on the Sea House I've had much time to concentrate
on the Word of God. And there's one verse I remember in
Romans 11:33. It goes something like this:

> O the depth of the riches both of the wisdom
> and knowledge of God! how unsearchable are
> His judgments, and His ways past finding out!

And somehow, I believe, however we end our life here on
this earth, God will understand the circumstances under
which you received The Mark...for He is all-seeing and all-
knowing. And in His infinite mercy He will provide the
answer."

After a time of Bible reading and prayer they again began

to talk. Faye asked, "How did this Mark idea come about in the first place?"

"The Mark is not an original idea, Faye," George replied trying to comfort her. "Other ruling powers have adopted a Mark in their day. Nazi Germany had its *swastika;* the Soviet Union its *hammer and sickle.* Both were universally recognized. I've done a little research on this. In Daniel 7:4 we are told that Babylon was symbolized by God in a vision given to Daniel as a lion with eagle's wings. The Medo-Persian empire was portrayed by a bear's rising up with three ribs between its teeth in Daniel 7:5. And in Daniel 7:6 the Graeco-Macedonia influence was pictured as a four-headed leopard with wings. Royal families and dynasties eve˙ had their own marks.

In the late 1960's and early 1970's a common Mark was the Broken Cross or Peace Symbol, as some called it. It was first used as a peace symbol by marchers in England, led by Lord Bertrand Russell in the late 1940's. It was developed by superimposing the *semaphore code signs* for N and D and stood for nuclear disarmament. As far back as the Middle Ages this symbol was a common symbol used by godless forces with the cross reversed and broken."

"Is the word MARK actually in the Bible?" Faye questioned. "Yes, it occurs eight times in the Bible. And all are found in the book of Revelation and all pertain to antichrist. The word comes from the Greek *charagma.* It means etching or stamp such as a badge of servitude."

Brother Bartholomew was busy making great plans for the Garden Tomb execution site. "Everything must work like clockwork," he warned Prophet Arthur.

If BB were aware of what was occuring in the Space Exploration department his mind would have been on more important things. Dr. Curter who had become a liaison officer to Brother Bartholomew was summoned to the Space Exploration briefing room. The news was not good. Quickly he raced to Brother Bartholomew's office, and dashed in apologetically. "Why so flustered, Curter?" Brother Bartholomew questioned. "I'm afraid I have some bad news, sir. The tidal drag of the moon is slowing the earth's rotation. Recent nuclear explosions combined with air pollutants have caused some sort of cosmic chaos. The moon's rotational period is now matching that of the earth and this is eliminating the tidal drag."

"What does all this mean, Curter?" Brother Bartholomew asked.

"Simply this. The *sun* is continuing to exert tidal pull, further slowing down the earth. The sun also may cause the moon to reverse direction and move closer to the earth until the moon is torn apart at a distance of 10,000 miles. Earthquakes, enormous tides will result...but even more catastrophic, the expansion of the sun in its dying throes will cast off an intense heat...a heat so intense that it might kill everything on earth."

"When will this occur?" Prophet Arthur asked.

"Our Space Exploration laboratory was not prepared for such an ineventuality and therefore their research of this area of phenomenon was not conducted until just a few days ago."

"What are you trying to say, Curter, speak up and stop this mumbo jumbo!"

Curter stammered, "What I am trying to say, sir, is that this catastrophe could strike at any moment!"

Frantically, Brother Bartholomew began pushing buttons, flipping switches shouting into his control console to alert all units to prepare for a catastrophe of the sun, urging everyone to take cover.

And even as he spoke it appeared as though the axis of the earth was turning, the sun coming closer. The oppressive heat closed in like a suffocating blanket.

The scene was beyond description. The hot rays of sun broke through the polluted screen of dust and grime that had so long covered the earth and these rays seemed to lick up this barrier like a flame licking up particles of chipped wood. It came searing, hotter, and hotter, and hotter. Screaming, agonizing screaming even penetrated the deep shaft where Faye and George were imprisoned. Those who but for a moment glanced up at this holocaust of horror were instantly and permanently blinded.

> And the fourth angel poured out his vial upon the sun; and power was given unto him to scorch men with fire.
> And men were scorched with great heat, and blasphemed the name of God, which hath power over these plagues: and they repented not to give him glory. (Revelation 16:8-9)

And then as suddenly as the oppressive heat and brilliant light of the sun had appeared... it just as suddenly disappeared! And the earth was plunged into a terrifying DARKNESS.

> And the fifth angel poured out his vial upon the seat of the beast; and his kingdom was full of darkness; and they gnawed their tongues for pain.
> And blasphemed the God of heaven because of their pains and their sores, and repented not of their deeds. (Revelation 16:10-11)

Dr. Curter was a genius. And having great scientific insight, he was prepared against any

The earth was plunged into a terrifying DARKNESS.

problem he thought might occur. Patiently he had obeyed every command of Brother Bartholomew. He was among the first to have The Mark 666 imprinted on his forehead. But as the years passed, his closeness to this power brought some revelations...revelations that Dr. Curter felt were chinks of weakness in the character of this man who would be God. God was supposed to do good, Dr. Curter reasoned. But this man was a mixture of good and evil and now leaned heavily to doing simply everything evil.

Dr. Curter realized he had already taken his position with Brother Bartholomew. There was no backing out now. But in his last days the least he could do was to contribute some good to humanity...even if it would cost him his life. Perhaps in so doing, he reasoned, he might gain the peace of knowing that he had caused Brother Bartholomew also to pay and suffer. Bring BB to grief...he who had grieved millions. That was it!

He made up his mind. He would have his vengeance. He would help Faye and George escape.

Faye and George were praying. It was pitch black. George, in his prayer was quoting II Corinthians 4:6...."For God, who commanded the light to shine out of darkness..."

The sound of the elevator descending interrupted them. They looked up. In the pitchblackness of the surroundings, they heard the elevator door open. And coming towards them...a thin ray of light!

As the light came closer they heard a voice: "Don't be afraid, it's me!"

"Dr. Curter," Faye shrieked in fear.

"Quiet," Dr. Curter urged. "I am not your enemy. I am come as your friend. I have watched your testimony through these years. There's not much I can do, but I can set you free. Your Lord will have to do the rest. A short time ago Brother Bartholomew gave me my own private heliojet...as a reward. It's waiting up above. It won't be missed for an hour. Tell me where you want to go in Palestine. It can take you anywhere in Palestine and be back within the hour. No one will know it. I'll program the control mechanism to fly you there automatically."

"Praise God," George replied.

"Take us to GIHON!"

"Why Gihon?" Dr. Curter questioned. "That's right outside the inner city walls of Jerusalem. It's just a dried up spring. I thought you would want to get farther away from this place than that."

"But as you wish, George, but I can't go with you. The heliojet will land you on the spot, then it will take off again and return here to the Mount of Olives all within the necessary hour. It won't be missed."

Brother Bartholomew was listening to a geophysical report from aides in his office. Things had quieted down to a point where he could proceed with his planning.

And the sixth angel poured out his vial upon the great river Euphrates; and the water thereof was dried up, that the way of the kings of the east might be prepared. (Revelation 16:12)

The aide was speaking: "Sir, something unusual is occurring. The intense heat from the sun has caused vast destruction. Fortunately its course has been changed to give us temporary relief. But reports indicated that the river Euphrates is drying up."

"Why is this so drastic?" Brother Bartholomew demanded.

"For as long as we can trace," the aide continued, "the Euphrates River has been a formidable barrier to East-West transportation and communication. The River is nearly 1800 miles long, a thousand feet to a mile wide at some points, and it is as deep as 57 feet at the average depth. While modern day weaponry can cross this with ease, nevertheless, it has been a subtle dividing line. I know the Bible is a fabled book but Dr. Curter pointed out to me Isaiah 11:15. It's quite prophetic sir...

> 'And the Lord shall utterly destroy the tongue of
> the Egyptian sea; and with his mighty wind shall
> he shake his hand over the river, that is, the
> Euphrates, and shall smite it in the seven streams,
> and make men go over dryshod.'

This drying up of the River, the Euphrates, may be just the sign to encourage China or Russia to begin another invasion."

Brother Bartholomew gazed at the aide and spoke sharply, "Nonsense, you've been reading too many fairy tales. Get me Dr. Curter!"

Within moments Dr. Curter arrived.

"Curter, what have you been babbling about? Have you also outlived your usefulness? Should I set up 3 guillotines for tomorrow? What a picture that would make—the 3 Wise Men!" With that he flipped a switch to light up a video screen. "Let's look in on our God-fearing duet down below. Perhaps I'll send you down to keep them company."

The screen was lit. Brother Bartholomew looked at it in shock. The picture showed an empty room!

He turned to Dr. Curter enraged...about to speak. Just

then Prophet Arthur rushed in with a video communique.

"Brother Bartholomew. There's trouble in the South. The Egyptian-African coalition of nations is on the march. Their war cry is 'TO THE SEA WITH BROTHER BARTHOLO-MEW...FORCE HIM TO THE SEA!'"

Another aide rushed in, "Brother Bartholomew, the armies from the North are marching down from Russia. They are headed towards Jerusalem!"

Brother Bartholomew was visibly moved. "From the South, from the North. It's a pincer movement. Those traitors. Like a clever mousetrap they hope to close in on us and snap us into oblivion. But they are not wise enough. Once and for all, we'll demolish them. Prophet Arthur launch MIRV on our scheduled contingency battle plan."

The aide shuddered. MIRV, the Multiple Independently-targeted Re-entry Vehicle, had devastating nuclear power. No nation had dared to use it before. Even though countries went to war, this was one international treaty they always had respected.

Prophet Arthur pushed the ignite button. The sequence began. There was no reversing now. It was too late. Soft, silent whistles were heard. All knew what it was. The MIRV's had been launched. Soon they would take their deadly toll.

But some of the invading forces had already reached Jerusalem. The city was being invaded. The prophecy of Zechariah 12:2,3 was becoming a reality.

> "Behold, I will make Jerusalem a cup of
> trembling unto all the people round about,
> when they shall be in the siege both against
> Judah and against Jerusalem.
>
> And in that day will I make Jerusalem a burdensome
> stone for all people: all that burden themselves
> with it shall be cut in pieces, though all
> the people of the earth be gathered together
> against it."

The MIRV's did their deadly work and Brother Bartholomew beamed at their amazing ability to change the enemy's mind. It was easy to force Egypt and her coalition from the South and the Russian coalition from the North to come to terms. Brother Bartholomew even convinced them that they should not be fighting each other, but should merge together to fight an even greater enemy...those who believe they are Kings from the East...the Chinese!

Leader Chou was infuriated. His hopes for victory over the dynasty of Brother Bartholomew were crushed. He had cleverly encouraged the Egyptian and Russian coalitions to fight in a pincer movement to wipe out the United States of Europe's stronghold in the Middle East. Then, their energies spent, Leader Chou had planned to rush in with his hordes of soldiers and quickly overtake the two victors and make them subservient to China and his leadership. He would have become the Leader of the World.

But the humiliating defeat by Russia and Egypt washed out those dreams. "Why didn't they win?" he gasped. "Those traitors marched to defeat...But...If they couldn't do the job, I must march in myself and once and for all conquer the world. The yellow hordes of China will wipe the white man from the face of the earth. We are in the majority anyway. It would be an easy accomplishment," Leader Chou believed.

He had a plan...a clever plan that would bring his armies marching down from Turkey, in an armada of inconspicuous sailing ships across the Mediterranean to Haifa. This would not start as an obvious attack. This would be a Chinese Trojan Horse!

The heliojet had landed them safely. Under the cover of darkness it had deposited them at the place called GIHON. George took Faye's hand and slowly they descended the 32 steps to the spring called the Virgin's Spring. While it was still dark, they could yet feel that the spring bed was dry. But in a few feet they were soon wading in cold water. Faye stumbled on the stony floor. She removed what was left of her sandals. Both Faye and George, parched from going so

long with so little water, knelt in the cool spring and drank slowly and thankfully.

George spoke first.

"Faye, perhaps we should stay right here, just for a little while. I somehow feel the Lord wants us to be still and not move anymore."

"How did this tunnel come about, Dad?"

"This is called Hezekiah's tunnel," George replied. "This is a water shaft dug in solid rock. It's described in II Kings 20:20. It was constructed by King Hezekiah's engineers when the Jerusalem water supply was threatened by the approach of Sennacherib's army in 701 B.C. He built what is called by some the 'Siloam tunnel' to convey water from Gihon, where we are now, to the new upper pool of Siloam."

Suddenly the stillness was broken by the amplified sound of Brother Bartholomew...carrying his voice over the many Video lampposts that covered the city. His voice was loud and ominously clear...

For they are the spirits of devils, working miracles which go forth unto the kings of the earth and of the whole world, to gather them to the battle of that great day of God Almighty. (Revelation 16:14)

ALL ELEMENTS OF THE ARMY. EMERGENCY. REPORT TO DIVISION HEADQUARTERS. PREPARE TO MARCH ON MEGIDDO!

Chapter 15

Search for Tomorrow

MEGIDDO!

A dreaded name.

Megiddo, a city situated on the Great Road, which linked Gaza and Damascus, and controlling the principal pass through the Carmel Range, connecting the coastal plain and the Plain of Esdraelon. Megiddo was important because of its domination of the intersection of two vitally important trade and military routes. One of the best recorded and most interesting military operations of ancient times took place at Megiddo when Thutmose III defeated an Asiatic coalition headed by the King of Kadesh. The importance of this area is reflected in the statement of the Egyptian king that the capture of Megiddo was the capture of a thousand towns.

"Har Megiddon" in the Hebrew; the "Mountain of Megiddo." At the foot of this mountain lie the Valley of Jezreel and the Plain of Esdraelon...the entire valley-plain region being together called, ARMAGEDDON! This was the scene of many decisive battles.

Here in this valley-plain region Gideon defeated Midian (Judges 6:33). Here Saul met death at the hands of the Philistines (I Samuel 31). In 1918 the then Allied forces under General Allenby entered northern Palestine through the Megiddo Pass to wrest it from Turkish forces. Subsequently he was named Viscount Allenby of Megiddo.

The sailing sloops went undetected as they entered the Haifa harbor. Brother Bartholomew's men were too preoccupied with the other fronts of attack which the Chinese had already started.

The world had never witnessed such a vast array of men and arms. The mass destruction leveled by the MIRV's had convinced Brother Bartholomew that to insure the survival of his own army this war with China would have to be fought with conventional weaponry.

Brother Bartholomew was kept busy directing the plan for conquest from his war operations office atop the Mount of Olives.

Prophet Arthur looked at him amazed as he entered with a report and found Brother Bartholomew poring over a Bible.

"A Bible? The world is falling apart! Why are you reading the Bible?" Prophet Arthur asked:

"This fabled book has some good object lessons in it...and some good plans for ambushes are in the Book of Joshua. It's excellent for the geography of this land. Who knows, the clue to once and for all defeating the Chinese might be right within its pages?"

Prophet Arthur began to give the information which he had just received, "I have word that soon the Chinese army will be near Mount Tabor. Our generals say that even though it is only 1843 feet high, if captured it would make a good command post for our enemy. They surprised us at Haifa. Innocent looking sloop sailing ships came into harbor. Our men thought them nothing but old sailing vessels. But on command, their holds opened, landing platforms extended down to the ground and a large array of tanks overran

Haifa leaving a wake of dead in their path. They, too are headed for Megiddo."

"Are you sure of that information?" Brother Bartholomew questioned.

"Yes," Prophet Arthur replied, "Our videoscopes confirm this."

"Good! That may be their biggest mistake. In Judges 5, the army of Sisera with 900 chariots moved near the entrance to the Esdraelon Plain to attack Israel. In the meantime a storm caused the Qishon River to overflow its banks, turning the fields into a quagmire. The chariots became hopelessly stuck in the mud...and the Israelites won an overwhelming victory!"

"But it is not raining, Brother Bartholomew, and no rain is predicted." Prophet Arthur revealed.

"Prophet Arthur, how long have you been close to me and yet still not realize that I control the heavens and the earth? It will be a simple matter to send rain over the Plain of Esdraelon and, in fact, to restrict the deluge to that area and to that area alone!"

Hezekiah's tunnel was a welcome relief from the unbearable heat of the last few hours. Faye and George had proceeded further into the tunnel to escape the hot air.

At some places it was necessary for them to crawl on their hands and knees, sometimes flat on their stomachs. The tunnel seemed full of twists and turns.

"How long is this tunnel?" Faye questioned.

"In a straight line it would be some 750 feet but this tunnel does not follow a straight line...but rather a circuitous route and it's over 1700 feet in length."

"Where does it lead to, Dad?"

"It goes through the High Rock, the Ophel, to the reservoir called the Pool of Siloam. This is the same pool to which Jesus sent the blind man with the command 'Go, wash in the pool of Siloam.' That was in John 9:7. The blind man went in, washed, and came out seeing!"

Turning another very sharp corner suddenly a streak of light broke through. Far in the distance they could see an opening. Faye was bruised and weary. The long days of running were catching up with her. She was exhausted.

"Let's rest here just a moment, Dad," she begged.

"Good idea, Faye. And with this little light, we can sit down and give thanks to God for bringing us safely this far."

"What is happening outside, Dad? The shouting, the screaming, the noise of explosives? Does the Bible give any clues to what is happening?"

George took the well-worn Bible from his coat pocket. "Yes, Faye, the Bible tells us much about His plan for tomorrow. Like many we were fools thinking Revelation and portions of Daniel and Jeremiah and Zechariah were just imaginations of men long ago. Even many clergymen passed these truths off as mere symbolism, and not as events which would actually come true. Yet God's prophecies have all been accurate up to this point. There is no reason to doubt that the rest of His Word will not prove accurate as well. Let's look at God's Timetable."

Turning the pages, he continued, "The Fourth Vial, the scorching sun as revealed in Revelation 16:8-9 and the sudden darkness which is the Fifth Vial described in Revelation 16:10-11 have already occurred. With the March to Megiddo now occurring, we must assume that the drying of the Euphrates River in the Sixth Vial judgment has come to pass, too. This would bring us up to the present time when the Armies of the East and the Armies of Brother Bartholomew, Antichrist, meet at Armageddon. And if I remember a very vivid statement on that is found in Joel 3:9-11...

> 'Proclaim ye this among the Gentiles; Prepare war,
> wake up the mighty men, let all the men of war
> draw near;
> let them come up;
> Beat your plowshares into swords, and your

pruninghooks into spears: let the weak say,
I am strong.

Assemble yourselves, and come, all ye heathen, and
gather yourselves together round about: thither
cause thy mighty ones to come down, O Lord.'
This truly presents the scene that is now taking place."

"You know what I wish, Dad? I wish I could be up in
Heaven looking down on this battle. Wouldn't it be wonder-
ful! But what about those Israelites who bear the seal of
God, the 144,000. Where are they??

"God will deliver them. He
says so in His word. And also
Gentiles like us who have accepted Christ as our Messiah
will be safe — safe with Christ
whether we live or die. And
after this judgment, at Armageddon Christ will come down
with His armies from Heaven to
slay the wicked and redeem the
saved. We'll meet Helen and
Sue and Tommy and Bill and
Tom Malone. It won't be long
now, Faye. What a grand and
glorious reunion that will be!"

And I looked, and lo, a Lamb
stood on the mount Sion, and with
him an hundred forty and four
thousand, having his Father's
name written in their foreheads.
(Revelation 14:1)

After this I beheld, and, lo, a
great multitude, which no man
could number, of all nations, and
kindreds, and people, and tongues,
stood before the throne, and
before the Lamb, clothed with
white robes, and palms in their
hands:
...These are they which came
out of great tribulation, and have
washed their robes, and made
them white in the blood of the
Lamb. (Revelation 7:9, 14)

"Oh, Dad," Faye cried, "it's going to be so wonderful...so
wonderful. If only God would remove the Mark from my
head. I would be so ashamed to face him hearing the mark
of antichrist!"

"God will do it Faye, I am sure God will do it."

Brother Bartholomew stood on a hill looking down over
the Plain of Esdraelon. Before him the mightest armies in
the world were massing...and slowly approaching the point
of contact.

An ominous cloud of dust seemed to hang heavy over the
miles and miles of flat plain. The noise of approaching armies

The Plain of Esdraelon...ARMAGEDDON!

thundered and echoed against the hills.

Leader Chou who claimed via radio to have with him some 200 million troops assembled felt confident of victory as his heliojet soared above his advancing tank columns. Almost 15,000 tanks were proceeding across the hot desert floor.

Brother Bartholomew smiling, as though he had the situation well in hand, stood watching the mass of millions at the point of confrontation. With him Prophet Arthur, hands on hips, watched as though he were to see a dream come true.

Suddenly Brother Bartholomew raised his arm, and removed the protective cap from the ruby laser ring.

Through the din of tanks and armor he shouted to Prophet Arthur, "Now you will see the heavens themselves empty every drop of rain on the Plain of Esdraelon. Then Leader Chou will be like putty in my hands."

Just as he finished speaking, the very heavens opened, like a scroll being rolled back. What appeared to be a mysterious cloud formation from high in the sky was descending.

Brother Bartholomew knew his Scriptures well. And the sign in the sky revealed to him that the Army of the Lord was descending. This was no time to be fighting the Chinese.

> And I saw heaven opened, and behold a white horse: and he that sat upon him was called Faithful and True, and in righteousness he doth judge and make war. (Revelation 19:11)

Quickly by picturephone he contacted Leader Chou who was in his heliojet. The heliojet of Leader Chou soon landed bearing a white flag of truce. It then picked up Brother Bartholomew and Prophet Arthur, and whisked them away to the Mount of Olives!

Atop the mountain headquarters both Leader Chou and Brother Bartholomew hastily signed an agreement. Prophet Arthur called in Defense Strategy Command and together they mapped a plan of attack against the armies of God.

Bishop Arthur anxiously spoke to Leader Chou. "We must work together. With your 200 million army combined with my millions not even God will withstand our assault. We will win the victory. They raised their glasses in a diabolical toast to victory. Then quickly Brother Bartholomew issued orders to the armies in the field to prepare for the onslaught that was to follow.

Faye and George rested, and then decided to continue again what seemed an endless crawling and walking through the tunnel of King Hezekiah towards its termination point at the top of the hill.

Like two happy children finally reaching the top of a verdant green hill...they literally ran the last few feet and fell on the ground gazing up at the sky.

After a few minutes, Faye jumped up. Weary and bruised she saw a pool of water.

"There it is, Dad...there it is...THE POOL OF SILOAM!" Without hesitation she jumped in the pool, and swam in the cool refreshing waters. It was as though she had found an oasis after walking in a parched, sun-baked desert. The sparkling clear waters seemed to give her new life.

As quickly as she dove in she emerged, happy and laughing.

George looked at her stunned.

"Dad," her face looked suddenly worried, "what's the matter? Why are you staring at me like that?"

"Your face, Faye, your face," he shouted as he jumped up and pointed hysterically happy.

"What's wrong with my face, Daddy, what's wrong with my face?"

"The Mark, Faye, The Mark is GONE. DISAPPEARED. The 666 has DISAPPEARED! It's not there!"

Faye cried tears of joy as they ran into each other's arms with Faye shouting, "God answered my prayer, Daddy... God has answered my prayer!"

"Faye," George replied, "Scriptures had made it very plain to me that accepting The Mark was an unpardonable sin. Yet I believed God would provide an answer. And now I remember Tom telling us that he used a fade-out temporary dye on his forehead. It's funny how things come back. It was Bishop Arthur who told me a long time ago that no one can be privileged to wear The Mark unless they desire it voluntarily. So now it is clear. Brother Bartholomew, in his sinister planning, used a temporary fade-out Mark on you. And when you plunged into the Pool of Siloam it washed away!"

Faye beamed with happiness. "And you know Dad, one thing puzzles me...Brother Bartholomew issued plaques to everyone with the inscription PRAYER CHANGES THINGS. But you said the plaque in his office was THINGS CHANGE PRAYER. Why the difference?"

"That almost slipped my mind, Faye. Isn't it odd how these relatively insignificant things all fall together. Let's see...THINGS - that's 6 letters...CHANGE...that's 6 letters and PRAYER...why that, too, is 6 letters! If only we had known then..."

On the Plains of Esdraelon the armies had received their orders. Quickly they merged as one.

Who were they fighting? There was mass confusion. Here they were one moment ready to tear each other apart...the next moment joining forces against what seemed to be an invisible force.

Suddenly all eyes focused on the sky. What appeared to be a mysterious white cloud way off in the distance was now becoming clearly visible.

It seemed unbelievable. Men everywhere were rubbing their eyes...for they believed that what they saw must be some hallucination...a mirage because of the desert heat.

There in front was a Rider, a magnificent, stately, Kingly rider...a rider on a WHITE HORSE and armies of people were following him; they too on white horses.

His eyes were as a flame of fire, and on his head were many crowns; and He had a name written, that no man knew, but He himself.

And He was clothed with a vesture dipped in blood: and His name is called The Word of God.

And the armies which were in heaven followed Him upon white horses, clothed in fine linen, white and clean.

And out of his mouth goeth a sharp sword, that with it he should smite the nations: and he shall rule them with a rod of iron: and he treadeth the winepress of the fierceness and wrath of Almighty God.

And he hath on his vesture and on his thigh a name written, KING OF KINGS, AND LORD OF LORDS.

(Revelation 19:12-16)

There was a loud thunder. Then silence. Brother Bartholomew and Leader Chou fell to their knees along with Prophet Arthur. From their vantage point atop the Mount of Olives they could see the entire Plain of Esdraelon on their life-size video screen.

Suddenly there was a loud voice speaking...a voice never before heard by mortal man. The voice of God!

Soon their eyes were directed to the Mount of Olives.

And the entire army of men, multiple millions, fell to the ground dead, as one. THE BATTLE WAS OVER.

Circling overhead it seemed like all the birds of earth were gathered. And as if by command, they swooped down on the inert bodies, gorging themselves with the flesh of men.

Then the greatest earthquake man has ever known suddenly erupted. Cities of all nations around the world collapsed. Giant hailstones, weighing as much as 100 pounds each, fell in an avalanche of death.

And the remnant were slain with the sword of him that sat upon the horse, which sword proceeded out of his mouth: and all the fowls were filled with their flesh. (Revelation 19:21)

And the seventh angel poured out his vial into the air; and there came a great voice out of the temple of heaven, from the throne, saying, It is done.

And there were voices, and thunders, and lightnings; and there was a great earthquake, such as was not since men were upon the earth, so mighty an earthquake, and so great.

And the great city was divided into three parts, and the cities of the nations fell: and great Babylon came in remembrance before God, to give unto her the cup of the wine of the fierceness of his wrath.

> And every island fled away, and the mountains were not found.
> And there fell upon men a great hail out of heaven, every stone about the weight of a talent (100 pounds): and men blasphemed God because of the plague of hail; for the plague thereof was exceeding great. (Revelation 16:17-21)

From their vantage point at the Pool of Siloam Faye and George could see the entire action. They were stunned as the reality of all their hopes began to formulate into victory.

Ahead of them a yawning chasm opened. Fire and smoke gushed forth as the earth opened. Almighty God on His White Horse summoned an angel. With him the angel brought a large key and a ghastly chain.

Soon their eyes were directed to the Mount of Olives. Coming from the fortress on top of the Mount were two defeated and humbled figures.. Brother Bartholomew (antichrist) and Prophet Arthur (the false prophet). The angel led them to the awesome chasm. Bound in chains they were thrown into what appeared to be a bottomless pit.

> And the beast was taken, and with him the false prophet that wrought miracle before him, with which he deceived them that had received the mark of the beast, and them that worshipped his image. These both were cast alive into a lake of fire burning with brimstone. (Revelation 19:20)

The Lord was off his White Horse now. And his feet were coming to rest on the Mount of Olives. Just as his feet touched the hallowed Mount it split in two, leaving a great valley through the center, with springs of water gushing out of the earth in two directions, part towards the Mediterranean, and part toward the Dead Sea. With the water came many bodies...among them that of Leader Chou.

> And His feet shall stand in that day upon the mount of Olives, which is before Jerusalem on the east, and the mount of Olives shall cleave in the midst thereof toward the east and toward the west, and there shall be a very great valley; and half of the mountain shall remove toward the north, and half of it toward the south.
> And it shall be in that day, that living waters shall go out from Jerusalem; half of them toward the former sea (Dead Sea), and half of them toward the hinder sea (Mediterranean Sea): in summer and in winter shall it be. (Zechariah 14:4, 8)

Both Faye and George were crying...crying tears of joy at what they saw. And as they looked up God's Army on white horses, clothed in fine linen, white and clean were coming into view. There through the moisture of their tears...there they could see HELEN, little SUE, TOMMY, BILL and TOM MALONE, waving and singing praises to God.

Faye and George held hands, tears streaming down their face...looking up at that wonderful sight...their choking, tearful voices sang in unison...

> It's not the first mile
> > That's so important.
> It's the last mile
> > When day is done.

> Then we'll see Jesus
> > In all His splendor
> And He will have for us
> > The Crown we've won.

It was going to be a grand reunion. Their search for tomorrow had ended.

There in front was a Rider, a magnificent, stately, Kingly rider...a rider on a WHITE HORSE and armies of people were following Him; they too on white horses.

What Will You Do With Jesus?

You have just read 666.

It may seem just too fantastic to be true. While it is written in novel form the facts of the RAPTURE (when believing Christians meet Christ in the air)...the Tribulation Period and its judgments...these facts are true! You can find them in the book of Revelation and in other places in the Bible.

Take any Bible...the King James Version, the new revised versions, even the Duoay Version. Those who do not accept the New Testament will find these same prophecies substantially made in the Old Testament book of Daniel.

The main question however is this:

WHAT WILL YOU DO WITH JESUS?

Will you state that He never existed?

Will you simply say He was a good man who did good things?

Will you say His message is not relevant to our enlightened age?

Would you buy a car without first finding out the facts relevant to that car?

Would you invest money in a venture without first finding out details of that organization?

Would you get married without first finding out more about the individual with whom you pledge your entire life?

Your answer would probably be NO to each of these three questions.

Then WHAT ABOUT JESUS? WHAT ABOUT HEAVEN? WHAT ABOUT HELL? WHAT ABOUT ETERNAL LIFE? WHAT ABOUT ETERNAL DAMNATION? WHAT ABOUT YOUR FUTURE AND THAT OF YOUR CHILDREN?

First, I am sure you will agree that your life here on earth will not go on and on. Any funeral director can attest to that fact. Any nurse or doctor can tell you that physical life on this earth someday ceases for each of us.

Second, if you have examined world conditions very carefully, you will admit that the world is certainly not getting better and better. Scientists even acknowledge the fact that the next 30 years will give us more complex problems in population growth, in famine, in crime, and in war.

Third, money (or the lack of it) will not cure your ills nor the ills of the world. Even if the wealth were spread out more evenly it would not resolve the problems. In actuality the spread of wealth worldwide on an even basis would make almost all Americans far poorer than they are now.

Fourth, if you look at it honestly, the permissive use of drugs and sexual freedom from the moral code will not build a better world.

Then what can you do?

Well, you can simply choose to ignore Christ and the Scriptures...go on living your life, doing the best you know how to meet your problems, work and provide an income for your family, set aside a nest egg for retirement...

But THEN WHAT?

What happens when it comes time for you to depart from this earth?

Then WHAT WILL YOU DO WITH JESUS?

It takes NO DECISION on your part to go to Hell!
It does take a DECISION on your part, however, to go to Heaven!

> He that believeth on Him is not condemned:
> but he that believeth not is condemned already,
> because he hath not believed in the name of the
> only begotten Son of God. (John 3:18)

Here are five basic observations in the Bible of which you should be aware:

1. ALL SIN

> For all have sinned, and come short of the glory of God. (Romans 3:23)

2. ALL LOVED

> For God so loved the world, that He gave His only begotten Son, that whosoever believeth in Him should not perish, but have everlasting life (John 3:16)

3. ALL RAISED

> Marvel not at this: for the hour is coming, in which all that are in the graves shall hear his voice,
>
> And shall come forth; they that have done good, unto the resurrection of life; and they that have done evil, unto the resurrection of damnation. (John 5:28,29)

4. ALL JUDGED

> ...we shall all stand before the judgment seat of Christ. (Romans 14:10)
> And I saw the dead, small and great, stand before God; and the books were opened....(Revelation 20:12)

5. ALL BOW

> ...at the name of Jesus every knee should bow... (Philippians 2:10)

Right now, in simple faith, you can have the wonderful assurance of eternal life.

Ask yourself, honestly, the question....

WHAT WILL I DO WITH JESUS?

Will you accept Jesus Christ as your personal Saviour and Lord or will you reject Him?

This you must decide yourself. No one else can decide that for you. The basis of your decision should be made on God's Word—the Bible.

God tells us the following:

"...him that cometh to me I will in no wise cast out. (37)

Verily, verily (truly) I say unto you, He that believeth on me (Christ) *hath* everlasting life" (47)—(John 6: 37, 47).

He also is a righteous God and a God of indignation to those who reject Him....

"...he that believeth not is condemned already, because he hath not believed in the name of the only begotten Son of God"—(John 3:18).

"And whosoever was not found written in the book of life was cast into the lake of fire"—(Revelation 20:15).

YOUR MOST IMPORTANT
DECISION IN LIFE

Because sin entered the world and because God hates sin, God sent His Son Jesus Christ to die on the cross to pay the price for your sins and mine.

If you place your trust in Him, God will freely forgive you of your sins.

"For by grace are ye saved through faith; and that not of yourselves: it is the gift of God: (8)

Not of works, lest any man should boast" (9)— (Ephesians 2:8, 9).

"...He that heareth my word, and believeth on Him that sent me, *hath* everlasting life, and shall not come into condemnation: but is passed from death unto life" —(John 5:24).

What about you? Have you accepted Christ as your personal Saviour?

Do you realize that right now you can know the reality of this new life in Christ Jesus. Right now you can dispel the doubt that is in your mind concerning your future and that of your loved ones. Right now you can ask Christ to come into your heart. And right now you can be assured of eternal life in heaven.

All of your riches here on earth—all of your financial security—all of your material wealth, your houses, your land will crumble into nothingness in a few years.

And as God has told us:

"As it is appointed unto men once to die, but after this the judgment: (27)
So Christ was once offered to bear the sins of many; and unto them that look for Him shall He appear the second time without sin unto salvation" (28)— (Hebrews 9:27, 28).

Are you willing to sacrifice an eternity with Christ in Heaven for a few years of questionable material gain that will lead to death and destruction? If you do not accept Christ as your personal Saviour, you have only yourself to blame for the consequences.

Or would you right now, as you are reading these very words of this book, like to know without a shadow of a doubt that you are on the road to Heaven—that death is not the end of life but actually the climactic beginning of the most wonderful existence that will ever be—a life with the Lord Jesus Christ and with your friends, your relatives, and your loved ones who have accepted Christ as their Saviour.

It's not a difficult thing to do. So many religions and so many people have tried to make the simple Gospel message

of Christ complex. You can not work your way into heaven—
heaven is the gift of God to those who believe in Jesus Christ.

No matter how great your works—no matter how kind you
are—no matter how philanthropic you are—it means nothing
in the sight of God, because in the sight of God, your riches
are as filthy rags.

"...all our righteousnesses are as filthy rags..."—
(Isaiah 64:6).

Christ expects you to come as you are, a sinner, recognizing your need of a Saviour, the Lord Jesus Christ.

Understanding this, why not bow your head right now
and give this simple prayer of faith to the Lord.

Say it in your own words. It does not have to be a beautiful
oratorical prayer—simply a prayer of humble contrition.

My Personal Decision for CHRIST

"Lord Jesus, I know that I'm a sinner and that I
cannot save myself by good works. I believe that
you died for me and that you shed your blood for my
sins. I believe that you rose again from the dead. And
now I am receiving you as my personal Saviour, my
Lord, my only hope of salvation. I know that I'm a
sinner and deserve to go to Hell. I know that I cannot
save myself. Lord, be merciful to me, a sinner, and
save me according to the promise of Your Word. I
want Christ to come into my heart now to be my
Saviour, Lord and Master."

Signed.....................................

Date...............................

If you have signed the above, having just taken Christ

as your personal Saviour and Lord...I would like to rejoice with you in your new found faith.

Write to me...Salem Kirban, Kent Road, Huntingdon Valley, Penna. 19006...and I'll send you a little booklet to help you start living your new life in Christ.